This nation is sick and tired of the politics of personal destruction.
This nation is looking for an administration that
will appeal to our better angels, not our darker impulses.
George W. Bush

If men were angels, no government would be necessary.
If angels were to govern men, neither external nor
internal controls on government would be necessary.
James Madison

There's such a difference between the way we really live
and the way we ought to live that the man who neglects the real
to study the ideal will learn how to accomplish his ruin, not his salvation.
Niccolò Machiavelli

Wall Street on Trial

Wall Street on Trial

A Corrupted State?

Justin O'Brien

WILEY

Published by John Wiley & Sons Ltd, The Atrium, Southern Gate, Chichester,
    West Sussex PO19 8SQ, England
    Telephone (+44) 1243 779777

Email (for orders and customer service enquiries): cs-books@wiley.co.uk
Visit our Home Page on www.wileyeurope.com or www.wiley.com

This publication is designed to provide accurate and authoritative information in regard to
the subject matter covered. It is sold on the understanding that the Publisher is not engaged
in rendering professional services. If professional advice or other expert assistance is
required, the services of a competent professional should be sought.

Other Wiley Editorial Offices

John Wiley & Sons Inc., 111 River Street, Hoboken, NJ 07030, USA

Jossey-Bass, 989 Market Street, San Francisco, CA 94103-1741, USA

Wiley-VCH Verlag GmbH, Boschstr. 12, D-69469 Weinheim, Germany

John Wiley & Sons Australia Ltd, 33 Park Road, Milton, Queensland 4064, Australia

John Wiley & Sons (Asia) Pte Ltd, 2 Clementi Loop #02-01, Jin Xing Distripark, Singapore
129809

John Wiley & Sons Canada Ltd, 22 Worcester Road, Etobicoke, Ontario, Canada M9W 1L1

Wiley also publishes its books in a variety of electronic formats. Some content that appears in
print may not be available in electronic books.

British Library Cataloguing in Publication Data

A catalogue record for this book is available from the British Library

ISBN 0-470-86574-1

Project management by Originator, Gt Yarmouth, Norfolk (typeset in 11/15pt Goudy)
Printed and bound in Great Britain by Antony Rowe, Chippenham, Wiltshire
This book is printed on acid-free paper responsibly manufactured from sustainable forestry
in which at least two trees are planted for each one used for paper production.

Contents

To
Peter Blake – For Believing

Foreword

For many months now the world has been both entertained and alarmed by reports of the excesses of a number of key actors on Wall Street. The various ways in which investors, pensioners and ordinary working people have been shamelessly exploited have created a wave of revulsion across the United States, and incredulity abroad. There have been promises of stern action from politicians. The so-called "rotten apples" have been labelled a disgrace to their society and as being deserving the prison time.

This book both explains and lifts the veil on these sagas. It examines how it was that regulatory bodies were deliberately weakened at the behest of Wall Street and shows how it is that those very same financial institutions have been able – and continue to be able – to blunt the politicians' promises of meaningful reform.

The picture that emerges is one familiar to those working to strengthen national integrity systems of governance around the world: voracious money-grabbers empowered by networks of lawyers, bankers and accountants only too willing to do their bidding for a fee; weak and deliberately under-resourced official regulators; well-connected individuals appointed to public posts regardless of their obvious unsuitability; and a political class devoid of the will necessary to push for effective change through being hopelessly compromised by its dependence on "the Street" for the financing of political campaigns.

What may be less familiar is the growing realization that legislation in the United States designed to check the operation of the Mafia – the RICO[1] laws – is a perfect fit for both the operation of Wall Street and as a potential mechanism to catch political operatives who extract donations in return for favours, long delayed and difficult to link directly. Given that RICO prosecutions are made easier to bring because of problems otherwise inherent in obtaining evidence against Mafia godfathers, this development becomes all the more intriguing. Justin O'Brien presents an instance of this process starting to get under way – albeit against an independent mayor in a small American city. Could this be the first sign of a wider clean-up driven by determined and ethical prosecutors? Or will it simply provoke a review of RICO by politicians who feel threatened, leading to a radical toning down of what they would prefer the expression "organized crime" to mean?

He further demonstrates how it was that the Wall Street scandals came to be investigated and exposed, much against the wishes of the federal body responsible for regulation – the somnambulant Securities and Exchange Commission (SEC) – through a process driven by the Attorneys General of three states that provoked a vicious turf war. Those who argue the case for overlapping jurisdictions in the fight against corruption are presented with a classic case where this has worked, however unintentionally.

The overarching lesson that emerges from the crisis is the unarguable importance of strong, independent and professional official regulation. The major contribution made by this book to the debate on the corporate scandals is the manner in which it tracks the dynamic and complex interactions between the economic and political sectors, providing an astute analysis that gives equal credence to corrupted actors and to a corrupted system. O'Brien argues persuasively that ideology has been allowed to swamp logic and common sense and that the origins of the scandals lie not in the mendacious character of the individuals who have so gleefully pocketed other people's

---

[1] RICO, Racketeering and Corrupt Organization Act.

money, but in the blind faith of ideologues who believed that deregulation of any kind was necessarily a "good thing" – and who swung the stable doors wide open by repealing long-standing regulatory legislation and downgrading the capacity of the SEC to handle its tasks.

None of these problems is unique to the United States. What makes them close to many around the world is more than their familiarity. It is the fact that Wall Street is an essential driver of the global economy, but has been shown to lack integrity and so has forfeited confidence; it is the fact that two or more generations of unsuspecting savers have suffered irreparable harm; and, moreover, it is the fact that the scandals have come at a time when there is a global consensus that sustainable development, and so the reduction of poverty in the developing world, can best be achieved through private sector – rather than state-led – development. It is thus imperative for the global community that the model on which so many countries are encouraged to base their market economies is one that can be relied upon to guard against the excesses and abuses presented to us here.

The market economy has faced and overcome major challenges in the past and has survived by adapting to new norms and expectations – ranging from the distant abolition of slavery through to the contemporary curtailment of undue market dominance, involving the blocking of mergers and the breaking up of major corporations. Invariably, reform has been achieved by defusing threats through strong and incisive regulation, not by way of deregulation and voluntary compliance.

As in the past, the market economy will doubtless overcome its present difficulties. But as Justin O'Brien makes plain, these will only be dealt with effectively when there is sufficient political will to recognize that the problems are structural and not the isolated actions of individual "rotten apples". When there is an acceptance that these threats must be countered by strengthening systems, not simply by prosecuting those who step out of line. And when ideologues forsake their unquestioning mantra that deregulation improves all things in favour of a mindset that accepts the eternal fallibility of humankind. Then, and only then, will political institutions endorse the consequential and continuing need for strong, independent and effective regulation, the more so in the money marketplace. Government can actually be good for you.

Jeremy Pope[2]
Executive Director
Transparency International Centre for Innovation and Research
London
April 2003

---

[2] Jeremy Pope wishes to make it clear that the views expressed in this foreword are his own and not necessarily those of the Transparency International Centre for Innovation and Research.

Acknowledgements

This book owes its origins to a research project undertaken at the Institute of Governance, Public Policy and Social Research, Queen's University, Belfast. I am grateful to its Director, Professor Elizabeth Meehan, for her unstinting support. My colleagues at the Institute provided a collegial and intellectually stimulating place in which to work. I wish to place on record my appreciation to Gina Inglis, Dr Alex Warleigh, Dr John Barry at the School of Politics, John Morison at the School of Law and Istemi Demirag at the School of Management and Economics.

John Barry, Istemi Demirag, Elizabeth Meehan and Robert Miller read early drafts of this book. Their insights, from diverse intellectual backgrounds, helped guide the interdisciplinary framework adopted and improved the argument immensely. My former tutors, now colleagues, Professor Paul Bew and Professor Richard English continued to provide unstinting encouragement. My colleague and friend, Bronagh Hinds, was an exceptionally patient sounding board. Her enthusiasm and words of wisdom are gratefully acknowledged. Trevor Newsom and Sir George Bain have been exceptionally supportive of the need to emphasize the governance component of corporate governance.

Transparency International has been very supportive of the project from the beginning. I am particularly grateful to Jeremy Pope for his unwavering belief in the need to focus on systems, not actors.

Gillian Dell in Berlin opened a number of avenues, not least the Seoul International Anti-Corruption Conference, as did Fredrick Galtung in London.

At Wiley, Rachel Wilkie confidently broke all production time-scales to put the book into print in record time. As an editor, she has proved invaluable. Bruce Shuttlewood at Originator was a pleasure to work with, polishing the text and inserting late additions with professional ease.

As every author will testify, professional support alone is not enough to ensure the transformation from idea to completed project. Friends and family once again provided me with unrivalled encouragement. Michael Scallon provided an endless supply of anecdotes and an unforgettable time in New York, awakening old memories and providing wise counsel. Kevin and Joan Gilmartin were always on hand in Irvinestown's own Central Station to discuss the latest machinations of corporate excess. Peter Blake instilled a fascination for the world of finance that has paid dividends. Both Peter and Mary Blake provided encouragement at every juncture. But this book would not have been possible at all without the forbearance of my long-suffering wife, Darina. Yet again, she had to put up with my shouts from the study that I would be finished shortly. That we both knew that it would be hours, days, weeks and months before normal life resumed is testament to her patience. To her, and my beautiful children, Jack and Elise, I owe the greatest debt.

Introduction:
The corruption cycle

The malaise in the capital markets is not merely the result of venal personalities – although there are many in this story – but also of a system that allows for full expression of those characteristics. The central argument of this book is that the "rotten apple" theory, positing the problems in corporate America as merely the result of deviancy by an individual or a single firm, is an intellectual deceit not supported by the facts. Looking beyond the undoubted greed exhibited by corrupted actors, the book critically examines the structural imbalances within the contemporary American regulatory framework, the reasons for the failure of federal oversight and the long-term political implications of the erosion of confidence. If, as argued, the corruption of the market – and the political structure that underpins it – has systemic flaws, then the corrective action needed to restore confidence necessitates a far more radical approach than that conceived or articulated by Republican and Democrat alike. As the list of those implicated moves out of the boardroom in concentric circles to indict the operation of the entire business and political model, this task has become imperative. Unless the extent of the crisis is identified, codified and explained, the search for solutions will be compromised from the start. In the absence of paradigmatic change, while optical illusion will provide the appearance of reform, the underlying fundamentals will remain intact, awaiting another bull market to unleash a further speculative orgy with equally dangerous consequences.

The politics of business has become the business of politics. Across the world the lesson is clear: just as too much governmental interference leads to dysfunctional economies, left to its own devices the market is incapable of adequate self-regulation. Crony capitalism in East Asia destroyed the glittering façade of the emerging markets in 1997–8. The selling of state assets in much of Europe throughout the 1980s and early 1990s spawned a privatization wave that has failed to provide compelling evidence that the market alone offers better services than public utilities. Deregulation and decentralization in former planned economies, particularly Russia, without an adequate institutional framework has resulted in a skewed market, which served merely to legitimize organized crime. The corporatization of communism in China has also failed to improve the efficiency of former state-owned industries, in large measure because of a failure to allow market forces to work because wider societal needs preclude the allowance of bankruptcy.[1] By means of contrast, a reliance on the efficacy of the market alone has also brought Latin America to crisis point, most recently in Argentina. While the triggers for the collapse in each jurisdiction differ, a common failing has been an imbalance in the wider corporate governance structure. Now, the exposure of that shortcoming has migrated to the United States with devastating effect.

Off-balance sheet loans, accounting irregularities and deliberate misleading of investors were dysfunctions not simply confined to emerging markets. The most advanced financial system in the world is not, in itself, an antidote to the corrosive effects of deregulation ceded on terms conducive to the corporate interests that controlled it. Centred on an excessive, and ultimately misguided, belief in the efficacy of the market, the economic and political roots of the crisis lie in the deregulation policies adopted in the Reagan era. This ideological aversion to the role of government in driving the

---

[1] See Jean Jinghan Chen, "Corporatisation of China's state-owned enterprises and corporate governance", paper presented at the *Third International Conference of the British Accounting Association Special Interest Group on Corporate Governance*, *Queen's University, Belfast, 16 December 2002*.

economy, embedded within the political system a disdain for regulation and led to the dismantling of legal restraints. In the context of a
fundamental weakening of the role to be played by the state in
policing the economy, the asymmetrical relationship between the
three pivotal actors – regulators, corporations and politicians –
became even more pronounced, lowering, in the process, the "moral
cost" of corruption.[2]

Despite periodic outbreaks highlighting the negative consequences,
including the insider-trading allegations of the late 1980s, this reliance on the market to police itself retained its potency. In the United
States, indicative of how far the power relationships had changed was
the decision to repeal Depression era legislation without simultaneously updating the regulatory framework to take due cognizance
of the newly designed complex financial architecture.[3] Striking out
the Glass–Steagall Act in 1999, ostensibly to allow for a strengthening of the banking sector, sowed the seeds for the conflicts of interest
that were to consume the integrity of the system after the euphoria of
the boom subsided.

The traditional banking sector sought to enhance its position by
tying commercial lending to the utilization of its nascent investment
services; by contrast the traditional investment banks sought to
replace commercial lending with debt financed by equity. Both
methods carried inherent risks of abuse. A survey for the Association
of Financial Professionals, published in March 2003, revealed that
56% of firms with over $1bn in revenues alleged that attempts were
made to illegally force tie-in arrangements to secure capital.[4] In order
to retain their competitive advantage, for the first time since the 1929

---

[2] See Yves Meny, "Fin de siècle corruption: Change, crisis and shifting values",
International Social Science Journal, Vol. 149, September, pp. 309–20.

[3] This blurring of oversight, coupled with the changed expectations was central to the
insider trading scandals of the 1980s. See N. Reichman, "Breaking confidences:
Organizational influences on insider trading", *Sociological Quarterly*, Vol. 30,
pp. 185–204.

[4] See Riva Atlas, "Corporation in survey say banks tie loans to other business", *New
York Times*, 19 March 2003.

stock market crash, the financial powerhouses of Wall Street were allowed to offer a single service to their clients under the rubric of "structured finance". Although there had been a gradual reduction in the strict rules governing this combination of services, following repeal all restrictions disappeared.[5] Under the new deregulated system, fears over conflicts of interest were casually disregarded and the merchants of Wall Street proclaimed that the excesses of the past would never be repeated.

As Jack Grubman, the senior communications analyst for the Citigroup subsidiary, Salomon Smith Barney, pithily described it, "what used to be a conflict are now synergies."[6] Yet a mere three years later, the entire structure is in ruins, along with the reputations of the star analysts like Grubman who had talked up the market in a deliberate and misleading manner that bordered on criminal behaviour. Investment banks produced unsustainable research to boost the bull market and gain lucrative underwriting and consultancy fees. Proving the efficacy of the market, in effect, proved the cyclical nature of corruption on Wall Street. Repealing Glass–Steagall, without adequate institutional safeguards to police a much more complex structure was, therefore, in retrospect, an unmitigated disaster. Among other unintended consequences, explored in detail throughout this book, it opened the door to the provision of corporate advice on how to reduce tax liability that, at times, transgressed the fine dividing line separating legal avoidance from illegal evasion. Stock value was improved by shifting debt off the books through the manipulation of accountancy rules based on laws, not principles, with the fiduciary trust of auditors and legal counsel systematically traduced as a direct consequence.

The systemic failure reached its apogee in the role played by the investment banks in the rise and fall of Enron. Over the course of its development into one of the most powerful corporations in the world, Enron itself mirrored the growing financialization of the American

---

[5] For a historical overview see Charles R. Geisst, *Wall Street, A History* (Oxford University Press, New York, 1997), pp. 328–69.

[6] Arianna Huffington, *Pigs at the Trough, How Corporate Greed and Political Corruption Are Undermining America* (Crown, New York, 2003), p. 161.

economy. Enron transformed itself from a purveyor of gas through a national pipeline network into the architect of the most innovative financial derivatives available on the market. Taking advantage of its dominant position in a deregulated playground, with no credible supervision, the Enron fiasco is a talisman for a wider and more fundamental failure. Given the global reach of Enron and the complexity of its operations, it is not surprising that its collapse has injected a new urgency to understanding the nature of modern capitalism and the dangers inherent in leaving untreated the conflicts of interest.

In January 2003, a panel from the Senate Permanent Subcommittee on Investigations called on the regulators to restrict the operation of mercantile-provided, structured finance because of the abuses encountered at Enron. In a statement to accompany the report, the chairman of the committee, Senator Carl Levin, noted: "Enron's deceptions were shocking, and equally shocking was the extent to which respected U.S. institutions like Chase, Citigroup, and Merrill Lynch helped Enron carry out its deceptions and mislead investors and analysts ... These financial institutions weren't victims of Enron; they helped plan and carry out Enron's deceptions in exchange for large fees or favourable consideration."[7]

Asking regulators to look again at strengthening rules after the market has lost trillions of dollars strikes one as either hopelessly naive or hopelessly inept.[8] Given that the market had simply reverted to type, Senator Levin would have been better advised to look at the reasons why his predecessors banned merchant banks from those activities in 1934 and why it only took three years of repeal to again bring the market into disrepute. The banks' response to the unfolding crisis in the securities market spoke volumes. They

---

[7] Quoted by Kevin Drawbaugh, "Senate panel seeks 'structure finance' crackdown", *Reuters*, 2 January 2003, carried on www.forbes.com/newswire/2003/01/02/rtr836580html

[8] The General Accounting Office issued a final report into the role played by the investment banks in March 2003. See GAO, "Investment banks, the role of firms and their analysts with Enron and Global Crossing", March 2003, GAO-03-511. Full text available online at http://www.gao.gov/cgi-bin/getrpt?GAO-03-511

claimed they did not do anything illegal, even if the result was illegal, and when the Securities and Exchange Commission (SEC) belatedly brought civil actions, they settled in order to prevent further investigation, exposing just how corrupted the operation of the market had become.

While it is important to point out at the outset that the vast majority of those working for corporations, investment houses and the wider financial services industry are honest, the integrity of the system itself has become increasingly problematic because of the skewed relationships inculcated by a business culture that preached a gospel of untrammelled market dominance. The problem is intensified because the distribution of power within the industry itself favoured profit over cost centres. Internal risk management systems, developed by legal and compliance departments, were subservient to the profit centres, most notably the investment banking divisions. The vast sums involved created further conflicts of interests for those providing professional services, most notably the accountants. Throughout the 1990s, for the major accountancy firms, the audit function was supplanted by valuable consultancy business. The collapse of the Savings and Loans industry due to financial incompetence, rapacious selling by Wall Street of junk bonds to greedy and unprincipled executives and a betrayal of fiduciary trust by auditors had revealed the dangers of weak regulation, but, despite the warning signs, Congress not only failed to legislate but also maintained blind faith in the ideological doctrine. The question is why?

This, in turn, suggests that much more serious attention needs to be paid to the intersection between politics and economics, especially in the developed world. In 1995 the World Bank defined good governance as "the practice by political leadership of accountability, transparency, openness, predictability and the rule of law."[9] Much early, original research into corrupt networks tied the process to modernization. This cosseted assumption was falsified following the implosion of the entire Italian political system in a welter of revela-

---

[9] A. W. Goudie and David Stasavage, "A framework for the analysis of corruption", *Crime, Law and Social Change*, Vol. 29, p. 113, 1998.

tion over the existence of corrupt networks. The Elf scandal in France proved instrumental in providing further data linking governmental contracts to party funding.[10] In the Republic of Ireland, no less than 10 tribunals of inquiry are now investigating deficiencies in every aspect of political and economic life.[11] As this book will demonstrate, in the United States the networks that define policy had rendered the entire system dysfunctional. Despite, or perhaps because, of a reliance on interpreting political and economic mores via a narrow application of carefully defined legal safeguards, the ethical component of public and corporate life was fatally undermined. By mapping the political economy of corruption in the securities markets, using the key variables determined by the World Bank – transparency, accountability and legal process – one can track how all but the rule of law broke down with devastating effect on the American securities exchanges, in the process exposing the powerlessness of the regulators to affect meaningful enforcement.

In large part, therefore, the excesses of the 1990s can be traced to the increasing financialization of the American economy. The result has been the creation of a model of business success based not on solid foundations but suspect financial engineering, which, in turn, fostered a climate that denigrated oversight. Much more seriously, the continual ebb and flow of allegations surrounding the corrupt nature of the market in the 1990s ensured the indelible rendering of the taint of scandal on the very foundations of the securities markets. Dissecting the roots of the scandal, in turn, implicates very major actors: from the boardroom to the outside legal counsel, from the auditors to the federal regulators, from the self-governing policing of the markets to the politicians who ostensibly guard the guardians.[12]

---

[10] See the perceptive treatment provided by Paul Heywood, "Political corruption: Problems and perspectives", *Political Studies*, Vol. XLV, pp. 417–35, 1997.

[11] See Justin O'Brien, *The Modern Prince: Charles J. Haughey and the Quest for Power* (Merlin, Dublin, 2002); Colm Kenna, *Haughey's Millions* (Gill & Macmillan, Dublin, 2002) and Paul Cullen *With a Little Help from My Friends* (Gill & Macmillan, Dublin, 2002).

[12] See John Nofsinger and Kenneth Kim, *Infectious Greed, Restoring Confidence in America's Companies* (Prentice Hall, Upper Saddle River, NJ, 2003).

For many in the financial services industry, the most important body to weaken has been the SEC. With George Bush's accession to the presidency in 2000, the lobbying was more finely calibrated. Bush appointed the most powerful lobbyist within the accountancy cartels to chair the SEC just as the organization was about to deal with a succession of irate investors looking for answers as to why the SEC had not protected them from egregious conflicts of interest. Usefully, for the politicians, the perception of the flawed pedigree of Harvey Pitt has served merely to transfer the spotlight away from their culpability; with him now gone, blaming the regulator for a wider failing for which they share corporate responsibility may not be so easy. As the true cost of the crisis in the United States becomes apparent, increasingly questions need to be asked about the fundamental reasons behind the wider political failure to deal with the systemic nature of the problems.

Trust, an essential ingredient for the smooth operation of the market, remains in short supply. The revelations of how warped the financial system had become in the late 1990s and the colossal greed that underpinned it was truly shocking to many who believed in the rhetoric of equality of opportunity in the marketplace. This erosion of faith is both widespread and deeply rooted in fact as well as perception – unpalatable realities belatedly accepted by the corporate world. Among those now expressing revulsion at the structure they had created are the primary architects of the contemporary system. The former Chairman of the Federal Reserve, Paul Volcker, summed up the unease when he commented, "corporate responsibility is mainly a matter of attitudes, and the attitudes got corrupted. In the 1990s, we went from 'greed is good' being said as a joke to people thinking 'greed is good' was a fundamental fact."[13]

While deception undermines trust, greater transparency – in this case acknowledgement of conflicts of interest – does not in itself restore confidence. President Bush has vowed to prosecute the war on corporate crime with the same vigour as that deployed against the

---

[13] *Business Week*, 24 April 2002.

scourge of international terrorism. In the President's estimation, both were crimes against the American way of life perpetrated by deviants. In the folksy rhetoric so beloved by the former Texas governor, both sets of outlaws need to be hunted down in order to protect the homestead. Left unanswered in this simplistic analysis is the charge that the crisis facing corporate America is not the result of deviance, but rather the inevitable outworkings of a political and economic system, which pivots on the malign power of money to distort the deliberative process. It is the system itself that now stands accused of creating the circumstances for the morally challenged executives to thrive. It is not in the interests of the system to draw attention to this failure: better then to create the impression of decisive action to dispense with "the rotten" element, the deviants who demean the American dream.

As the scandals unfolded, the indictment of the professional classes for their role in facilitating that attitudinal ethos prompted further erosion in fiduciary trust. It is this wider breakdown that poses the most serious questions of legitimacy. In a probing account of the consequences of the breakdown in social trust, the philosopher Onora O'Neill has commented that unless transparency is accompanied by a genuinely enforceable sense of obligation not to deceive, the conditions for the maintenance of distrust remain untreated:

> We can only judge whether there is deception, hence reason not to place trust, when we can tell whether we have been fed deliberate falsehoods. But how can we do this when we cannot tell who has asserted, compiled or endorsed the supposed information? In a world in which information and misinformation are "generated", in which good drafting is a vanishing art, in which so-called information "products" can be transmitted, reformatted and adjusted, embroidered and elaborated, shaped and spun, repeated and respun, it can be quite hard to assess truth or falsehood.[14]

It is indicative of the climate of suspicion inculcated by corporate malfeasance crises that investors continue to take money out of

---

[14] Onora O'Neill, "Trust and transparency", *Reith Lectures 2002*, 24 April 2002, p. 4. BBC full text available at http://www.bbc.co.uk/radio4/reith2002

liquid assets, further weakening the capital investment necessary to boost manufacturing. It represents a crisis of confidence that the administration has singularly failed to address beyond rhetorical demands for the jailing of corporate malefactors. Even the much-vaunted Sarbanes–Oxley legislation on corporate responsibility, passed with such fanfare in July 2002, is being undermined. Michael Oxley, the co-sponsor of the act, has served notice that its provisions are not cast in stone. While the legislation does go some way in addressing the problem of corrupt actors within the firm, the wider issue of the operation of the financial model itself at systemic level are not meaningfully addressed, a failure that can be traced, in part, to the expenditure of $41m in lobbying by the securities industry.[15] For prosecutors like John Moscow, Deputy Chief of Investigations at the New York District Attorney's office, there is a recognition that the heart of the matter has yet to be addressed:

> Where is George Orwell when we need him? Many people have used corrupted language in an attempt to justify actions that are simply not justifiable in plain English. Securities filings are required in the interests of disclosure. [But] we have new laws proposed that [have the effect of making them] more compli-cated. I think we need to simplify them. I think that we should go back to [proper] disclosure. Not a line for this and a line for that, but actual disclosure. It would be a sea change if at the end of reading the document a careful reader would know what happened as opposed to the current status where a careful reader knows there are questions that he cannot answer by reading the docu-ment because [the requisite facts] are not disclosed. Seeing a footnote that says something happened is not the same as disclosing what actually happened.[16]

The difficulties in breaking open the inner machinations of the cor-porate world centre on internal and external factors. Hierarchical reporting structures within the managed corporate model, coupled with an unwillingness to challenge privately condoned, if publicly proscribed behaviour because of fear of retaliation or spurned advancement, have long been recognized in case study analysis. As Pound has argued, not only is bad news "filtered out" as one moves

---

[15] For a scathing critique see John Nofsinger and Kenneth Kim, *Infectious Greed, Restoring Confidence in America's Companies* (Prentice Hall, Upper Saddle River, NJ, 2003), pp. 218–19.

[16] Interview with John Moscow, New York City, 9 April 2003.

up the reporting chain, but at the highest level – that of the board – there "tends to be a bias in favour of collegiality and consensus. For one, it is easier than provoking a conflict. For another, although they may suspect that a particular decision is wrong, directors in most cases have little evidence on which to base a debate ... The managed corporation model plays into the weakness of human and organizational behaviour and allows mistakes to go uncorrected until they become catastrophic."[17] Enron provides a case in point. As early as 1977, the SEC in the United States mandated the establishment of audit boards made up of independent directors to ensure that effective oversight was carried out. Delegating this authority to a stacked board, handsomely rewarded for inaction, was a disaster for Enron and its shareholders and was, in part, responsible for the failure of the company.[18]

The confluence of systemic internal and external flaws – the inability to detect illicit management decisions and the pathological capacity of firms to retrospectively cover their tracks – and the ending of the euphoria associated with the boom have made the task of disentangling causes and consequences of wider failure exceptionally problematic.[19] Conflicts of interest over audit and consultancy business, somnolent boards, subservient audit committees

---

[17] John Pound, "The promise of the governed corporation", in *Harvard Business Review on Corporate Governance* (Harvard Business School Press, Boston, 2000), pp. 85–7. For Pound one of the key deficiencies in the managed corporation model is that "boards do not prod managers when performance is not a disgrace" (p. 90). This was precisely the problem in the 1990s boom, during which overvalued stock masked less than robust performance, performance that could only be sustained by increasingly meretricious accounting.

[18] Similar problems plagued the board of RJR Nabisco during the tumultuous machinations surrounding a Leveraged Buy Out (LBO) in 1988. For full details see Bryan Burrough and John Heylar, *Barbarians at the Gate* (Random House, London, 2001).

[19] See Bill Witherall, "Corporate governance and responsibility", *Observer*, OECD No. 234, October 2002, pp. 7–9. The writer, head of the OECD Directorate for Financial, Fiscal and Enterprise Affairs, concludes that "the role of good governance and corporate responsibility in helping to assure the well-functioning markets needed for economic growth and development cannot be taken for granted ... [W]e are falling short: the systems may be there – the US had, on paper, one of the best – but evidently they have not worked. Fixing them will require both private initiative and strong government action" (p. 8).

that rubber-stamped managerial pay packages, asymmetrical imbalances that relegated the power of cost centres (such as legal and compliance departments) to enforce change, innovative financial instruments that have left the legislative and regulatory frameworks hopelessly outdated and, most importantly, a reliance on accounting standards based on principles rather than rules were all contributory factors that invited an erosion of business integrity. The danger inherent in not calibrating reputational risk, in part because the lack of credible enforcement informed corporate decision-making, has exposed fundamental weaknesses that are only now being addressed in comprehensive enterprise risk management. Furthermore, while it is important to demonstrate how actors have deviated from established internal codes of practice, it is also necessary to examine the dysfunctional realities inherent in the model. The result is an erosion of the efficacy of voluntary codes and self-policing paradigms, thereby proving the truth of Machiavelli's warning: "There's such a difference between the way we really live and the way we ought to live that the man who neglects the real to study the ideal will learn how to accomplish his ruin, not his salvation."

The debate on corporate governance has traditionally centred on ensuring a balance between the tripartite relationship between the board, management and shareholder; less attention has been placed on the wider issue of the role played by corporations in society and its unique power to distort the deliberative agenda by setting the stage for socially and politically acceptable behaviour.[20] The recent wave of scandals in the United States has rendered such an approach unsustainable. It is therefore necessary to begin the analysis with an examination of what corporate governance entails. The definition of corporate governance utilized in this book is that formulated by the British entrepreneur Adrian Cadbury. He refers to corporate governance as "the system by which companies are directed and

---

[20] This is central to the Sarbanes–Oxley Act on corporate responsibility. For a concise assessment of the regulatory changes entailed by the act see "Special report: Corporate governance", *Wall Street Journal*, 24 February 2003.

controlled" – an interpretation that allows for a wider investigation of the interlocking processes and shifting boundaries at work.[21]

The exercise of power without responsibility has long been recognized as a feature of the legal status of the corporation in society. In 1932, in the middle of the Great Depression, a judgment provided by a US Supreme Court Justice Louis Brandeis encapsulated the unease felt about the inordinate power that incorporation can give an entity. It is a warning that retains its power. Brandeis argued that, traditionally, incorporation is in the gift of the state to bestow, depending on "an instrumentality of business which will facilitate the establishment and conduct of new and large enterprises deemed of public benefit." For Brandeis, fear of the corporation was well founded. He concluded with a jaded acceptance of the powerlessness to reverse the relentless expansion of the corporate model: "There was a sense of some insidious menace inherent in large aggregations of capital, particularly when held by corporations. ... The later enactment of general corporation laws does not signify that the apprehension of corporate domination has been overcome."[22]

The international retraction of the role played by the state in the direction of the economy as a consequence of privatization policies has significantly enhanced the concern about the state's ability to regulate corporate life. The collapse of the British-based Maxwell empire in a welter of recriminations over the systematic looting of the corporation's pension funds and the gargantuan failure of the Bank of Credit and Commerce International highlighted problems of control long before the clarion call of the Seattle protestors brought the social and economic consequence of globalization onto the world arena. The conflicts-of-interest investigations on Wall Street have injected new impetus to the need for systematic analysis that reaches beyond self-policing models.

---

[21] Adrian Cadbury, *Corporate Governance and Chairmanship* (Oxford University Press, Oxford, UK, 2002), p. 1.

[22] Cited in Robert Monks and Nell Minow, *Corporate Governance* (Blackwell, Oxford, UK, 2001), p. 8.

In this regard, the emphasis on dealing with corrupted actors – while necessary – falls short of identifying the circumstances in which malfeasance can occur and the systemic problems that result from the pivotal role that is played by the corporation model itself.[23] More importantly, the trillions of dollars lost as a consequence of misguided belief in the integrity of the system has also occasioned a partial realignment of the balance of power between the corporate sector and wider society, a process that throws into stark relief the hidden architecture of the corporate model.

The success of the populist campaign for paradigmatic change espoused by the New York State Attorney General, Eliot Spitzer, lay in the fact that, as an outsider, he operated at one remove from the network. Capitalizing on or, as his critics would suggest, fomenting revulsion at the excesses associated with the collapse in confidence, the investigations ordered were pivotal

---

[23] See Gerald Vinten, "The corporate governance lessons of Enron", *Corporate Governance*, 2 April 2002, pp. 4–9. For a dissection of economic crime, arguing the need to situate it with the context of systems rather than actors see R. T. Naylor, "Towards a general theory of profit-driven crimes", *British Journal of Criminology*, Vol. 43, pp. 81–101, 2003. Naylor develops a typology based on three distinct forms of economic crime: predatory, market-based offences and commercial offences. Naylor's key argument is that an inordinate emphasis on tackling predatory crime misses the point. In the other categories "the harm is harder to assess, the identity or even the existence of victims more problematic and the borderline between the responsibilities of economic regulator, tax authority and police no longer clear" (p. 85). It is precisely the disconnect between political emphasis on actors and the reality of market-based and commercial criminal activity that accentuates the crisis of confidence in the probity of the entire system. For our purposes, the significance of Naylor's typology is the implicit notion of fair market value being routinely flouted and structured finance deals being allowed for systemic tax and regulatory evasion, creating in the process what he terms "fiscal contraband" (p. 86). For Naylor the difficulty is further magnified because fair market value "usually boils down more to an ideological rather than an operational construct" (p. 89). Naylor concludes that in defining three forms of crime the key characteristics are: "predatory crimes involve the illegal redistribution of existing wealth, market-based crimes involve the illegal earning of new income and commercial crimes involve the illegal redistribution of legally earned income" (p. 90).

in prising open the closed network that controls corporate finance.[24]

Network theory can play a pivotal role in understanding the extent to which the problems associated with corporate America are best described as the outworking of systemic flaws. The theoretical basis for network analysis lies in the fact that interaction with others reveals not only the existence of social groups but also how these groups form, develop into clusters, mutate and grow into complex, interconnected networks with the capacity to extend their influence. In a recent seminal contribution by the physicist Albert-Laszlo Barabasi, it is argued that independent actions combine to form "spectacular emergent behaviour" that, while conforming to a self-replicating fundamental structure, is contingent on complex interactions with other networks. Detailing the make-up of Fortune 100 company boards, Barabasi demonstrates "how the interlocked small world nature of corporate directorships determines most major appointments in corporate life."[25] Precisely because board membership tends to be drawn from the same gene pool – other CEOs – the emphasis is not only on congeniality rather than confrontation, it also creates powerful interconnections.[26] The linkages across the entire corporate sector from board directors to the market via professional "brokers" – accountants, auditors, lawyers – has resulted in the

---

[24] For an assessment of network theory see Albert Laszlo Barabasi, *Linked: The New Science of Networks* (Perseus, Cambridge, MA, 2002). See also Nigel Coles "It's not what you know – it's who you know that counts: Analysing serious crime groups as social networks", *British Journal of Criminology*, Vol. 41, pp. 580–94, 2001.

[25] Albert-Laszlo Barabasi, *Linked, The New Science of Networks* (Perseus, Cambridge, MA, 2002), pp. 205–6.

[26] A separate analysis carried out by Jerry Davis using "small-world" theory argued that corporate boards are separated by only 3.5 degrees, substantially less than the 5.5 degrees separating any two people in the United States. According to Davis, "One could hardly design a setting more conducive to contagion than this. It is literally true that an especially contagious airborne virus would spread quite rapidly through the corporate elite" (quoted in Phyllis Plitch, "Ready and able", *Wall Street Journal*, 24 February 2003).

creation of an extraordinarily powerful network, capable of exacting significant influence over political, economic, social and cultural life:

> Real networks are not static ... instead, growth plays a key role in shaping their topology. They are not centralised as a star network is. Rather, there is a hierarchy of hubs that keep these networks together, a heavily connected node closely followed by several less connected ones, trailed by dozens of even smaller nodes. No central node sits in the middle of the spider web, controlling and monitoring every link and node. There is no single node whose removal could break the web. A scale-free network is a web without a spider.[27]

Central to Barabasi's mapping of corporate reality is the argument that reference to an exchange between competitors is a myth. Rather, the relationship in contemporary capitalism is one between partners, trading on long-term linkages, indebtedness and support rather than immediate superiority. The implications are enormous and suggest that an inordinate emphasis on corrupted actors destroying the credibility of the market spectacularly misses the point:

> In reality, the market is nothing but a directed network. Companies, firms, corporations, financial institutions, governments, and all potential economic players are the nodes. Links quantifying various interactions between these institutions, involving purchases and sales, joint research and marketing projects, and so forth. The weight of the links captures the value of the transaction, and the direction points from the provider to the receiver. The structure and evolution of this weighted and directed network determine the outcome of all macroeconomic processes.[28]

The existence of socially embedded networks imbues the business culture with a malignant virus that thrives in an environment in which ethics play a secondary consideration to short-term success, whatever the wider consequences. Just as the clash of egos destroyed

---

[27] Albert-Laszlo Barabasi, *Linked, The New Science of Networks* (Perseus, Cambridge, MA, 2002), p. 221. In developing the theory Barabasi provides a persuasive case that the Al Qaeda network is a typical example of the validity of network analysis, arguing that "Al Qaeda is so scattered and self-sustaining that even the elimination of Osama bin Laden and his closest deputies might not eradicate the threat they created. It is a web without a true spider ... If ever we want to win the war, our only hope is to tackle the underlying social, economic and political roots that fuel the networks growth" (pp. 223–4).

[28] Ibid., p. 209.

the utility of many LBOs in the late 1980s, so a decade later did the thrill of gaming the system undermine the fundamental rules governing the marketplace. Networks exert powerful socialization processes across the corporate landscape both within firms and between corporations and those in whom fiduciary trust is placed. The central question is whether the process is reversible. The call of the Chairman of the SEC, William Donaldson, for a change in the DNA structure of American business necessitates a profound cultural shift in corporate culture. It is based on the optimistic belief that reindoctrination can cleanse the corporate body. Recent advances in gene theory posit that the emphasis on an unchanging blueprint model to understand the complexity of how cellular structures mutate leads one into an intellectual cul-de-sac. Ridley, for example, argues that structural changes are determined at least in part by experience.[29] It is, therefore, theoretically possible for change to occur. This belief in ethical change is also central to the solutions put forward by the Conference Board Chairman Peter Peterson: "If these recent scandals are not simply to be just another episode of corporate misconduct, we will need business leaders with a steady moral gyroscope and business leaders with personal, internal, self-imposed, and, yes, absolute standards."[30]

Internalizing that belief system would require a mass Pauline conversion, an enormous undertaking with only a partial chance of success. Shifting the balance of power within the corporation from executives to the board in itself will not be enough to effect meaningful change. Unless the nodal links that make up the interlocking networks internalize the value of dissent, the result will be an emphasis on confirming the bureaucratic process to the letter. As Jeffrey Sonnenfield, Dean of Executive Education at the Yale School of Management, has argued, "the key isn't structural, it's social. I'm always amazed at how common group-think is in corporate boardrooms. Directors are almost without exception intelligent,

---

[29] Matt Ridley, *Nature Via Nurture: Genes, Experience and What Makes Us Human* (Fourth Estate, London, 2003).

[30] Peter Peterson, "A personal postscript", *Conference Board Commission on Public Trust and Private Enterprise*, 12 March 2003, p. 16.

accomplished and comfortable with power – but if you put them into a group that discourages dissent, they nearly always start to conform."[31]

The row over Sandy Weill's short-lived nomination to the Board of Directors of the New York Stock Exchange (NYSE) in March 2003 indicates the limits of corporate proselyte. Weill, the chairman of the financial conglomerate Citigroup, had presided over a corporation in receipt of the biggest fine levied for regulatory violations as a consequence of the conflicts of interest investigations. Yet the NYSE accepted his nomination to the board. In effect, Weill was being corporately absolved without the discomfiture of penance. The nomination provoked outrage from the New York Attorney General. Weill withdrew the nomination to avoid further embarrassment. The incident itself was exceptionally revealing about the network process. As a leading investment banker, Weill has undoubted managerial skills that make him a valuable addition to any board. The fact that the nominating committee of the NYSE contemplated his suitability for such a sensitive post at such a sensitive time was a very public sign of support to the beleaguered chief executive that for the leading manifestation of the market partnership at least, Sandy Weill was judged absolved from corporate sin. This raises even more disturbing questions about whether the socialization process has so conditioned the major players in the corporate power game that appeals from regulators have little more than rhetorical appeal. It also demonstrates an arrogant contempt for public opinion, a further indication of the unstoppable rise to dominance of corporate America as forecast by Justice Brandeis in his 1932 judgment.

The scale of the malfeasance in the United States has comprehensively falsified the canard that corruption, particularly in the private sector, is best tackled through the placing of an inordinate emphasis on tackling predatory crime, such as the payments of bribes to low-level officials. The most insidious form of corruption has been in the systematic evasion of regulatory oversight. Overloaded and under-

---

[31] Quoted in Carol Hymowitz, "Changing the rules", *Wall Street Journal*, 24 February 2003.

staffed, the regulatory authorities are compromised from the beginning because of the need to rely on the accuracy of the information provided, the constant exchange between regulatory bodies and those who are being invigilated without a cooling off period and the political support given to corporations. Corporations therefore "influence directly through campaign contributions and lobbying of politicians, and indirectly through information designed to mould public opinion, both the shape of regulatory legislation and the degree of enthusiasm with which it is enforced."[32]

Corporate governance has become one of the most important political issues in the United States, a fact acknowledged by Paul Atkins, a commissioner in the SEC: "Sarbanes–Oxley contains many advances for corporate governance, although it represents what formerly would have been an unimaginable incursion of the US federal government into the corporate governance arena."[33] Commissioner Atkins' stresses not only the importance of what he terms the tone from the top, in terms of inculcating a corporate culture, but he also

---

[32] Ibid., p. 94.

[33] Paul S. Atkins, "The Sarbanes–Oxley Act of 2002: Goals, content, and status of implementation", *International Financial Law Review*, 25 March 2003. In a previous speech, Commissioner Atkins maintained the inability of the market to police itself left the government no alternative: "My first inclination is to encourage reasonable self-regulation, rather than government-imposed mandates. Yet I recognise that self-regulation alone may not always be sufficient. Consistent with my market-oriented philosophy, my preference would have been for the profession [accountants] to regulate and police itself. Yet because the professionals fell down on the job – after they had ample warning from regulators and the marketplace – Congress called upon us to act." Atkins, however, made clear that he was going to invigilate the enforcement department of the SEC to ensure that "enforcement actions do not serve as an alternative means of rule making. I intend to assess enforcement actions to ensure that the alleged illegal conduct *does* clearly violate the law and to verify that the action is not an inappropriate extension of the law" (remarks by Paul Atkins at the conference *The SEC Speaks in 2003, Washington, DC, 28 February 2003*). Both speeches are heavily influenced by Robert Higgs, *Crisis and Leviathan* (Oxford University Press, New York, 1989), a seminal tract that argued that governments traditionally use crises to extend their own power, a development that was counterproductive to economic growth. The full texts of both speeches are available online at http://www.sec.gov/news/speeches.html

recognizes explicitly that "morality and ethics cannot be legislated into existence. Government controls alone – too often paternalistic – will never be a solution if individuals and individual firms are not upholding their own end of simple business ethics through their own effective compliance. Internal controls and the culture of an organisation are basic structural aspects to reinforce the inherent nature of most people to do the right thing." This a crucial insight. The failure of effective oversight and the fascination with meeting the Wall Street "number" created the circumstances for a culture of impunity to take hold. Financial engineering was an accepted reality. No-one, except the short-sellers who profited from betting that a firm will decline in value because of unanswered questions in the publicly available information, probed the consequences of a system that rationalized profoundly irrational behaviour, a process that led to a yawning gap between projected earnings and underlying fundamentals.[34] The fall of Enron and the forced restatements of earnings suggest that several hundred billion dollars were artificially added to profits, a development that added to the boom. Indeed, after the NASDAQ crash, the pressure to meet the numbers became more, rather than less intense. This in turn suggests an urgent need to unpack the various components of the corporate network.

Economic crime necessitates what Naylor terms "a complex series of interrelated actions in which various participants perform a host of different roles that have different degrees of importance and show different degrees of awareness and involvement."[35] For Naylor it is necessary to define whether the activity constitutes a crime, identify who was responsible and, thirdly, create more efficient legislative and regulatory rules to ensure deterrence and prevention. Unless such a

---

[34] See Alex Berenson, *The Number, How the Drive for Quarterly Earnings Corrupted Wall Street and Corporate America* (Random House, New York, 2003), p. 205. The author, a financial investigative reporter with the *New York Times*, concludes, "the ideal of transparency and disclosure enshrined in the securities laws had been forgotten; 10-Qs and 10-Ys [compulsory quarterly and yearly returns filled with the SEC] had become a funhouse mirror" (p. 209).

[35] R. T. Naylor, "Towards a general theory of profit-driven crimes", *British Journal of Criminology*, Vol. 43, p. 83, 2003.

systematic approach is taken to map the terrain, an over-reliance on outdated legislation will allow for the continuance of bad practice. In this sense Naylor is undoubtedly correct in noting that the real poison of corruption centres not on the payment of bribes, but rather on "regulatory offences, often quite distinct from those enumerated in the criminal codes of most countries, in which case it takes a form particularly difficult to root out."[36] In essence then, effective corporate governance involves rendering the exercise of power accountable in a system whose defining characteristic is the separation of ownership from control. The essential difficulty in ensuring compliance became apparent with the $1.4bn restatement of accounts by the health provider HealthSouth in March 2003. It demonstrated that the pressure to meet Wall Street expectations remains a crucial determinant of corporate policy, despite the legislation passed after the first wave of scandal necessitating executives to vouch for the accuracy of company accounts.[37]

In the longer term, the financial crisis has profound implications for the interchangeable political and economic elite, a grouping denigrated by the financial historian Niall Ferguson as "the new CEOcracy."[38] In some respects, both President George Bush and his Vice-President Dick Cheney personify that new sociological grouping. On the face of it, 2002 was an excellent year for George W. Bush. After a shaky first nine months in office, during which international treaties were torn up and his economic programme produced desultory results, the taint of an interloper appeared indelible. When coupled with unease before the microphones, unless heavily pre-scripted and choreographed, he displayed the attributes of an accidental president: a dangerous dilettante who occupied the White House by default. All that was transformed, totally, by the events of September 11, 2001. The terrorist attacks on New York and Washington DC offered the 43rd president of the United States an opportunity to prove his critics

---

[36] Ibid., p. 94.
[37] See Andrew Hill, "Corporate scandals back in the headlines", *Financial Times*, 25 March 2003.
[38] Niall Ferguson, "Full Marx", *Financial Times*, 17 August 2002.

wrong. Not only did he rise to the challenge posed by the most serious assault on the defences of the country in its history, but in the process displayed a level of political acumen hitherto unacknowledged. The implosion of corporate America and the questions surrounding his own involvement in shady business practices, now decried for turning American business into the raw material for scandal sheets, were brushed aside as the presidency sought to define itself by reference to foreign policy, first in Afghanistan, now in Iraq. As the war on terrorism lost its nebulous intellectual underpinnings in favour of a tangible, if tangentially implicated foe, resolute action and the rhetoric of a president at war fundamentally transformed the administration.

In a calculated campaign, Bush turned the November 2002 midterm elections into a referendum on his post-9/11 leadership. All the political capital raised during the traumatic aftermath of the terrorist attacks was risked in a battle for the popular legitimacy so lacking in 2000, when his opponent won the popular vote and a controversial Supreme Court decision precluding the count of disputed votes in Florida gave victory to the Republican candidate. On a parallel track, Bush introduced massive economic restructuring through a $1.4bn tax reduction. Designed to act as a stimulus to a depressed economy, it also had the effect of disproportionately benefiting corporate America. Corporate donors responded with a major increase in campaign funding for the Republicans, which in turn rendered the economy subservient to the need to support a wartime president. Breaking campaign finance records, Bush personally raised and spent over $140m in securing control over all three branches of government in November. What the president intends to do with his increased mandate once the winds of change settle is another matter entirely. Looking ahead, the outlook at home and abroad looks far from certain.

The true extent of the catastrophe facing the American financial markets has been – and continues to be – masked by the pursuit of the war against terrorism. The defenestration of Saddam Hussein has provided a tangible target on which to vent America's undiminished rage. As a palliative to the uncertainty, the Iraqi doctrine based on a pre-emptive strike and a stated willingness to breach international law, if circumstances deem it necessary, served, therefore, a very clear purpose. This is not to suggest that the war was deliberately concocted. Rather, the rhetoric contained within it an inexorable escalation imperative that alienated international partners and made unilateral military engagement inevitable. Simultaneously, the emphasis on high-profile arrests and exemplary punitive sanctions provided visual cover for a decided unwillingness to tackle the pressing, intractable systemic problems on the home front. Inability to cut the Gordian knot with interested money curtailed the possibility of the change necessary to restore integrity to corporate America.

The subservience of the Democrats to the same sources of money, as vividly demonstrated by the catholic dispersal of Enron largesse, ensured the cry for reform sounded increasingly hollow.[39] To make matters worse, the tinge of political scandal impacted most of all on two high-profile Democratic politicians. James Trafficant, a representative from Ohio was expelled from Congress in July, following his conviction three months earlier in Cleveland on petty racketeering charges.[40] On the west bank of the Hudson, overlooking the epicentre of American finance, a much more debilitating scandal centred on Bob Torricelli, a highly ambitious senator from New Jersey, over campaign finance violations dating back to 1996. Until

---

[39] Given the similarity, the American political system displayed the attributes of a cartel. As Michael Johnston has pointed out, "colluding parties are never wholly on or out of power, there's little to gain and potentially much to lose (both legitimate and illegitimate) by disrupting the linkages and deals that sustain the cartel." See Michael Johnston, "Party systems, competition and political checks", in Arnold Heidenheimer and Michael Johnston (eds) *Political Corruption: Concepts and Contexts* (Transaction Books, Brunswick, NJ, 2002), p. 786.

[40] Robert Pierre and Juliet Eilperin, "Trafficant is found guilty", *Washington Post*, 12 April 2002; Juliet Eilperin, "House votes 420 to 1 to expel Trafficant", *Washington Post*, 25 July 2002. Trafficant was one of the most colourful characters in Congress. Staggeringly, he was elected in 1984 after successfully rebuffing charges that he was in hock to organized crime. He accepted he had received $169,000 from mob sources while a sheriff, but claimed he was conducting a single-handed sting operation.

his resignation weeks before polling, the Democratic leadership gave him considerable support, making allegations of Republican graft difficult, if not impossible to sustain. For Mark Elias, a political lawyer who defended Torricelli, the New Jersey senator was simply a victim of unfortunate timing and an unacceptable conflation of incommensurable events:

> The timing cut Torricelli in different ways. While the allegations had nothing to do with Enron, he found it impossible to get his message out. In political science terms the dependent variable was press coverage. In 1996–97 after the DNC investigation, any contribution from an Asian was worthy of investigation. Likewise today a lot of the people covering the Wall Street scandals live in the same state that Torricelli hails from. The morphing of coverage was not coincidental even though the underlying conduct is not connected.[41]

While neither politician had any direct involvement in the corporate scandal, the guilt by association severely limited the efficacy of any attempt to raise fundamental questions about ethical behaviour in accepting corporate contributions. Beyond the specifics, however, lies the central issue of influence peddling. Neither party was prepared to face the logical conclusion. There was a limit to the official investigation into contemporary links, even when executive connections, such as Dick Cheney's links to Halliburton, placed the issue firmly in the media spotlight that paralleled the later investigation into attempts by Michael Oxley to place a Republican lobbyist in the heart of a K Street (the thoroughfare housing most lobbying operations in Washington) office.[42] Ultimately, it was the combination of executive stonewalling, the reluctant acceptance of this state of affairs by the wider media and, by extension, the agenda forged by the White House that destroyed the Democrats' electoral strategy.

With tactical brilliance that owed much to the acute political strategic skills of his chief advisor, Karl Rove, Bush invigorated his presidency by ensuring that foreign policy dominated the media

---

[41] Interview with Mark Elias, Washington, DC, September 2003.

[42] Cheney's links to Halliburton resurfaced in March 2003 when it emerged that Halliburton was awarded a lucrative contract to extinguish fires on sabotaged oil wells in Iraq. The contract was not subject to public tender.

agenda, while simultaneously downgrading the importance of the corporate governance crisis by divesting it of its structural nature. The cynicism has prompted former Republican pollster turned historian Kevin Phillips to conclude in his impressive political history of the American rich that the Achilles heel in American capitalism is its increasing reliance on finance, both as a motor of economic growth and as the main net contributor to political funding. "Patriotism and *rage militaire* are a second track along which Middle American radicalism and frustration can vent itself. But the economics will out."[43]

The collapse of Enron, therefore, it is argued, served to open a Pandora's Box. It revealed that the corruption was not simply the result of corrupted individuals manipulating their companies, outside auditors, general counsel and the market itself. Enron is a symptom of the corrupting tendencies endemic in the business and political model, not the cause; a point underscored by the fact that of the 248 senators and representatives now investigating Enron, 212 received contributions from the Houston conglomerate.[44] So sophisticated had Enron's lobbying operation become prior to its collapse that it had developed a software programme, internally termed "the Matrix". The programme tracked every proposed change in federal legislation and automatically produced a cost–benefit analysis for the firm. The economist who developed the programme that computed the bottom line and provided detailed information as to whether or not to deploy Enron's formidable lobbying machine told the *Washington Post*, "it was a new thing to be able to quantify the regulatory risk."[45]

Quantifying the political cost of this enormous power to influence, or more accurately distort, the deliberative process is a much more complicated affair. Despite a number of high-profile arrests and impending prosecutions, scant attention has been paid to the underlying malaise, a phenomena identified by the American sociologist, Edward

---

[43] Kevin Phillips, *Wealth and Democracy, A Political History of the American Rich* (Broadway Books, New York, 2002), p. 401.
[44] Mark Green, *Selling Out* (HarperCollins, New York, 2002), p. 202.
[45] Joe Stephens, "Hard money, strong arms and 'Matrix'", *Washington Post*, 10 February 2002.

Ross, in an article for the *Atlantic Monthly* in 1907. Coining the phrase "criminaloid" to characterize corporate crime, Ross's polemic retains its vividness and essential truth:

> Secure in his quilted armour of lawyer-spun sophistries, the criminaloid promulgates an ethics, which the public hails as a disinterested contribution to the philosophy of conduct. He invokes a pseudo-Darwinism to sanction the revival of outlawed and bygone tactics of struggle. Ideals of fellowship and peace are "unscientific." To win the game with the aid of a sleeveful of aces proves one's fitness to survive. A sack of spoils is nature's patent of nobility ... The criminaloid is really a borderer between the camps of good and evil, and this is why he is so interesting. To run him to ground and brand him, as long ago pirates and traitors were branded, is the crying need of our time. For this Anak among malefactors, working unchecked in the rich field of sinister opportunities opened up by latter-day conditions, is society's most dangerous foe, more redoubtable by far than the plain criminal, because he sports the livery of virtue and operates on a Titanic scale.[46]

The first difficulty to overcome is how to define corruption. At what stage does an action become corrupt and how do you stop the entire fabric of politics from itself being labelled as corrupt as opposed to being susceptible to corruption?[47] This is particularly the case in a political system like the Unites States, where the combination of an executive presidency and the ever-increasing demands to secure financing to run for office have resulted in the atomization of the party structure.[48] American political parties are weak facsimiles of their European counterparts. "The traditional distinctions between the roles of political parties and interest groups have almost disappeared as interest groups have sought to determine the choice of candidates and the outcome of elections. The dependence of

---

[46] Edward Ross, "The criminaloid", *The Atlantic Monthly*, January 1907, pp. 44–50.

[47] Mark Philp, "Defining corruption", in Paul Heywood (ed.) *Political Corruption* (Blackwell, Oxford, UK, 1997), pp. 20–46.

[48] One manifestation of this weakening of the party structure and the increasing dominance of individual campaigns is the expansion of ticket splitting. For survey evidence see Martin Wattenberg, *The Decline of American Political Parties 1952–94* (Harvard University Press, Boston, 1996), pp. 17–28. It is precisely because the Republicans bucked the trend by capturing all three branches of the executive in November 2002 that merits attention. See Chapter 6.

politicians on private contributions mean that they are not well placed to resist the demands of institutionalized lobbyists. Empirical evidence by political scientists suggests that 'electoral performances seem increasingly to be the product of their own situations, opponents and campaigns'."[49] Given the increasing reliance on negative campaigning, the cost of taking positions at variance with the conventional wisdom or world view associated with the corporate sector is one few candidates are prepared to take. With the agenda skewed in advance, the consequences for the quality of political discourse and the interrelationship between the various actors – corporate, political and civil society – are profoundly disturbing.

It is therefore necessary to factor into the analysis a systematic examination of the structural bias in American politics. This addition raises fundamental questions about the validity of traditional models used for measuring corruption. Apportioning responsibility for the crisis in the capital markets is therefore increasingly problematic without providing an overview of the way in which formal and informal networks combine to discretely ensure that any legal or regulatory change will not lead to a diminution of power and influence. Three major paradigms, or theories, have been developed to describe the circumstances in which corruption thrives: public office, public interest and market models. While each provides a useful lens to examine the nature of the corruption in the American political and business circles, none on its own offers full explanatory power. There is therefore an imperative to place the analysis within a broader theory of the role of the state and the mechanism through which power is exercised.

The most widely used definition of political corruption comes from the American political scientist Joseph Nye:

> Corruption is behavior which deviates from the formal duties of a public role because of private-regarding (personal, close family, private clique) pecuniary

---

[49] Susan Welch and John R. Hibbing, "The effect of charges of corruption on voting behaviour in congressional elections 1982–1990", *Journal of Politics*, Vol. 59, No. 1, February, p. 228.

or status gains; or violates rules against the exercise of certain types of private regarding influence. This includes such behavior as bribery (use of a reward to pervert the judgement of a person in a position of trust); nepotism (bestowal of patronage by reasons of ascriptive relationship rather than merit); and misappropriation (illegal appropriation of public resources for private regarding purposes).[50]

This framework, positing that corruption results from the malign manipulations of debased individuals, has certain obvious benefits for the economic and political elites. According to this view, officials – elected and bureaucratic – who subvert the public good for private gain destroy public confidence in the efficacy of the state's ability to be an independent arbiter of competing claims. In the process, limited but corrosive actions destroy the legitimacy of an essentially rational political system. This explanation has the advantage of being both limiting and self-serving: it diverts attention from questions surrounding the systemic nature of the problem and minimizes the responsibility of the system itself for contributing to or exacerbating the extent of the malaise.

It was a world view self-consciously put forward by the political elite in Washington at the early stages of the corporate meltdown in 2001 and 2002. But, as the list of corporate failures grew and the complex mechanisms used in the financial engineering were progressively exposed, the drawback of relying on this model became ever more apparent. Much to the chagrin of the interchangeable business and political elite in the United States, it is necessary to look more deeply for the fundamental causes of the problem, a search that inevitably leads one to the financing of the political system itself. As Robert Williams has pointed out, "if private money in public elections is the major source of sleaze where elected politicians are concerned, the appointment of political executives raises other difficulties. Clearly if appointees come from the world of business or corporate law, they will have a variety of contacts and connections which may

---

[50] Joseph Nye, "Corruption and political development: A cost benefit analysis", *American Political Science Review*, Vol. LXI, No. 2, p. 419.

raise questions of conflicts of interest."[51] The revolving of the door back and forward is almost certainly bound to create what Wilson terms "ethical confusion".[52]

The expansion of the reporting of corruption has enhanced considerably the literature, but a catch-all definition of what political corruption entails beyond the bureaucratic sphere has proved maddeningly elusive. Although the public office definition retains its potency in dealing with inappropriate behaviour within the bureaucracy, its relevance is devalued when attempts are made to apply it to situations where the law itself is either silent on the activity being analysed or in understanding the political dynamic by which laws are actually framed. Determining what is corruption on the basis of legal definitions without giving due cognizance to how legislation is enacted, amended or repealed may have the benefit of precision, but lacks explaining the actual operation of power.[53] Attempting to broaden the definition, however, provides a separate set of conundrums for the researcher. This is particularly the case when the gain is party political rather than personal. Just as a public office solution is too narrow, definitions based on a public interest defence are too elastic and prone to manipulation to have meaning.

The third major school of thought in relation to corruption is that of economic models. Economic theory has opened useful avenues with principal agent theory. Its main exponents are the economists Susan Rose Ackerman and Robert Klitgaard. Klitgaard argues "this approach defines corruption in terms of the divergence between the principal's or the public's interests and those of the civil servant: corruption occurs when one agent betrays the principal's interest in pursuit of her own."[54] Seen from this perspective, the operation of American

---

[51] Robert Williams, "Private interests and public office: The American experience of sleaze", *Parliamentary Affairs*, Vol. 48, No. 4, October 1995, p. 646.

[52] Ibid., p. 646.

[53] Stephen Lukes, *Power, A Radical View* (Macmillan, London, 1974).

[54] R. E. Klitgaard, *Controlling Corruption* (University of California Press. Berkeley, CA, 1988), p. 24. See also Susan Rose Ackerman, *Corruption and Government* (Cambridge University Press, Cambridge, UK, 1999).

capitalism in the dispensation of stock options is clearly an example of this definition in action. The executives (agents) charged with managing the firm in the best interests of the shareholders (principals) were excessively rewarded to the detriment of shareholders, and the artificially boosted profits provided added risk to the principal if and when the fraudulent manipulation of the books was discovered. The definition is equally useful in examining how the merchant banks manipulated the research to dupe institutional investors.

However, it does not take us to the level of the political market-place. Nor does it bring us closer to an adequate definition that reflects actual political practice, mainly because it is difficult to ascertain the roles of the political players. If a politician ensures legislative change after receiving payments from a particular source, union or corporate, but discloses the payment and argues the change is in the public interest, just who or what is the principal? If the party is deemed subservient to those who fund it, there is no conflict; if on the other hand the payment is disclosed and a cogent policy reason is given for the change, how does one differentiate a legitimate political preference from corruption. Thus, for Robert Williams, "principal–agent analysis identifies corruption as occurring when agents betray principals but it leaves open the question of how to determine what constitutes corruption by principals. The omission is a reminder of how concepts of corruption fit awkwardly with political practice."[55]

The difficulties are magnified precisely because everyone is doing it and, secondly, in the context of intense partisan debate "allegations of abuse are rife and, once made, tend to lead to counter-allegations". In this context, two avenues emerge: either the charge is rendered in-effective because of the existence of evidence that contributions were elicited from the same source, or a "puritan plague infects the body politic" and "forms of behaviour which were once acceptable are judged by new rules and found wanting. Politicians who fail to make a nimble enough transition from the old practices to the new

[55] Robert Williams, "New concepts for old?", *Third World Quarterly*, Vol. 20, No. 3, p. 509.

are those most likely to be identified as associated with sleaze. But this identification may well have more to do with the timing than the substance of their actions."[56]

This problem is minimized however by refocusing the problem of political corruption to incorporate the proactive role played by politicians themselves in creating and maintaining the system. It allows the analysis to move beyond the anecdotal to provide a systemic explanation. Crucially, it also demonstrates why reform has proved so elusive: political corruption is a two-way process in which the politicians themselves have exacerbated the role played by money in American politics by their constant attempts to extort it from the very industries with most to fear from government regulation. It is no coincidence that the sectors most affected by what the NYSE calls the "meltdown of significant companies due to failures of diligence, ethics and controls" are those that thrived because of changes in the legislative climate: in the 1990s telecommunications, banking and energy.[57] The corporate governance crisis therefore extends well beyond the boardroom and stretches inexorably to the nation's capital itself.

Central to its operation is a sophisticated "rent extraction process" developed by Fred McChesney, in which "politicians are seen not as mere brokers redistributing wealth in response to competing private demands, but as independent actors making their own demands to which private actors respond."[58] Seen from this perspective the operation of Congress has become a form of political extortion through which companies are as likely to pay up to prevent legislation as to introduce it. Rather than limited to spectacular but limited cases of malfeasance, the cost of electioneering in the United States has done much to inculcate and exacerbate the deleterious effects of a skewed

[56] Robert Williams, "Private interests and public office: The American experience of sleaze", *Parliamentary Affairs*, Vol. 48, No. 4, October 1995, p. 632.

[56] NYSE Corporate Governance Rule Proposals (1 August 2002), accessible online at http://www.nyse.comGuidelines/

[58] Fred McChesney, *Money for Nothing, Politicians, Rent Extraction and Political Extortion* (Harvard University Press, London, 1997), p. 157.

and corrosive system that, without paradigmatic change, is incapable of reform.

In this context, therefore, it is imperative the analysis provides a critical account of the pivotal role played by ideology as a cloak to disguise special interest pleading. Ideological battles are accentuated precisely because there is a consensus on the common core values but fundamental division over whether government is part of the problem or the solution. While the pursuit of equality, liberty and fairness before the law is central to American conceptions of the state, an innate distrust of politicians and government is deeply embedded in the fabric of society. As James Madison has pointed out, "If men were angels, no government would be necessary. If angels were to govern men, neither external nor internal controls on government would be necessary." Working from the assumption that man is inherently corrupt, the question to be addressed is how to control those who govern. This was to be achieved by a comprehensive separation of powers to curb any potential abuse emanating from a concentration of power. This in turn feeds into acute debate over the reach and extent of governmental interference. What the historian Samuel Huntington terms the "anti-power ethos" was, and remains, a key weapon in the ideological battle over regulation.[59]

One of the major reasons for Bill Clinton's ability to ensure that the Democrats could compete effectively in the 1992–2000 period was the Democratic acceptance of the hegemonic conception conceived by corporate America and delivered by a political system that ensured that the range of available options was delineated on its terms. In a subtle reworking of Gramsci, the "Modern Prince" is conceived, not as a political party, but as corporate manipulation.[60] It is precisely for this reason that Gramsci offers a powerful lens to examine American politics.

Ideological disputes are by definition constant with battles of

---

[59] Samuel Huntington, *American Politics, The Promise of Disharmony* (Harvard University Press, Cambridge, MA), pp. 33–8.

[60] Antonio Gramsci, *Selections from the Prison Notebooks* (Lawrence & Wishart, London, 1998), p. 133.

position waged over the legitimacy of current practice. The scale of the problems exposed on Wall Street has ensured that legislative change is both necessary and inevitable. It also raises fundamental questions about political legitimacy.[61] Following the limited response by the political establishment to the corruption of the marketplace, opportunities existed for ideological entrepreneurs, most notably the combative Attorney General for New York, Eliot Spitzer, to carve out ideological space that is deeply threatening to the established order. While it is also true that the probes into the operation of Wall Street provided the Attorney General with a populist crusade, which served to provide him with a bespoke political base, there can be little doubt at this stage that the systemic conflicts of interest point to a criminal conspiracy to defraud the market.

As such, it warrants a potential prosecution under the draconian Racketeering and Corrupt Organization Act (RICO), seminal legislation designed to combat the influence of organized crime in the United States. Under the terms of RICO, prosecutors merely have to demonstrate a pattern of activity. Prosecuting the investment banks, however, raises deeply disturbing questions about the probity of the entire system, hence the attempts to circumscribe the extent of the investigation and the desire to settle in order to preclude the mounting of a criminal case. This *ex post facto* criminalization of once-accepted practice provides a textbook example of how conceptions of corruption change over time. This in effect makes the search for definitions a political as well as an analytical process and feeds back into Gramscian wars of position.[62]

Politicians themselves remain exceptionally reticent about admitting any wrongdoing, or even unethical behaviour. There has been no serious investigation into the role played by the politicians themselves in inculcating the business model in the first place owing to their subservience to "interested money", or the corrosive effect of what

---

[61] Ian Lustick, *Unsettled States, Disputed Lands* (Cornell University Press, Ithaca, NY, 1993), pp. 123–4.

[62] Michael Johnston, "The search for definitions: The vitality of politics and the issue of corruption", *International Social Science Journal*, Vol. 149, September, p. 321.

Scott terms "corruption as influence".[63] This was underscored by the allegation that the Chairman of the House Finance Committee, Michael Oxley, had attempted to persuade a mutual fund trade association to sack its chief lobbyist in Washington and replace her with a Republican candidate.

A report in the *Washington Post* suggested the decision was linked to a calculation that the money expended by the industry should reflect the new political realities following the Republicans' success at the mid-term elections.[64] In return, aides to the committee chairman were alleged to have suggested that a congressional inquiry into mutual fund industry practices might cease. According to the *Post*, the heavy-handed attempt, which Oxley's office rejected as rumour-mongering, was part of an attempt by the Republicans to establish its own "Matrix", tracking the political leanings of lobbyists. The data provided by the "K Street Project" were to be used to gain or curtail access to policy-makers. Attempts by public integrity watchdogs such as Common Cause to get the issue investigated by the House Ethics Committee failed because of a truce between the two parties, which precluded each side from tabling ethics violations. In an email alert posted on 5 March 2003, the Common Cause Acting President, Don Simon, complained vociferously at the failure of the Democrats to lodge a formal complaint. "A system in which there is no enforcement unless a complaint is filed, but the two parties have colluded to avoid filing complaints, is a system that badly disserves the public interest," he wrote.[65] The primary reason for the Democrats' reluctance to file a complaint was that it could ignite a destabilizing turf war, bringing both parties into higher levels of disrepute. The matter was to be quietly swept under the plush carpets of Capital Hill. The Oxley row was indicative of the inability of Congress to deal with potential

---

[63] James C. Scott, *Comparative Political Corruption* (Prentice Hall, Englewood Cliffs, NJ, 1972), p. 21.

[64] Kathleen Day and Jim VandeHei, "Congressman urges Republican lobbyist, Oxley staff pressuring mutual funds", *Washington Post*, 15 February 2003.

[65] Common Cause, *CauseWire*, 5 March 2003.

egregious complaints, a situation that occurs even when the Ethics Committee meets.

The reliance on legally enforceable edicts to ensure compliance is a pivotal part of the American political process and the operation of the Ethics Committee. At stake therefore in any investigation of wrong-doing is whether the act complained of transgressed the requisite statute. To be effective it requires "an institutionalized system of standards, investigation and sanction."[66] The effectiveness of the system is reduced, however, if enforcement is ruled out because of a political truce. Interested money is the oil of politics, and the elimination of legislative independence is at the heart of the conflict-of-interest problem. "The main weakness of the edict system is that it does not encourage much reflection on the content of these rules. Having overcome the obstacles to producing a body of rules in the first place, legislators are reluctant to then subject them to detailed scrutiny or to evaluate their contribution to political morality."[67]

This delineated approach risks inculcating the attitude that what is not prescriptively prohibited is acceptable. As noted above in relation to the corporate world, disclosure does not in itself end conflict. Thus the pursuit of investigations based on whether disclosure has been made spectacularly misses the point. If the working assumption is that once these criteria are satisfied the content of disclosures becomes a matter to be judged by constituents, the wider public and a vigilant media, ethical underpinning remains absent. In determining how to guard the guardians, the Senate Ethics Committee provides a salutary lesson in political failure.

The book begins with an investigation of the causes of the rot on Wall Street and extends to provide evidence that Enron should be viewed as a symptom rather than the cause of the problem in the financial marketplace. Chapter 3 takes us into the political world, examining a political corruption trial in Rhode Island that has

---

[66] Michael M. Atkinson and Maureen Mancuso, "Edicts and etiquette: Regulating conflict of interest in Congress and the House of Commons", *Corruption and Reform*, Vol. 7, 1992, p. 3.

[67] Ibid., p. 14.

profound implications for the policy-makers. Chapters 4 and 5 then assess whether the conflicts of interest on Wall Street demonstrate the hallmarks of a "criminal enterprise", as defined by RICO, and provide a critical analysis of political interference in the judicial plane. Chapters 6 and 7 provide an assessment of the political economy of corruption in the United States.

The implosion of corporate America in the aftermath of the fall of Enron has demonstrated the pressing need for cross-disciplinary research in which the forensic capabilities of management, accountancy, law and business are married with political science in order to maximize our understanding of the macro- and micro-picture. In the process, the research becomes not only more relevant but also more focused. In short, we are entering a difficult and intellectually challenging period, in which the quality of new cross-fertilized research has the potential to fundamentally determine policy outcomes. This book is a first step in that direction.

1

Assessing guilt:
the Wall Street shakedown

A life-size, cast bronze bull stands incongruously in the heart of the New York financial district, poised as if to charge past the skyscrapers enveloping Wall Street and escape up Broadway, the arterial centre of Manhattan. For many of the tourists taking photographs of each other draped on the rippled bronze, the flared nostrils and aggressive stance are symbolic of the underlying strength of the American political and economic systems. The architecture that frames the shot, while dramatic, is immaterial. For the corporate and political elite, the positioning of the bull has a much darker meaning. It underscores the short distance between success and failure, honesty and graft, confidence and crisis in American governance. The fallout associated with the corporate malfeasance that has destroyed the credibility of financial reporting since the collapse of Enron in October 2001 has been subject to unprecedented investigation in two buildings in the shadow of the bull: the office of the New York State Attorney General and the Federal Bankruptcy Court.

The potential impact of the inquiries cast a heavy pall over the hubris associated with the extraordinary growth of the American economy on the cusp of the 21st century. When combined with a class action involving a claim for $25bn currently being adjudicated in Enron's hometown of Houston, it is clear that the nature of American capitalism itself is facing an unprecedented assault. The bull market has not only been tamed but humiliated by the exposure of the sharp practice and conflicts of interest that had become integral, but hidden, weapons in the armoury of the corporate matadors.

One of the most combative class action lawyers in the United States William Lerach, a partner with Milberg Weiss Bershad Hynes and Lerach, put the point succinctly in a recent address to Stanford Law School. The collapse of Enron, he intoned, was simply a manifestation of the unsavoury reality of the bull market: "Even in those halcyon days, there were a few of us – viewed as cranks at the time – who warned that underneath this veneer of prosperity and profit actually lay widespread accounting rot, falsified profits, inflated asset values, and executive chicanery which would collapse the system. What happened did not happen by accident, and a full accounting is owed to the people who were fleeced."[1]

The sudden decline and fall of Enron, from symbol of strength and innovation to talisman for organizational dysfunction was played out in real time to a disbelieving world. It provided evidence that something was very seriously wrong in corporate America. How wrong would take a further year to reveal. Blue-chip companies became chipped; behind the thin veneer of respectability lurked an interlinked business and political culture that placed greater store on maximizing revenue than in revealing the sources of that generation. Spreading outward from the corrupted core of Enron and replicating like an uncontrollable virus, the integrity of the American corporate model has been seriously undermined. Responsibility for the malaise

---

[1] Quoted in Carl Cannon, "Letter from Washington: Suits vs. suits", *Forbes*, 7 October 2002. Lerach's methods raised the ire of many in the corporate world. See, for example, Editorial, "Lerach's Enron gambit", *Wall Street Journal*, 6 February 2002, which likens the decision by Caplers, the Californian public pension fund, to retaining his services as a "wildebeest hiring hyenas as bodyguards". A second editorial in April warned the Regents of the University of California that in dealing with Lerach, "when you lie down with lawyers, you catch ethical fleas." Castigating the lawyer, the editorial asked rhetorically of the California Regents, "Do they really want to patronize Mr Lerach's latest effort to engulf corporate America in a tide of lawsuits primarily for the benefit of the lawyers. This can't be a good thing for the rest of the University of California's stock portfolio." See Editorial, "Lerach's Enron sweep", *Wall Street Journal*, 17 April 2002.

goes much further than the board of Enron and the other spectacular cases of material and moral corporate bankruptcy.

Faced with accusations from the New York State Attorney General Eliot Spitzer that the leading investment banks in the country effectively ran a criminal enterprise designed to mislead individual investors, a co-ordinated investigation was belatedly established among the disparate regulators of the most sophisticated securities market in the world. The wider investigations were launched in April 2002 after Spitzer had secured a $100m settlement from Merrill Lynch for issuing "buy" recommendations for stocks that its senior Internet analyst Henry Blodget had decried in private emails as "a piece of junk", a "dog" or, with vulgar precision, "crap". The skill in bringing the case catapulted the issue of regulating Wall Street to the top of the agenda and the grudging admiration of senior compliance officers in the merchant banks. As the head of the legal department at one major investment bank in New York explains, there is no doubt that the Merrill case marked a watershed:

> Every so often a case comes up that you just know is so important and it's so attention grabbing, so monumental that it is at the heart of something big. He found those emails, he brought this case. Everybody knew that everyone was going to get investigated and that laws were coming. It doesn't surprise me. He should get a lot of credit for it. He brought a great case back then.[2]

The investigation into Merrill had provided prima facie evidence that not only was there a direct connection between recommending stock for companies that already had investment business with the firm but the obverse was also true. Stock ratings could be reduced if the firms did not utilize the mercantile facilities. Much more seriously, ratings could change if the companies changed mercantile facilities, an effective form of blackmail. Merrill settled without admitting liability, but the release of the documents ensured that a wider investigation needed to be carried out. The potential implications of exposing the rot within Wall Street were spelled out in an address to the New York

---

[2] Interview, New York City, 7 February 2003.

judiciary in May 2002. Spitzer complained that there has been "a gradual dissipation of standards and ethics ... driven by an obsessive desire to get quarterly numbers up." For Spitzer, who has chosen negotiation rather than prosecution to clean up Wall Street, the malaise occasioned by conflicts of interest, deceit and fraud can be traced directly to "the pressures of competition", which were exacerbated precisely because of "a lack of definable boundaries of acceptable behaviour."[3]

In an attempt to redress the balance, Spitzer joined forces with the Securities and Exchange Commission (SEC) and other regulatory bodies to assess the extent of the problem and determine a "global settlement". The investigation proved pivotal in providing a revealing glimpse of the reality behind the rise to dominance of finance as the primary motor of economic growth. It also served to expose how dysfunctional the system had become because of the asymmetrical balance of power within the corporate sectors and between it and the regulators and politicians. Just before Christmas (2002), the financial powerhouses of Lower Manhattan settled in a $1.4bn deal designed to bring closure to the issue and to a calamitous year for the American financial services industry.

In 2002, a total of $2.9bn was paid in regulatory fines and court settlements – enough to buy 108 of the Forbes 500 companies. The publication of the details of the joint investigation is likely to increase the legal challenge dramatically. Even if court appearances are, in all likelihood, years off, the ongoing damage to the credibility of the largest brokerage and investment banking firms in the market, in terms of further disclosure and negative headlines, is both ongoing and significant. Already Citigroup, one of the most powerful corporations in the world, has made a provision for $1.5bn to fend off future court actions, as has JP Morgan Chase, one of the banks most exposed by Enron's collapse.

On the same day as the regulators and the corporations sued for peace in New York, 2,000 miles to the west a decision by a federal

---

[3] Mark Gimein, "The enforcer", *Fortune*, 16 September 2002.

judge threatened to undermine the deal before the ink had dried. The judge ruled that confidential documents relating to the investment decisions made by Wall Street to support Enron should be disclosed to lawyers running the class action suit. The consequences are immense. That single decision will add substantially to the pressure on an already strained system. A consortium of those with most to lose by disclosure, including the remnants of Enron, its auditors Arthur Anderson and major banking institutions – such as JP Morgan Chase, Citigroup and Credit Suisse First Boston – had claimed that the documents were privileged under client confidentiality. In rejecting the argument, the federal court not only provided significant ammunition for the class action lawyers but also raised exponentially the economic, political and financial stakes. The conflict of interest investigations and the Enron case are further intertwined because of a further aspect of the Houston challenge.

Lerach and his colleagues claimed that the structured finance deals provided by Wall Street to Enron's top executives allowed for the legitimization of tax avoidance and other forms of financial alchemy that distorted the true financial health of the company to the detriment of individual and institutional shareholder alike. At the stroke of a pen, the Houston judge had opened the floodgates to a whole new wave of litigation that threatens to deluge the financial district crammed into Lower Manhattan. With class actions securities lawyers given clearance to enter the inner sanctums of the firms, the cost in both reputational and financial terms increased dramatically.

With Enron itself bankrupt, it is Lerach, through his role as lead plaintiff in the multibillion dollar lawsuit claiming damages against Enron and its bankers, who will reap the benefit.[4] One sensed that the lawyer could almost hear the cash registers when he spoke to reporters outside the Houston court. "This decision confirms the validity of our legal claims against the major defendants, and leaves in the case

---

[4] For full details of the claim against the investment banks see *Mark Selby et al. vs. Enron Corp*, Consolidated Claim against Violation of Securities Law, pp. 340–401. The claim alleges that the banks actively colluded in insider-dealing (p. 343).

defendants with resources to pay substantial compensation to the class. It also should open the way for discovery, which has been stayed pending the decision to commence."[5] A leading New York bank managed to escape the opening of discovery, enabling one of its senior legal officers to provide this telling assessment of the likely outcome:

> Once the judge turns down the motion to dismiss and allows discovery you settle. If the judge dismisses, you uncork the champagne and have a party; if it rules discovery you have to start talking settlement because you cannot afford — whether you are liable guilty or not — to have these plaintiff lawyers raid your offices.[6]

Two diametrically opposed possibilities therefore present themselves: a new beginning or a recurring nightmare? How this pivotal question is answered will help determine, in part, the future of American politics. If the system was as corrupted as the extent of the fine hammered out in New York implied, how did it become so? This in turn leads to a much more destabilizing query: To what extent can the failure to regulate the economy effectively be traced back to partial and self-serving decision-making made with due cognizance of the views of the corporate interests that fund the American political system?[7] For William J. Flynn, the influential Chairman of Mutual of America, one of the country's most powerful pension providers, the crisis is one of the systematic corruption of the American ideal:

> An enormous tragedy has befallen capitalism. It is the most serious crisis in its history. It is the consequence of a calamitous collapse of trust in our tax system, fueled, quite frankly, by corporate greed. There is a lack of faith in our investment banks, executives, our accountants and law firms and ultimately Congress, which repealed the legislation that allowed it to happen. No one

---

[5] Dan Ackman, "Big banks must still reckon with Enron", *Forbes Online*, 23 December 2002: http://www.forbes.com/2002/12/23/cx_da_1223 topnews. html (accessed 4 January 2003).

[6] Interview, New York City, 7 February 2003.

[7] See John Nofsinger and Kenneth Kim, *Infectious Greed, Restoring Confidence in America's Companies* (Prentice Hall, Upper Saddle River, NJ, 2003), pp. 248–53.

trusts people in the corporate boardrooms. Regulation has failed and the result is clear: The system has been systematically corrupted.[8]

As the diverse threads of the Enron scandal further unravel, it is impossible to avert one's gaze from the fundamental nature of the system that has caused the ruination of so many. Deeply embedded within the machinations of a complex structure are the internal contradictions that have done much to erode confidence. Reprising the chicanery that had fuelled the speculative excesses of the 1920s, the perennial character flaws of modern American capitalism are once again exposed. "Wall Street," remarked the influential economist J. K. Galbraith in his seminal study of the 1929 Great Crash, "is like a lovely and accomplished woman who must wear black cotton stockings, heavy woollen underwear, and parade her knowledge as a cook, because, unhappily, her supreme accomplishment is as a harlot."[9] By the end of the century the financial devices deployed by the tease merchants in Lower Manhattan to lure the greedy and the incautious were significantly more advanced than trading on margin. The basic premise of the oldest profession, however, and the forbidden fruit it promised, remained substantially unchanged.

Galbraith wrote his classic account of the 1929 Crash to mark its 25th anniversary. He reasoned that understanding why the calamity occurred was "our best safeguard against the recurrence of the more unhappy events of those days."[10] But just as the New York speculators in 1929 failed to internalize the lessons of previous collapses, for contemporary investors in the same market the passage of time had served to dull memories. The immunizing effect of past failure had become defective in the face of an avaricious bull market, nurtured and manipulated by those who controlled the market. What differentiated the crisis, progressively revealed from 2000 onward, from previous waves of scandal, such as the junk bond and asset-stripping mania of the 1980s, was the revelation of the structured and sustained

---

[8] Telephone interview with William J Flynn, New York, 6 March 2003.
[9] John Kenneth Galbraith, *The Great Crash 1929* (Penguin, London, 1992), p. 46.
[10] Ibid., pp. 28–9.

involvement of some of the most respected corporate names in the financial firmament.[11] As such, the consequences, for the equities market in particular, extend well beyond the collapse of Enron.

The susceptibility of the sober investment houses to stoking the irrational giddiness in the marketplace is one of the key defining elements of the American crisis. Suspension of disbelief by those consumed with greed did not mean that the laws of gravity could equally be ignored by reputable funds, which charged a premium for their knowledge. The consequences of the investment decisions made through ignorance, or negligence, about the underlying reality are profound: auditors had signed off fantasy figures to protect lucrative consultancy business; merchant banks provided public analysis that differed sharply from internal communications; regulators failed to regulate; and the politicians, in need of the corporate backing required to fund increasingly expensive electoral campaigns, feted corporate financiers who, in turn, distributed largesse to a supplicant legislative class. It represented a sordid marriage of self-interest and wilful neglect in which decency was replaced by greed and confidence by betrayal.[12]

The recent publication by Transparency International of the Global Corruption Index rightly emphasizes the importance of the Enron scandal in highlighting the global importance of corruption within the private sector.[13] Enron represents, however, much more than that. It is symptomatic of the problem rather than the cause. It underscores the need to combat the ability of major corporate interests to impact on governance through a corrosive compact that distorts the deliberative process by virtue of its financial contributions to the political system. With the 10 biggest economies in the world

---

[11] The most detailed account of the junk bond scandal is to be found in James B. Stewart, *Den of Thieves* (Touchstone, New York, 1992).

[12] See Margaret M. Blair, "Post-Enron reflections on comparative corporate governance", Working Paper 316663, Georgetown University Law Centre, http:// papers.ssrn.com/paper.taf?abstract_id=316663

[13] Jermyn Brooks, "A large dose of Enronitis", in *Transparency International, Global Corruption Report 2003* (Profile Books, London, 2003), pp. 80–2.

today belonging to corporations rather than countries, it has become increasingly clear that the mechanics of international contemporary capitalism are themselves potentially seditious to the needs of domestic governments. Nowhere is the case more pressing that in the United States, the prime exporter of the model.

Institutional investors in the United States control 59.7% of total equity investment; pension funds alone control 35.1% of the market, making the investment decisions taken by the fund managers crucial to the financial health of all those with defined pension benefits.[14] A survey of institutional investors, published after the corporate scandals had reached their apex, demonstrated the extent of deterioration in confidence. Greenwich Associates polled 51 institutions with a combined investment portfolio of $775bn, while the investment banks and American regulators were negotiating a global settlement on conflicts of interest with Wall Street's major players in December 2002. According to Greenwich, the general response to the crisis and the ability of reforms to change the situation was "marked by disillusionment, cynicism, even despair."[15]

This sullen acceptance can be traced back to the power of corporate interests to reduce the range of effective enforcement options available. By successful lobbying of Congress, vested interests can prevent the introduction of new legislation. More insidiously, legislators, whose world view correlates with the special interests that contribute to their campaign war chest, can threaten the budgets of regulatory agencies if the result of systematic investigation is a further decline in confidence in the probity of the market. For John Moscow, Deputy Chief of Investigations at the office of the District Attorney of New York, two key regulatory changes paved the way for systemic failure of oversight:

---

[14] See Marco Becht, Patrick Bolton and Ailsa Roell, "Corporate governance and control", European Corporate Governance Institute Finance Working Paper No.2/02, October 2002, p. 11 (accessible online at http://www.ecgi.org/)
[15] Quoted in Gary Silverman, "Investors unmoved by analyst reforms", *Financial Times*, 17 December 2002.

The securities industry persuaded Congress to concentrate regulatory power with the SEC in 1996 taking a lot of regulatory power away from the states. Having concentrated with the Commission and having made enforcement exclusive to the Commission, they then cut the Commission's budget, Then the securities industry obtained the repeal of Glass–Steagall. Our regulators were used to dealing with commercial banking or with securities or with investment banks and they all felt differently. It got to the point where I don't think that the regulators had the manpower trained in each discipline in sufficient numbers to deal with the problem.[16]

The complexity of the modern business world and the growing financialization of the post-industrial economy, oiled by deregulation, is an ancillary driving motor of the cynicism. "I think there was an awful amount of game playing. I don't know if it was impossible to control the markets but they weren't controlled."[17] Globalization and the international migration of finance have further weakened the ability of regulators to enforce compliance. The massive expansion in the use of offshore holdings has not simply reduced the tax liability of major corporations, it also ensures that enforcement is all but impossible to achieve in the absence of a corporate meltdown, forcing a fundamental reappraisal of how the system actually works as opposed to how it should work.[18] In a perceptive analysis of the threat posed by financial muscle to the power of the nation state to preserve its tax base, John Plender has recently argued that modern capitalism is facing a profound crisis of legitimacy. For Plender, the Enron fiasco is symptomatic of "the whole culture of Anglo-American finance [which] is increasingly subversive of regulation, taxation and democratic values, even where it remains within the law."[19] Nowhere was this challenge more acutely exemplified than in the Congressional Joint Committee on Taxation report into the financing of Enron, released in early February 2003.

---

[16] Interview with John Moscow, New York City, 9 April 2003.

[17] Ibid.

[18] A. Larry Elliot and Richard J. Schroth, *How Companies Lie* (Nicholas Brealey, London, 2002), p. 77.

[19] John Plender, "The hijack that made Enron happen", *Financial Times*, 28 January 2003. The theme is further developed in John Plender, *Going off the Rails, Global Capital and the Crisis of Legitimacy* (John Wiley & Sons, Chichester, UK, 2003).

The report was scathing in its deconstruction of the tax strategies adopted by the corporation. "Enron came to view the role of its tax department as more than managing its Federal income tax liabilities. Rather, Enron's tax department became a source for financial statement earnings, thereby making it a profit centre for the company."[20] Citing a systematic breakdown in ethics, the report suggested Enron "excelled in making complexity an ally." The corporation had "an incentive and the ability to engage in unusually complicated transactions in order to preclude meaningful review." This aggressive and essentially duplicitous approach to corporate reporting, designed to minimize tax liabilities, presents major problems that extend well beyond the corporation:

> Corporations like Enron have an inherent advantage over the IRS [Internal Revenue Service]. Enron relied on advice from sophisticated and experienced lawyers, investment bankers, and accountants. Assertions of attorney–client privilege hinders the ability of the IRS to obtain many of the most instructive documents, which impedes the IRS's ability to audit the transaction. Enron's activities shows [sic] that the IRS cannot minimize the importance of loss [making] companies because to do so would ignore a breeding ground for tax-motivated transactions that also could be used by taxpaying companies.
>
> Enron's aggressive interpretation of business purpose, the cooperation of accomodation parties, the protection provided by tax opinions, the complex design of transactions, advantages over the IRS – all were factors that contributed to Enron's ability to engage in tax-motivated transactions. Until the costs of participating in tax-motivated transactions are substantially increased, corporations such as Enron will continue to engage in transactions that violate the letter or the spirit of the law.[21]

The aim of the structured transactions was quite simple: the subversion of the tax code to enhance revenue, which in turn was translated on the bourse as a higher stock price, setting in motion a classic pyramid scheme. None of these transactions served bona fide business

---

[20] Joint Committee on Taxation, *Report of Investigation of Enron Corporation and Related Entities regarding Federal Tax and Compensation Issues, and Policy Recommendations*, JCS-3-03, February 2003, p. 8.
[21] Ibid., p. 16.

purposes, but were constructed to generate income through the manipulation of financial accounting. According to the congressional investigation, "nearly all of the reviewed transactions are vulnerable to attack under judicial or administrative anti-abuse and anti-avoidance doctrines." The conclusion reached by the committee was devastating. "Enron's behaviour illustrates that a motivated corporation can manipulate highly technical provisions of the law to achieve significant unintended benefits. Remarkable in many re-spects was Enron's ability to parse the law to produce a result that was contrary to its spirit and not intended by Congress or the Treasury Department."[22]

The collusion of leading investment banks, lawyers and accoun-tants in the provision of tax shelters was central to the evasion that enabled Enron to book over $2bn in immediate profits while under-estimating its federal tax exposure by a similar amount over a six-year period. Bankers Trust, a firm now controlled by Deutsche Bank, was paid $40m for its work in helping to establish shelters, which were routed through the Caymans. Some of the most eminent legal firms in the United States signed off on the transactions, despite the suspicion that the structures were primarily designed as accountancy ruses. The combination of complexity and speculative mania gripping the markets successfully hid the alchemy throughout the boom years. In 2000 and 2001, Enron, despite booking revenue of $2bn, paid just $63m in federal tax. This degradation of tax revenue has raised serious structural questions about the role of the corporation in modern American society, a fact acknowledged by the highly influential District Attorney for New York, Robert Morgenthau. Speaking at the Brookings Institution last June, the Attorney argued that the risks of tax havens undermined the rule of law:

> In a democracy such as ours, where we rely largely on voluntary compliance with the tax laws, the tax system must not only be seen to be fair, it must be perceived to be fair. The unfairness of allowing citizens to avoid paying their fair share of taxes erodes confidence in the tax system and the voluntary

---

[22] Ibid., p. 22.

compliance on which the system is based. In addition, permitting some businesses to gain unfair tax advantages in offshore venues destroys the level playing field on which our system of free enterprise depends ... Finally, and perhaps most important, the obvious inequity of a system that allows certain individuals and companies to hide their financial affairs in offshore havens undermines respect for government and the rule of law.[23]

Senator Charles Grassley, Chairman of the Senate Committee on Financing, noted that the report read like "a conspiracy novel, with some of the nation's finest banks, finest accounting firms and some of our best attorneys working together to prop up the biggest corporate farce of this century."[24] Senator Grassley stated that "the unbridled greed and blatant disregard for the law of fairness" was staggering.[25] The lack of moral fibre demonstrated by Enron, its executives and the coterie of advisors paid over $87m in fees, was, however, merely the visible manifestation of a wider viral problem of corporate greed inculcated in the boom and facilitated by systematic tax evasion strategies, according to John Moscow, Deputy Chief of Investigations at the District Attorney's Office in New York:

Tax laws provide that certain things are legal and certain things are illegal. Tax laws operate without morality. You pay what is due, not a cent more. If a lawyer or an accountant says, "if I interpret the tax code correctly you can do this transaction," the implication is you can do anything within the code. However, we have had a collection of wise guys who say, "As I understand the Internal Revenue Service they will not be able to follow this trail if you do the following things." Therefore you can violate the tax code with impunity. That is not the same thing as a tax shelter, that is mischievous. And when people's deference to the law is whether they will be caught and whether there will be means to defeat ... not to justify legally the conduct ... but to defeat the investigation, that is what I am talking about – gaming the system. You are engaging in conduct, which you know to be

[23] Cited in Frank Vogl, "The U.S. business scandals: Perspectives on ethics and culture at home and abroad". Paper presented to the *TransAtlantic Business Ethics Conference*, September 27, 2002, Georgetown University, Washington, DC.

[24] Deborah Solomon, "Enron report urges penalties for corporate tax abuse", *Wall Street Journal*, 14 February 2003.

[25] David Cay Johnston, "Wall St. firms are faulted in report on Enron's taxes", *New York Times*, 14 February 2003.

unlawful, where your strategy is to defeat the investigators, regulators, criminal justice system, whatever. When that is done by powerful multinational corporations, it brings the law into disrepute and makes a hash of corporate governance.

The confluence of systemic flaws – the inability to detect illicit management decisions and the pathological capacity of firms to cover their tracks – and the ending of the euphoria associated with the boom have made the task of disentangling causes and consequences exceptionally problematic.[26] The official explanation for the largest stock market bubble in history was that coined by the Chairman of the Federal Reserve Alan Greenspan, who, as early as 6 December 1996, referred to it, somewhat euphemistically, as "irrationally exuberant". Greenspan's warning came when the New York Stock Exchange (NYSE) index was less than half the level at which it eventually ran out of altitude. In reality, it was a confidence trick that played on what psychologists term "cognitive dissonance". The official history of the period, which posits the positive role played by the stock market in incubating a technological revolution that allowed the United States to escape global recession, is falsified by economic data. The increasing dominance of financial instruments served to hide a multitude. According to an analysis carried out by Robert Brenner, when the boom is measured based by output levels, productivity and unemployment, rather than the price of equities, "performance in the supposedly sensational five-year period between 1995 and 2000 barely matched the levels achieved in the twenty-five year period between 1948 and 1973. The growth of labour productivity, the most important indicator of economic dynamism, was a full 20% lower. Taking into account the whole business cycle of the decade 1990 to 2000 and not just the five good years at the end, the average annual rate of growth of GDP per person was a meagre 1.6%, compared with 2.2% for the hundred-year period 1989–1999. Even by 2000, real hourly wages for production and non-supervisory

---

[26] See Bill Witherall, "Corporate governance and responsibility", *Observer*, OECD No. 234, October 2002, pp. 7–9.

workers were still palpably below, and the poverty rate above, their 1973 best."[27]

Perpetrated by the manipulation of a corrupted system, gullible investors and pension fund administrators who should have known better were divested of their money with consummate skill in a structure that was characterized by a devaluation of business and personal ethics. Risk was successfully transferred from investment banks and over-leveraged corporations to the pension funds with ongoing deleterious consequences. The result was what the leading British economist Will Hutton terms a Faustian bargain between US managers and Wall Street, "corporate America now no longer principally seeks to innovate, build and marshal resources over time to create value. It tries to extract value by financial engineering."[28]

Like any pyramid investment, the entire edifice relied on confidence and that was already weakening before Muhammad Atta and his colleagues boarded four airliners on September 11, 2001, to launch the most audacious terrorist attack in history against what they saw as the degeneracy of American economic and foreign policy. The physical ruination of the World Trade Center and its environs by the al Qaeda terrorist network served to obfuscate the obdurate reality that the financial system itself was already morally compromised from *within*. Six weeks later, the precipitate decline into bankruptcy of the seventh largest company in the United States provoked a similar sense of confusion.

The terrorist attacks in New York, Washington and Pennsylvania on 9 September may have demonstrated the vulnerability of the last superpower, but the betrayal of trust occasioned by the corporate governance scandals, progressively revealed as the country came to terms with the violation of once impregnable defences, therefore has exposed a wider and deeper malaise. The systematic evaporation of trust in corporations, the regulatory framework and the political

[27] Robert Brenner, "Towards the precipice", *London Review of Books*, 6 February 2003.
[28] "Wall Street's Faustian pact", *Investors Chronicle*, 30 May 2002. The theme is developed further in Will Hutton, *The World We Are In* (Little, Brown, London, 2002).

establishment has fundamentally weakened the three pillars of integrity upholding public trust.[29] The asymmetrical relationship inherent in "fiduciary trust" was skewed both by the corrupt behaviour of executives within corporations and the myopic rationality on behalf of the professional lawyers and accountants who did not question the ethical consequences of allowing egregious behaviour. Mutual trust between the corporation and its shareholders was comprehensively eroded, as was mutual trust between overworked and under-resourced regulatory bodies and corporations determined to evade rigorous policing at the same time as they inculcated a political culture in keeping with their world view. And social trust as a form of what Thomas terms "social capital" was devalued.[30] As such, the destruction wrought by corporate malfeasance is likely – in the long term – to have a more deleterious effect on the American political psyche than the fundamentalist delusions of the al Qaeda network.[31] Taken together, these two very different – but interlinked – seismic occurrences have transformed the political landscape in the United States, the aftershocks of which continue to be felt across the globe. The American response to the crises was scathingly condemned by the influential financier George Soros:

> I see a parallel between the Bush administration's pursuit of American supremacy and a boom or bust process or bubble in the stock market. Bubbles do not grow out of thin air. They have a solid basis in reality but reality is distorted by misconception. In this case the dominant position of the US, the pursuit of supremacy, is the misconception. Reality can reinforce the misconception, but

---

[29] Craig W. Thomas, "Maintaining and restoring public trust in government agencies and their employees", *Administration and Society*, Vol. 30, No. 2, May 1998, p. 170. For Thomas the three pillars of fiduciary, mutual and social trust are "interwoven and mutually supportive. Mutual trust, generated through microlevel and interpersonal relationships gives rise to and shapes the character of social trust. In turn, social trust enhances the ability of individuals to develop mutual trust. Social trust also buttresses the sense of moral obligation that sustains fiduciary trust" (p. 178). It is precisely for this reason that the forsaking of trust at all levels represents such a serious crisis for the entire financial model.

[30] Ibid., p. 176.

[31] See Paul Krugman, "The great divide", *New York Times*, 29 January 2001.

eventually the gap between reality and its false interpretation becomes unsustainable.[32]

The economic, political and security crises have served to reinforce each other: the result is increased global insecurity, a disastrous and self-replicating decline in confidence in the integrity of the stock market and the consequent erosion of trillions of dollars in share prices. In a country that boasts the world's highest percentage of small-time investors, the resulting collapse of confidence in the merchant banks, the regulators and, ultimately, the politicians has thrown into sharp relief the integrity of a system that is hard-wired to protect the interests of the top 1% of the population, who, in turn, still hold a controlling interest of 40% in the overall structure.

Statistics compiled by the Securities Industry Association demonstrate that 84 million Americans owned stock in 2002, double that of 1983. Many of these investors are unable to read complicated financial statements and are reliant on the stock picks of corporate analysts who have a vested interest in producing rose-tinted research in order to boost investment-banking clients.[33] Michael Lewis, a former broker with Salomon Brothers, once noted that sustained periods of growth in the stock and bond markets requires "a fool", whose ignorance or greed could be manipulated. In the context of the 1980s it was saving and loan chief executives who needed to remortgage billions of dollars of loans in order to keep their jobs.[34] In the 1990s the number of fools in the market had intensified exponentially.

With crucial design flaws inherent in contemporary capitalism, the destruction of the Twin Towers and the pre-eminent symbol of that system provided merely confirming evidence of an already structurally unsound blueprint. As David Ellis of Moneywise observed, on the first anniversary of the attacks, "this month, those who died in Washington and New York will be solemnly remembered, and the

---

[32] George Soros, "Bush's inflated sense of supremacy", Financial Times, 13 March 2003.

[33] Scot J. Paltrow, "The dark side of the Street, where scandals often erupt", Wall Street Journal, 23 December 2002.

[34] Michael Lewis, Liar's Poker (Coronet, London, 1990).

symbolism of the smoking, ruined financial power centre will never be forgotten. But as the history of the financial markets in the wake of the tragedy continues to be written, a bitter irony is emerging. In the end, old fashioned greed did for the markets what the terrorists never could."[35]

The excesses progressively exposed by the recent corporate governance scandals were distinguishable only by their size: greed has long been an essential feature of corporate practice. But greed alone is an insufficient rationale for the betrayal of trust occasioned by the collapse of Enron, WorldCom et al. and the interlinked crisis of confidence in the role played by market professionals, particularly research analysts. A corporate culture, inculcated during the long years of bullish growth, began to display its deadly symptoms only after the markets took a pummelling from those who hijacked the United and American airliners over the north-east coast. By that stage the condition of the markets was already terminal.

The collapse of the dotcom market in the two years prior to 9/11 was, in retrospect, a chronicle of a death foretold. The introduction of technology shares, created as a result of deregulation of the telecommunications market through the 1996 Telecommunications Act, created a displacement effect that prompted a change in the investing environment. In the scathing assessment of John McCain, a major promoter of campaign finance reform in the Senate, "all the interests were at the table except the public interest."[36] The rush to take advantage of the deregulation spawned the listing on the market of major new corporations, such as MCI, which later merged with WorldCom. The subsequent collapse of WorldCom, under $9bn in unsustainable debt, marked the nadir of the crisis. Its demise was an unthinkable prospect at the start of the boom, as the new economy produced prodigy after prodigy. As deregulation created new companies, mobile telephony created real-time communication and the introduction of broadband technology presented opportunities for a

[35] Cited in the *Guardian*, 14 September 2002.
[36] Elizabeth Drew, *Citizen McCain* (Simon & Schuster, New York, 2002), p. 3.

revolution on a scale to equal industrialization itself, Wall Street, Washington DC and Silicon Valley combined to offer investors ground-floor access to the citadels of wealth.

The cycle from boom to bust was exacerbated by the vast expansion in monetary supply, primarily through banking credit, which was then used to finance speculative activities. The touchpaper was lit by the irresponsibility of deregulating without introducing adequate institutional safeguards to prevent abuse. Nationwide gambling was decreed legal via the government's decision to allow pension holders to invest a larger percentage of their benefits on the stock market through corporate 401(K) pension plans than prudence would suggest. The introduction of this liquidity turned the entire bourse into an online casino, in which bets were taken on a corporation's daily positioning, rather than underlying performance. And none were more successful in tapping into the speculative zeitgeist than the mutual funds and hedging operations that sprung up to manage the vast increase in the money supply now locked into the securities market. In a remarkable but telling outburst, the chief executive of the British-based Threadneedle Investments, one of the largest retail schemes operating in the UK, suggested the avarice and stupidity of investors were as much to blame. "We encourage them to be even more stupid. I think the fire is already there: we've probably thrown a little bit of petrol – rather than water – but I think [the fire] does come from the greed of the individual."[37] In a staggering statistical survey, *The Economist* estimated that 90% of the venture capital distributed with such abandon during the boom years had been wasted on companies whose business models were untested and unworkable.[38]

Powered by hype and sold on the basis of past performance, mutual funds now account for 20% of all shares, with a capitalization greater than that held in the banking system. The shift to intangible assets managed by mutual funds, which even in the bull market failed to

---

[37] Simon Targett, "UK fund manager hits at 'greedy investers'", *Financial Times*, 3 February 2003.
[38] "The new-economy vultures", *The Economist*, 8 December 2001.

keep pace with the overall performance of the markets, was itself merely symptomatic of the wider problem. In a scathing letter to shareholders, Warren Buffet, one of America's shrewdest investors, castigated the mutual funds industry for its poor performance and the hypocrisy permeating the industry that front-loads costs to investors for undeserved executive pay. "For the most part, a monkey will type out a Shakespeare play before an 'independent' mutual-fund director will suggest that his fund look at other managers, even if the incumbent manager has persistently delivered substandard performance. When they are handling their own money, of course, directors will look to alternative advisors – but it never enters their minds to do so when they are acting as fiduciaries for others."[39]

Management fees and taxes were poorly explained, exit routes made difficult by restrictions on access without penalty, leaving investors little safeguard against corrections in the market. Agency problems abounded with fund managers buying personal stock and then using fund capital to drive up the price, making short-term profit for the manager. Across Wall Street, investors found similar pitfalls. Brokers, working on commission based on the number of trades rather than performance of the stock in a given portfolio, had a vested interest in maximizing trading activity, particularly in the issuance of secondary offerings where the level of commission was five times that of initial offerings. Internet trading and the running ticker on financial television served to add to the frenzy as the United States developed the attributes of a qualitatively different form of trading nation.

The situation was further exacerbated by the use of stock options to reward executives. The unhealthy relationship began to demonstrate

---

[39] *Berkshire Hathaway Annual Letter to Shareholders*, p. 17 (released 8 March 2003, full text available online at http://www.berkshirehathaway.com/letters/2002.html). Buffet announced that, despite major losses charged against its derivative business General Re, his fund posted earnings of $4.279bn and outperformed the S&P 500 by 32.1%. Buffet had the humility to point out, "there will be years in which the S&P soundly trounces us. That will in fact almost certainly happen during a strong bull market, because the portion of our assets committed to common stocks has significantly declined. This change, of course, helps our relative performance in down markets such as we had in 2002" (p. 3).

corrupting tendencies as early as 1992, in part occasioned as a result of a decision by the incoming Clinton administration to limit chief executive pay to $1m. The result was an exponential increase in stock options to reward executives, which, in turn, gave a rationale for fraudulent cooking of the books. If the corporate pay was determined by the rise in stock value, it was in the executives' own self-interest to boost share value by fair means or foul.[40] By the time of Enron's collapse, its chairman Ken Lay had options valued at over $168m. By way of contrast, the options package accrued by Sandy Weill, the chief executive of Citigroup, had risen to over $1bn. The consummation of this marriage of convenience reached its apogee in the financing facilities offered to Enron and the telecommunications giant WorldCom and the de facto bribery involved by the "spinning" of lucrative initial public offerings (IPOs) to executives in order to gain lucrative underwriting contracts.

Providing stock options, which did not appear as expenses, fundamentally warped any assessment of a company's real value. Designed to resolve what economists have termed the "principal–agent dilemma" by providing management with a vested interest in the profitability of a company, it succeeded only in boosting corporate pay while doing little to safeguard the interests of the shareholders. In 1992 average compensation for chief executives was $1.8m. By 2000, it had reached $6.1m. A survey by *Business Week* found that CEO pay rose by 340% over a 10-year period, compared with an average of 36% for employees.[41] The justification for such increases rested on the creation of a business etiquette that placed an inordinate emphasis on driving up the stock market valuation without paying due cognizance to the underlying economic performance.[42] This systemic

---

[40] See Peter Peterson, "A personal postscript", *Conference Board Commission on Public Trust and Private Enterprise*, 9 January 2003, p. 6. Paterson argues that setting limits on executive pay as a means of dealing with the crisis would risk repeating the "iatrogenic" failure of the Clinton administration.

[41] "How to fix corporate governance", *Business Week*, 6 May 2002.

[42] See Alex Berenson, *The Number, How the Drive for Quarterly Earnings Corrupted Wall Street and Corporate America* (Simon & Schuster, New York, 2003).

problem exacerbated the temptation to effectively cook the books, according to a former enforcement lawyer with the SEC and now a director at a leading European-controlled investment bank:

> The system in the US has evolved over recent years such that every quarter you put out earnings guidance and you have to make your numbers. If you don't make your numbers, if you don't meet what you projected you would meet for that quarter, if you miss it by as much as a penny a share, your stock will get hammered, absolutely hammered and it is a weird dynamic. I don't know if the system should function in that way. I don't know if it is artificial but our system has developed in such a way that it is. Corporate officers panic that they are not going to meet the quarterly numbers because if you don't make the quarterly numbers the stock price is going to plummet, so the incentive is built into the system that you meet the numbers, which drives people to become bad actors to meet the numbers.[43]

As a result, companies were grossly overvalued, saddled with wholly unrealistic price–earning ratios that created, in turn, irrational longer term profit expectations. To make matters worse, the extent of these stock options did not appear on company accounts, thereby precluding any real analysis of their impact on the true values of the company concerned and reducing the shareholders' knowledge of just how much profits the executives were siphoning off. Rather than solving the agency problem, the widespread use of stock options served merely to enhance the relative power of executives, whose recompense was determined by moving up the stock price by whatever means possible.[44] It is a point recognized in Wall Street:

> Incentive-based compensation is a second systemic problem. I don't think there is anything essentially wrong with incentive based compensation. I think it has a lot of benefits; it aligns the interests of senior management, and officers and directors with shareholders; it ensures that people stay around for a number of years, they don't leave promptly because if you do you forfeit these options, it

---

[43] Interview, New York City, 7 February 2003.

[44] See Gretchen Morgenson, "Time to look at stock options real costs", *New York Times*, 21 October 2001. For an extended analysis of the deleterious effect played on economic viability by the non-recording of stock options see Robert Brenner, "Towards the precipice", *London Review of Books*, 6 February 2003.

ensures that you have great motivation to think long term and to think long term to drive up the stock price because you will benefit economically. That is all good but the bad is your whole focus in life becomes that stock price can't go down because if the stock price goes down my options will expire valueless and I am going to loose x amount of dollars. So I think it has been another incentive that has been built into the system for CFOs or other officers to ensure that numbers are met, that their options and other incentive based compensation end up rewarding them handsomely.[45]

The pressure to meet those numbers was exemplified in February 2003 with the criminal and civil cases filed in Denver against mid-level executives working in the Global Business Markets Unit of the telecommunications company Qwest Communications International. The SEC brought a case alleging that the company inflated its earnings by $144m in two specific instances to meet quarterly numbers. The Justice Department simultaneously filed criminal charges against four executives in relation to the fraudulent booking of profits for one of the projects, which was designed to network the Arizona school system. The US Attorney for Colorado John Suthers termed the activity "true accounting fraud."[46] The firm is alleged to have delivered hardware to the School Board prior to its agreed delivery so that it could book profit. An email discovered in the course of the investigation suggested concerns about the facts of the plan "hanging together", an indication, according to the government, of a premeditated plan to deceive the market.

According to the SEC suit, "to support immediate recognition of revenue for the sale of the equipment, the defendants prepared false letter agreements for ASFB [Arizona School Facilities Board] and a fraudulent internal memorandum." The ficititious revenue allowed Qwest to meet its expected revenues. Without it, the company would have fallen short of its 12–13% growth forecast. The SEC suit provided further evidence of a concerted campaign to meet the market numbers, at whatever cost. A separate transaction involving

[45] Investment Bank counsel, New York City, 7 February 2003.

[46] Dennis K. Berman and Deborah Solomon, "Ex-executives are indicted in federal probe of Qwest", *Wall Street Journal*, 26 February 2003.

an Internet service provider Genuity Inc. ensured that the company "improperly recognized $100m in revenue" in two complex and interconnected contracts. The first involved Qwest charging inflated prices for equipment, which was then in a second contract bought back through Qwest assuming "all risk of loss and obsolescence on the equipment purportedly sold pursuant to the first contract."[47]

For the SEC, the activity was symptomatic of the aggressive strategy adopted by Qwest as it sought to redefine itself on the capital markets from a "stodgy, old-style telephone company" into a financial power-house. The court filing spoke of a business model that "placed extra-ordinary pressure on their subordinate executives, managers and employees to meet or exceed those earning objectives at all costs."[48] In a post facto indictment of the financial engineering im-perative, the Commission explicitly sought "an order pursuant to the equitable authority of the court requiring each defendant to disgorge all ill-gotten gains from their participation in the fraud including all benefits derived from their employment at Qwest such as salary, bonuses, stock and other remuneration."[49] In an attempt to gain the moral high ground, the prosecutions were accompanied by news conferences in Washington, DC. The Chairman of the SEC William Donaldson made clear that the prosecution marks the beginning of a process. "Accurate financials are the bedrock of our capital markets. This agency will pursue aggressively anyone and everyone who has participated in an illegal effort to misrepresent a company's financials and mislead the investing public."[50] This aggressive policy contains an escalation imperative that has profound implications for the reg-ulators and the Department of Justice itself. The unanswered question was whether the political will existed to move beyond individual

---

[47] SEC Press Release 2003-25 (accessible online at http://www.sec.gov/news/press.shtml).

[48] SEC vs. Joel M. Arnold et al., District of Colorado, Civil Action No. 03-Z-0328 (OES), p. 8.

[49] Ibid., p. 4.

[50] SEC Press Release 2003-25 (accessible online at http://www.sec.gov/news/press.shtml).

actors and indict the corporations that facilitated such egregious behaviour through the adoption of a policy of wilful ignorance.

Given that Qwest has already announced a restatement of $2.2bn, it is only a matter of time before responsibility for inculcating the model moves further up the corporate ladder.[51]

Tracking executive pay to the performance of the bourse rather than to individual company performance may have been illogical, but an unholy alliance militated against exposure until the bear began to roar, sending the corporate giants scurrying to the bank-ruptcy court, but not before the exercise of lucrative stock options, netting billions of dollars.[52] Insider-trading ensured that these "barons of bankruptcy" squeezed every droplet of profit before discarding their worthless companies.

Financial alchemy deployed by auditors, beholden to management for lucrative consultancy tenders, grossly overstated profits by utilizing dubious, and in some instances illegal, accountancy measures. The business model aggressively promoted by Bernie Ebbers, the Chief Executive of WorldCom, and his CFO Scott Sullivan rested on an uncomplicated manoeuvre that treated operating costs as capital in-vestment. As with Enron, the auditor was Arthur Anderson. The failure of the audit process, while not endemic, was however con-doned, infecting not just the voracious ambitions of Enron, World-Com and their ilk but also contaminating established corporations, including the pharmaceutical corporation Bristol-Meyers Squibb, which restated its accounts to the tune of $2.5bn because of what it termed, somewhat innocuously, "errors and inappropriate account-ing."[53] Outright fraud was alleged at the photocopying giant Xerox and its auditors KPMG.

---

[51] Barnaby J. Feder, "Charges filed in Qwest case", *New York Times*, 26 February 2003.

[52] A survey published by the *Financial Times* found that over $3.3bn in stock options were siphoned off by executives in the companies under investigation. See Ien Cheng, "Survivors who laughed all the way to the bank", *Financial Times*, 31 July 2002.

[53] Reed Abelson, "Bristol-Meyers lowers revenue by $2.5bn in restatement", *New York Times*, 11 March 2003.

In April 2002, Xerox agreed to pay a record $10m fine for posting more than $2bn in bogus profits in the period 1997–2000. On 29 January 2003 the SEC went further, filing a civil fraud complaint against its auditors KPMG.[54] One of those named in the suit was Michael Conway, a senior partner in the firm and one of the foremost auditors in the United States. According to the suit, "instead of putting a stop to Xerox's fraudulent accounting, the KPMG defendants themselves engaged in fraud. There was no watchdog at Xerox. KPMG's bark sounded no warning to investors; its bite was toothless."[55]

The censure of KPMG by the SEC was only the second time that a major accounting firm has been directly accused of fraud. The previous culprit Arthur Anderson has been consigned ignominiously to the history books. The partnership could not withstand the opprobrium heaped on the once-venerable institution because of its role in the obstruction of the Department of Justice investigation. Anderson was already on a final warning from the SEC because of major deficiencies in previous audits involving Waste Management in Chicago and Sunbeam in Florida. It fell on its own sword and dissolved itself rather than face SEC censure. KPMG called the suit "entirely unjustified" and claimed that "at the very worst, this is a disagreement over complex professional judgements." The firm proclaimed that it was pressure from the auditors themselves that forced Xerox to restate; an assertion disputed by the SEC.[56]

Crucially, little action was taken to address the systemic flaws at the time. In a bull market that fed the self-fulfilling myth of the efficacy of the American business and political model, none seriously questioned the implications of inaction[57] – until, that is, it was too late:

---

[54] For full details see *SEC vs. KPMG LLP, Joseph T. Boyle, Michael A. Conway, Anthony P. Dolanski and Ronald A. Safran*, Civil Action No. 03 CV 0671 (S.D.N.Y.) (29 January 2003), Litigation Release No. 17954/January 29 2003. See also Accounting and Auditing Enforcement Release No. 1709/January 29 2003 (available online at http://www.sec.gov/litigation/litreleases/lr17954.htm).

[55] Floyd Norris, "SEC says KPMG helped Xerox inflate profits", *New York Times*, 30 January 2003.

[56] Ibid.

[57] See John Cassidy, "The greed cycle", *The New Yorker*, 23 September 2002, pp. 64–77.

I knew during the bubble that we were going to be in trouble. I told Robert Morgenthau a year before the bubble burst that, if the market collapsed, if the prices went down thirty per cent, I would resign because I couldn't handle the kind of volume of complaints we were going to get. In fact the markets have gone down more than thirty. I haven't resigned, but I can't handle the volume of complaints that we have got, and some of them are well founded and that is separate from knowing about Enron or any one of them. You just know that at a time of unbridled growth ... uninhibited reporting of peculiar statistics ... you know that the fraudsters are going to make a killing, and when the thing comes tumbling down you will be left with a number of people screaming bloody murder. It was predictable that it was going to happen, we just didn't know which company it was going to be. In fact we were all shocked by how bad it was and how pervasive false accounting was, but we just missed it. I think that someone who knew the market better could have predicted it.[58]

The entire basis of modern American capitalism has been undermined by deficiencies in the key areas of accountability, openness and vigilance – the key areas identified by the World Bank as essential to good governance and economic growth. The paradox for the American economy is that the long years of bullish growth in equity value represented not only "the economics of the madhouse", it hid a multitude.[59] As Galbraith once remarked, recessions catch what auditors miss.

In a forlorn and belated attempt to restore confidence, the Conference Board (a trade grouping of CEOs) created a Commission on Public Trust and Private Enterprise to examine the fundamental causes for the explosion in corporate crime. The Commission released a number of reports examining the role played in the crisis by excessive compensation and lax corporate governance structures. Taking the title of a George Clooney disaster movie as a comparator, the Commission concluded that "there has been a *Perfect Storm* – a confluence of events in the compensation area which created an environment ripe for abuse ... These factors may have fostered what appears to be a vicious cycle of increasing short-term pressures to manipulate

---

[58] Interview with John Moscow, New York City, 9 April 2003.
[59] John Plender, *Going off The Rails, Global Capital and the Crisis of Legitimacy* (John Wiley & Sons, Chichester, UK, 2003), p. 43.

earnings in order to bolster stock price in order to cash in on stock options."[60] The Conference Board Commission concluded that greater use should be made of performance-related pay based on actual performance rather than stock market trends and endorsed a compensation formula that had "a clear correlation between the costs of the increased compensation and the expected benefits to the corporation."[61]

In short, the economic downturn has exposed a crisis in corporate governance of monumental proportions, which in turn makes it even more difficult to inject confidence into the system. Writing in the *Financial Times*, the paper's chief economics analyst Martin Wolf noted that "everything is made far worse by a plethora of conflicts of interest: financial conglomerates are more concerned with pleasing corporate management than with maximising the value of the funds they control; outside directors owe more loyalty to the managers who choose them than to the shareholders they represent; and accountants owe more to the people who employ them than to the investors who rely on their work."[62] Wolf could also add the role of the business press itself.

While the financial media has played a major role in analysing just what has gone wrong since the collapse of Enron, it remains remarkably silent about its own culpability in failing to provide non-institutional investors with any sense that the system was stacked against them at each end of the market.[63] Scepticism, the last refuge of the investigative journalist, was missing as it reported on the rollercoaster rise to dominance of Enron, a company that was making up the rules as it went along and disregarding them as the

[60] *Conference Board Commission on Public Trust and Private Enterprise Findings and Recommendations*, 17 September 2002, pp. 4–7 (available online at http://www.conferenceboard.org/).

[61] Ibid., p. 5.

[62] Martin Wolf, "Why it is so hard to fix the flaws of modern capitalism", *Financial Times*, 20 November 2002.

[63] A rare exception is Richard Lambert, former Editor of the *Financial Times*, who noted that Enron was also a failure of journalism. See Richard Lambert, "Enron and the press", *Prospect*, March 2002.

search for profit took ever more esoteric, if not ludicrous turns. In a scathing indictment of her own journalistic charges, the Chairman of Pearson, owner of *The Economist* and the *Financial Times*, told the *Royal Journal of Arts* in a recent interview that business reporting had failed: "We could have done a lot more digging. But business journalists often don't know a lot about business."[64]

The problem was that conflicts of interest ensured that outside the rarefied heights of the Wall Street skyscrapers, true knowledge of the impending change in the environment within the corporations affected was deliberately occluded. Those who relied on impartial analysis found that a dangerous admixture of pride and ignorance, deceit and greed, permeated the research departments of the brokerage houses who could not or would not admit to a failure to analyse the small print. Compensation packages within the major investment banks guaranteed the payment of bonuses to their specialist researchers according to their ability to rate stock and garner further investment business rather than assess specific intrinsic worth.

Nowhere was this corruption made more manifest than in the practice of "spinning" IPOs. Incestuous exclusivity determined access to the lucrative IPOs of market capitalizations, which were then heavily promoted, making those who invested initially substantial profits on the greed of those who wished to join the club. In return for hefty allocations, investment houses agreed informally to become what is termed "after-market players", meaning that they would actively trade the stock after its launch, which ensured that it was noticed and continued to rise. In August 2000 the SEC specifically banned the solicitation of after-market orders because of the danger that it manipulated the market. "Tie-in agreements are a particularly egregious form" of prohibited transactions that "undermine the integrity of the market." The then Chairman of the SEC Arthur Levitt told the *Wall Street Journal* that the linkage "erodes public confidence because it suggests that the process is rigged in favour of some over the interests of the individual." There was also a structural imperative

---

[64] Quoted in John Cassy, "Let's not do lunch", the *Guardian*, 6 January 2003.

for the underwriters. It artificially stimulated demand and therefore boosted prices and with it the underwriter's commission.[65]

This fraudulent manipulation was merely the tip of the iceberg. Not only was it common practice for firms to ramp up the share price, allocations were made to favoured clients on the basis of securing future underwriting business, and, in a particularly damaging case, brokers at Credit Suisse First Boston recouped some of the profit by charging exorbitant fees on trades, thereby making a mockery of legislation. In a settlement that was to do much to unleash the resentment at the activities of the investment banks, Credit Suisse agreed to pay a $100m fine to bring closure to an 18-month federal investigation into alleged abuses of the manner in which it allocated and valued initial offerings.[66] The fine represented less than 15% of the $717.5m the firm had earned in promoting IPOs in the period 1999–2000.

The avarice associated with the IPO market was fed by the "buy" recommendations from analysts working on the initial capitalization. The need to buttress the stock valuations occurred at every stage of the process: from the conception of a business plan to managing the slide into, or out of, bankruptcy. Fear of incurring the wrath of the issuer and therefore curtailing access to information was a further inhibiting factor according to Gary Lynch, Vice-Chairman of Credit Suisse First Boston and a former Head of Enforcement at the SEC:

> Retribution from issuers to analysts is also going on. They just cut you off from the flow of information. Unfortunately, all the focus has been on the invest-ment banks and regulating the investment banks themselves. On a daily basis companies and issuers are still punishing analysts who downgrade them. There are other things happening out there in the world that maybe regulators are powerless to act on that affect an analyst's view. Analysts are going to remain

---

[65] Susan Pulliam, "Seeking IPO shares, investors offer to buy more in after market", *Wall Street Journal*, 6 December 2000.

[66] Susan Pulliam, Randall Smith, Anita Raghavan and Gregory Zuckerman, "CSFB will pay $100 million to settle inquiry into firm's IPO distribution", *Wall Street Journal*, 11 December 2001.

reluctant to downgrade issuers rather than simply talk to them or express caution because if you put a sell on issuers they treat you differently than if you have a buy on them.[67]

While there is considerable merit in Lynch's argument it is also undoubtedly the case that investment banks stood to gain valuable consultancy fees from grandiose expansion programmes only if the stock market value and debt rating – that is, the corporation's ability to repay debt – remained high, an uncomfortable fact either not included or minimized in research reports. This was, in short, a very imperfect market in which power rested on knowledge, and knowledge was a chargeable commodity.

The analytical framework itself was fatally flawed from the outset. Too often reports merely recited the company figures rather than subjecting them to a thorough critique. Little attention, if any, was placed on "fundamental issues such as the corporation's liquidity and borrowing capacity; the adequacy of its lines of credit ratings on new or outstanding bond issues; and the contingent liabilities reflected in

---

[67] Interview with Gary Lynch, New York City, 7 February 2003. A graphic example of this pressure surrounded the treatment of Heather Jones, an analyst for BB&T Capital Markets during a tele-conference with Fresh Del Monte Produce. Miss Jones had recently downgraded the valuation of Del Monte from "buy" to "underweight". When she asked what were perceived to be hostile questions, the Del Monte executives cut the line. See Richard Gibson, "Del Monte flap is opposite of 'cozy analyst situations'", *Wall Street Journal*, 17 February 2003. Similar pressure was exerted on Christopher McFadden, a pharmaceutical analyst with Goldman Sachs. See Kate Kelly, "Goldman analyst learns that candor doesn't pay", *Wall Street Journal*, 5 February 2003. In the international arena, pressure from governments can also impact on investment banking capabilities. In March 2003, the Philippines government banned UBS for participating in future bond issues because of the release of a highly critical research report, timed to coincide with a rights issue. According to UBS the government has "banned it from all sovereign and sovereign-related fund raisings, which are expected to reach at least $3 billion this year; suspended its fixed-income, foreign-exchange and bullion dealings, which make up a big chunk of the bank's Asian revenues; and withdrawn about $180 million in central-bank funds from its asset-management arm." See Karen Richardson, "UBS banned in Philippines", *Wall Street Journal*, 26 March 2003.

the footnotes."[68] The use of pro forma company releases to enhance stock and the sports commentary style of financial television, in which profits were gained by advertising, inculcated a business media culture that mirrored the corporate ethos it fed off.

Its leitmotif was Consumer News and Business Channel (CNBC), a misnomer if ever there was one, and in particular its casino-style early morning programme *Squawk Box*. As the *Washington Post's* media consultant Howard Kurtz has commented, "back in the heady days of a stampeding bull market CNBC was a driving force, a cultural phenomenon, a ratings success, the play-by-play announcer for America's new pastime ... What CNBC did, along with the rest of the business press, was buy into an interlocking system – now widely viewed as flawed and in some cases corrupt – in which all the key players had an incentive to push stocks."[69] Those analysts who played the game, suggesting hot picks and feeding the gambling frenzy, were rewarded with repeat appearances, which in turn added to their fame and to their own marketability. Bluntly, there was a bias against understanding for corporate gain.[70] That gain was not inconsiderable. In 2000 the value of mergers and acquisitions and new share issues reached $3.5tn. This in turn generated no less that $28bn in fees for the mercantile class, who controlled access to the market.

American capitalism sailed into "the perfect storm" with the passengers unaware that the vessel had not been satisfactorily inspected to ensure its seaworthiness. As Lynn Paine, Professor of Ethics at Harvard Business School, pointed out to the *Financial Times*, the perfect storm analysis put forward by the denizens of corporate America usefully downplays structural weaknesses in the craft put to sea. "One of the most common explanations [for the scandals]

---

[68] Henry Kaufman, "A straighter path for Wall Street", *Financial Times*, 4 December 2002.

[69] Howard Kurtz, "On CNBC, boosters for the boom", *Washington Post*, 12 November 2002.

[70] For a further discussion on the role of the financial media see A. Larry Elliot and Richard J. Schroth, *How Companies Lie* (Nicholas Brealey, London, 2002), pp. 118–29.

is the perfect storm: a confluence of unusual forces. But when I look at it, I'm more inclined to go back to the underlying ideology that legitimised certain management practices."[71]

The perennial claims of monetarist economists that the markets act rationally and that destabilizing speculation is a contradiction in terms have been comprehensively falsified, technical justification by reference to "insiders" and "outsiders" notwithstanding:

> The insiders destabilize by driving the price up and up, selling out at the top to the outsiders, who buy at the top and sell out at the bottom when the insiders are driving the market down. The losses of the outsiders are equal to the gains of the insiders, and the market as a whole is a standoff ... But the professional insiders initially destabilize by exaggerating the upswings and the falls, while the outside amateurs who buy high and sell low are less price manipulators than the victims of euphoria, which infects them late in the day. When they lose, they go back to their normal occupations to save for another splurge.[72]

The corporate governance crisis demonstrates that one did not have to break the law to rake in millions of dollars from overvalued stock. Corporate accounts were rendered indecipherable because of opaque accounting that allowed firms to book potential future profits against losses, skewing the real bottom line:

> Bill Clinton came up with the greatest line to describe the kind of thinking that got us into this kind of trouble in the first place when he said, it all depends on what is, is. A friend of mine, a long time investment banker says you can't afford to teach the bean counters that it all depends on what is, is. The beans are either there or they are not there. When you start to get esoteric in fundamental accounting you turn out to be building unreal structures. When people get the idea that this word game is a sufficient substitute for economic activity you get the kind of bubble that we have had that we are now trying to clean up from.[73]

The accountancy revision was deemed necessary to value new technology companies, whose worth was measured not in equipment but

---

[71] Andrew Hill, "Has corporate America learned its lesson", *Financial Times*, 30 December 2002.

[72] Charles P. Kindleberger, *Manias, Panics and Crashes, A History of Financial Crises* (John Wiley & Sons, New York, 2000), pp. 29–30.

[73] Interview with John Moscow, New York City, 9 April 2003.

in intellectual capital. Over time, this gradually became the standard for all major publicly quoted enterprises. The move away from tangible assets was accompanied by a massive growth in the trading of complicated financial derivatives, ostensibly designed to help companies manage risk. The problem was that few understood either the nature of the risk or the complexity of the ruses: not the boards of directors, not the financial analysts, not the financial press and certainly not those at the bottom of the food chain who believed what they were told and suspended disbelief in the "irrationally exuberant" mania that gripped America. Enron was truly the epicentre of the perfect storm, prior to which the meteorologists had gone on strike.[74]

The quest to ascertain who was responsible for the malaise and to what extent its creation is owed to a wider failure of governance has been lost in the maelstrom surrounding the terrorist attacks on New York and Washington on September 11, 2001, an event seared into global collective consciousness. But as the list of corporate failures intensified, after Enron's collapse into bankruptcy on 2 December 2001, the initial temptation by policy-makers to blame individual greed looked increasingly like an acute manifestation of self-deception and self-preservation in equal measure. As a consequence, Wall Street itself is on trial.

---

[74] For a damning assessment of the risks associated with derivative trading see Warren Buffett, "Avoiding a mega-catastrophe", *Fortune*, 17 March 2003. The full text of Warren Buffet's annual newsletter is available online at http://www.berkshirehathaway.com/letters/2002.html

2

Power failure: the fall of Enron

The descent into bankruptcy of Enron and the disintegration of Arthur Anderson, once one of the most powerful accountancy firms in the world, for shredding documents relating to its controversial links with the Texan corporation, has spawned a multibillion dollar industry. The chicanery also raised fundamental questions about the power major corporations actually wield and the corrosive effect of money on the deliberative process in American politics. Given the complexity of the case, the Justice Department appointed an inter-agency task force, the first time that such an approach was taken to investigate white-collar crime within a single organization. From the beginning, there were problems. It was indicative of Enron's sprawling reach that the task force could not utilize local knowledge. Personal connections with former employees of the failed energy and trading leviathan ensured that Houston-based investigators were precluded from playing a major role in the direction of the enquiry. The company's links with the Washington establishment posed similar problems. The Attorney General John Ashcroft announced that he would play no role in the attempt to prosecute because of a potential conflict of interest. Enron had provided him with campaign contributions totalling $7,500.

Responsibility for unravelling the tentacles of corruption at the heart of the Enron enterprise fell on Leslie Caldwell, a securities fraud specialist from San Francisco. Caldwell made her name prosecuting organized crime figures in Brooklyn, before transferring to the securities fraud office in Manhattan. Recruited by Robert Mueller, now the Director of the FBI, she moved to San Francisco to open a similar operation on the west coast. Her credentials were impeccable, but the fact that an energy company had so comprehensively con-taminated all levels of the Justice Department indicates just what is at stake in the Enron debacle.[1]

The unit, which comprises agents from the FBI, the Internal Revenue Service (IRS) and 30 attorneys seconded from the Depart-ment of Justice itself, successfully prosecuted Arthur Anderson for destroying documents. Building its case slowly and methodically by a classic divide-and-conquer strategy, the focus is moving inexorably to the top of the management chain, unwrapping in the process the tissue of lies that held the company together. Former employees were made deals they could not refuse: in return for co-operation, reduced jail sentences and only partial forfeiture of assets. Pivotal to the success of the investigation has been the evidence provided by Michael Kopper, a middle-level executive who colluded with the CFO to establish the off-balance sheet partnerships that were at the root of the scandal.

These complex financial manoeuvres simultaneously defrauded the company and allowed it to continue to book the revenue increases that drove the share price upward. The scheme was so embedded in opaque structures that it was almost impossible to detect while revenue sales and, by extension, the stock price remained buoyant. But there was a fatal flaw in the arrangement. The company, in effect, was hedging against itself. In circumstances where Enron's own share price began to fall, even the most optimistic forecast could not stave off the inevitable slide into bankruptcy and exposure. For the Justice Department investigators, the central issue involved ascertaining whether this manipulation of arcane accountancy regulations was a corporate crime in which the company itself had acted as a criminal enterprise or whether Enron's directors were themselves, through

---

[1] For a profile of Caldwell see Stacy Finz, "Newsmaker profile: Leslie Caldwell", *San Francisco Chronicle*, 21 January 2002.

excessive and misplaced trust, unwitting victims of an audacious financial scam orchestrated by its CFO. In peeling back the corrupted layers, the prosecutors were also revealing agency failures at every level of responsibility.

Loyalty, so rooted in the publicy trumpeted corporate culture of Enron, was to be a further casualty as the search for scapegoats and justification intensified throughout the summer. Kopper's testimony in Houston that he paid substantial kickbacks to Fastow to participate in the partnerships has proved essential in building a prima facie case to charge senior management with fraud. Kopper pleaded guilty to wire fraud and money-laundering and agreed to repay $12m gained through criminal activity.[2] Attention has now turned to ascertaining who controlled the intricacies of the Enron operation – in particular, the machinations of Fastow and the CEO, Jeffrey Skilling, under the chairmanship of Ken Lay. Fastow is the most senior executive charged with criminal offences. On 31 October 2002 he was indicted on 78 counts of fraud, money-laundering and obstruction of justice. Freed on bail set at $5m, his trial is scheduled to begin in Houston in June 2003.

The announcement in January 2000 of a 20-year partnership between Enron and the video rental chain Blockbuster marked a potential watershed in the provision of home entertainment. Utilizing the geek language of the time, Ken Lay regarded the deal as "the killer app of the entertainment industry."[3] Like many of the ideas associated with Enron, in principle a sound business case could be made for the partnership. The problem was in the execution of the contract. Under the terms of the partnership, the Blockbuster chain would provide both the product and brand recognition, Enron would provide the infrastructure through the laying of fibre-optic cable along its gas pipeline network criss-crossing the United States. Within months,

---

[2] Kurt Eichenwald, "Ex-Enron official admits payments to finance chief", *New York Times*, 22 August 2002.

[3] For details of the Blockbuster deal see Rebecca Smith, "Blockbuster deal shows Enron's inclination to all show, little substance partnerships", *Wall Street Journal*, 17 January 2002.

the deal of a lifetime collapsed in a welter of recrimination over poor marketing, lack of demand and mutual distrust among the founding partners. This did not stop Enron from booking $110.9m in profits from the failed venture, nor did it prompt awkward questions either from Wall Street analysts or federal investigators. This failure of over-sight is rendered all the more remarkable because only 1,000 homes had access to the pilot project, and few of them actually paid for the service.

Enron's creative accounting was based on a separate transaction with the investment bank Canadian Imperial Bank Corporation (CIBC) World Markets. In return for Enron relinquishing the bulk of its share of the profits, CIBC, World Markets provided the Houston corporation with $115.2m. Significantly, the new partnership con-trolling the Enron stake had no additional staff seconded from CIBC, nor did ownership risk transfer to the Canadian bank. Enron promised to reimburse all money should the venture fail. Not only did the deal serve to occlude major losses in the broadband division, it also masked what amounted to a loan. On 12 March 2003 two low-level executives within the broadband unit at Enron were charged with securities fraud for their role in the improper booking of $111m in profits and obstruction of a federal investigation, in a move widely interpreted to put pressure on them to provide evidence against Skelling.[4]

The Securities and Exchange Commission (SEC) charges revealed that Fastow had knowledge of the transaction and had provided oral guarantees that there would be no risk to the bank's equity exposure.

---

[4] Rebecca Smith, "Enron executives face federal fraud charges", *Wall Street Journal*, 13 March 2003. The SEC filed similar charges, see *SEC vs. Kevin Howard and Michael Krautz*, Civil Action No. H-03-0905 (Harmon). According to the SEC complaint, "The Braveheart transaction and the earnings it generated were fraudulent" (p. 5). In its summary, the SEC painted a damning picture of orchestrated deception. "Project Braveheart was a sham from its inception. The transaction had no economic substance and was created solely for the purpose of generating earnings. The joint venture partner [CIBC] was an entity that never intended to participate as a partner, and its equity was not at risk because Enron guaranteed the entity a short-term take-out at a specified rate of return" (p. 2).

The court documents produce an email exchange between two CIBC bankers suggesting that senior executives in Enron were aware of the transaction and its purpose:

> Unfortunately there can be no documented means of guaranteeing the equity ... We have a general understanding with Enron that any equity loss is a very bad thing. They have been told that if we sustain any equity losses, we will no longer do these types of transactions with them. Not many institutions are willing to take such risks so it is important to Enron to keep us happy ... We have done many "trust me" equity transactions over the past 3 years and have sustained no losses to date. If there has been a case where the value of the asset has been in question, Enron has purchased the asset at par plus our accrued yield.[5]

The question of who ultimately was responsible for the fall of Enron reaches far beyond the narrow confines of the Enron boardroom, however, and therefore the Justice Department investigation. The bankruptcy of what was once the seventh most powerful corporation in America represents a failure at every level of political and economic responsibility. It is a fact acknowledged by the General Accounting Office (GAO) in its interpretation of the structured finance deals involving Enron and the nation's most prominent investment banks. While recognizing the difficulties faced by the SEC in bringing successful prosecutions for deliberately engaging in fraudulent activity, the GAO warned that greater oversight was necessary. "Since investment banks might be tempted to participate in profitable but questionable transactions when successful SEC prosecution is in doubt, it is especially important that regulators be alert to this possibility and be ready to use the rest of their enforcement tools to deter such actions."[6] This stark conclusion – suggesting the ever-present risk of deception because of poor oversight, vigorous competition for business and difficulties of proving fraudulent activity – is a far-from-ringing endorsement of the corporate model.

---

[5] *SEC vs. Kevin Howard and Michael Krautz*, Civil Action No. H-03-0905 (Harmon), p. 8.

[6] GAO, "Investment banks, the role of firms and their analysts with Enron and Global Crossing", March 2003, GAO-03-511, p. 39. Full text available online http://www.gao.gov/cgi-bin/getrpt?GAO-03-511

It is precisely for this reason that attention must be focused on an extraordinary civil action now under consideration in a Houston court. Even for a country obsessed with hyperbole, the scope of the litigation is staggering. The case is destined to become the most explosive economic and political trial in American history:

> Each of the defendants sued for fraud engaged in or participated in the implementation of manipulative devices to inflate Enron's reported profits and financial condition, made or participated in the making of false and misleading statements and participated in a scheme to defraud or a course of business that operated as a fraud or a deceit on purchasers of Enron's publicly traded securities between 10/19/98 and 11/27/01 ... This fraudulent scheme and course of business enabled defendants to pocket billions of dollars of legal, accounting, auditing and consulting fees, underwriting commissions, interest and credit facility payments, cash bonuses based on Enron's reported earnings and stock performance and illegal insider trading proceeds, such that each defendant was significantly enriched.[7]

The complaint, filed on behalf of the Regents of the University of California, represents a serious assault on the citadels of power in Wall Street and Washington. It extends culpability far beyond the now discredited management team. The class action asserts the masterpiece of deceit, lies and arrogance is essentially the intellectual copyright of American capitalism. Blowback, a term used by the CIA for the unintended negative consequences of arming those who then turn against their masters, could equally apply to the role played by the investment banks in the fall of Enron.[8] Driving the case is apportionment of motive and opportunity to the investment banks, critical

---

[7] *Mark Selby et al. vs. Enron Corp*, Consolidated Claim Against Violation of Securities Law, pp. 3–4. The initial complaint was lodged in October 2001, identifying the defendants as officers of Enron and its auditors. The extended complaint was lodged on 7 April. For press reporting see Katherine Kranhold and Jonathan Weill, "Enron holders' suit adds new defendants", *Wall Street Journal*, 8 April 2002.

[8] See Chalmers Johnston, *Blowback, The Costs and Consequences of American Empire* (Owl Books, London, 2000). "The term 'blowback', which officials of the Central Intelligence Agency first invented for their own internal use, is starting to circulate among students of international relations. It refers to the unintended consequences of policies that were kept secret from the American people. What the daily press reports as the malign acts of 'terrorists' or 'drug lords' or 'rogue states' or 'illegal arms merchants' often turn out to be blowback from earlier American operations" (p. 8).

components for a successful legal strategy. Following the bankruptcy protection filing from Enron, extending blame to the banks that funded the structure has practical as well as moral rationale: it provides the plaintiffs with defendants capable of paying the bill.

It is not simply individual directors of the corporation, its accountants and lawyers who are named as complicit in the fraud, therefore, but the investment powerhouses of Wall Street, including some of the most prestigious firms in the country, "This fraudulent scheme could not have been and was not perpetrated only by Enron and its insiders. It was designed and/or perpetrated only via the active and knowing involvement of ... Enron's banks, including JP Morgan, Citigroup, CS First Boston, Merrill Lynch, Deutsche Bank, Barclays, Lehman Brothers and Bank of America. Each of these actors directly violated the securities law and played an important role in the fraudulent scheme and wrongful course of action complained of."[9]

The complaint holds that the banks were responsible for structuring or financing the secret partnerships used to keep debt off the balance sheets at critical junctures to ensure that Enron's quarterly filings met, or exceeded, Wall Street's expectations. Investment banks "at key times advanced funds to help them to complete bogus transactions just before year- or quarter-end and helped create huge profits via transactions between Enron and those entities. The banks also provided loans that enabled Enron to preserve its liquidity and continue to operate while helping Enron sell billions of dollars of securities to public investors to utilize to pay down Enron's short-term commercial paper and bank debt, again to keep the Enron Ponzi scheme in operation and the banks also played an indispensable role in helping to inflate and support Enron's stock price by issuing research reports that contained false and misleading information about Enron's business, finances and future prospects."[10]

---

[9] Consolidated Complaint, p. 45.

[10] Ibid., pp. 45–47. Charles Ponzi was a notorious fraudster who pioneered a pyramid investment scheme in Boston in the 1920s, promising investors that he would double their capital within 90 days. When the scam collapsed following a federal investigation, Ponzi was imprisoned for securities fraud.

The complaint utilizes legal precedent concerning the role of underwriters to independently verify company accounts before offering securities to the market in order to build a case that asserts the banks "grossly violated these duties in their dealings with Enron."[11] The case law suggests that "an underwriter who does not make a reasonable investigation is derelict in his responsibilities to deal fairly with the investing public." Furthermore, that investigation must "not rely solely on the company's officers or the company's counsel." In a further case, the court has ruled that "tacit reliance on management assertions are unacceptable; the underwriters must play devil's advocate."[12]

In the course of charting Enron's rise to global dominance as an innovator, the investment banks were willing partners not only in the provision of loans but crucially also in the development of the complex financial architecture that was Enron's real claim to notoriety. Special Purpose Entities (SPEs), had long been used to provide a form of bridging finance for the motion picture business. Enron's manipulation of the system, with the connivance of Wall Street, was so gargantuan that it would have been rejected at pre-script stage in Hollywood as both implausible and incapable of execution. Yet, so successful was the financing that it was the market itself that faced the ultimate sanction when the complex structure began to show the strains.

Determined to stave off collapse and therefore exposure of their own responsibility, the banks kept the lifeline to the Houston firm and called in favours to the political elite in Washington. The growing financialization of the American economy and the revolving door policy that had seen top investment bankers and lawyers spend time in government service as a crucial part of the curriculum vitae building process was encapsulated in the actions of Robert Rubin, a former Treasury Secretary under Bill Clinton. Prior to his interregnum in Washington, Rubin was senior partner in Goldman Sachs, the most

[11] Ibid., p. 341.
[12] Ibid., pp. 340–1.

venerable investment bank in the country. After he resigned from his government position he returned to Wall Street to serve as a vice-chairman of Citigroup.

Rubin was, in effect, a troubleshooter for the financial services conglomerate. His combination of investment banking skills and political acumen were very marketable commodities as the bull market began to stumble. Although he had no specific dealings with Enron, Rubin initiated a telephone call to a senior civil servant who had served under him at the Treasury Department. Rubin warned the bureaucrat that if Enron collapsed, the impact on the world capital markets would be profound. Whether the call was a threat or a warning was immaterial. The fact that he prefaced his remarks with the comment that "this was probably not a good idea" indicated awareness that it was inappropriate for an investment banker to tacitly ask the government to prop up a private sector company, even one as well connected as Enron.

Further attempts were made to influence the judgement of the Chairman of the New York Federal Reserve William McDonough. Neither approach proved successful in provoking the government to act. Unlike a previous intervention in 1998 to stave off the collapse of Long Term Asset Management, a mutual fund whose imminent collapse threatened to provoke a meltdown of the entire corporate banking sector, Enron was deemed a corrupted company whose disintegration, although destabilizing, was not fatal. Armed with inside knowledge about how precarious Enron's position in reality had become, the emphasis by the banks was on minimizing their own individual exposure. It was a race against time, and time was running out. The continued slide in the stock market and the impact on global financial stability occasioned by the al Qaeda terrorist attacks on New York and Washington triggered further falls that even the most bullish analyst reports could not stem.

While Citigroup loaned the most money to Enron, the relationship cut across the major investment banking conglomerates, in large part because of the decision by the Houston company to enhance its leverage over investment houses by spreading its deals across Wall

Street. This strategy ensured that the banks actively competed for access to Enron's lucrative accounts and participated in schemes that clearly demonstrated enormous conflicts of interest. As Robert Roach, a senior investigator for Congress, pointed out: "clearly Enron was a big player on Wall Street at that period of time. They were doling out lucrative contracts for a lot of business to a lot of people. And Enron was not shy about telling potential suitors that if you want our business, you have to belly up to the bar."[13] For whatever reason – greed, avarice, an unwillingness to sacrifice a lucrative client – many of the major names in Wall Street joined in the off-shore partnerships cooked up by Andy Fastow, the CFO of Enron.

The most important of these called LJM2 was concocted by Merrill Lynch and promoted to a select group of investors at a meeting in the affluent Floridian resort of Boca Raton. The dual role played by Fastow in the deal should have sounded alarm bells. In fact, the Donaldson, Lufkin & Jeenrette Securities Corporation, in passing up on the offer to issue the securities, explicitly cited the perception of a conflict of interest.[14] But the doyens of Wall Street showed no such compunction. Offering a return of 30% a year on what Merrill described as an "unusually attractive investment opportunity", over $394m was raised: $16.6m came from Merrill's own executives, the company itself invested $5m and other contributors included Dresdner Kleinwort Wasserstein, Credit Suisse First Boston Corporation, JP Morgan Chase, Lehman Brothers and Citigroup.[15]

The prospectus for the offering made it quite clear that pivotal to its success was the active participation in the scheme of Enron's CFO. Investors were promised that Fastow would have day-to-day control of operations and the prospectus confidently proclaimed that it would

---

[13] Robert Roach Testimony, p. 24.

[14] William Donaldson, the founder of the firm is now the Chairman of the SEC.

[15] See William Powers, *Report of Investigation by the Special Investigative Committee of the Board of the Directors of Enron Corp*, 1 February 2002 (hereinafter *Powers Report*), pp. 72–3. See also Robert Bryce, *Pipe Dreams, Greed, Ego and the Death of Enron* (Public Affairs, New York, 2002), p. 223 and Loren Fox, *Enron, The Rise and Fall* (John Wiley & Sons, Hoboken, NJ, 2002), pp. 177–8.

be expected that "Enron will be the Partnership's primary source of investment opportunities." The conflicts of interest involved magnified when the prospectus notified prospective clients that the new partnership "expects to benefit from having the opportunity to invest in Enron-generated investment opportunities that would not be available to outside investors." In order to eradicate any doubt about whom the main beneficiary of the relationship would be, it specifically noted that Fastow's "access to Enron's information pertaining to potential investments will contribute to superior returns."[16]

It was the unravelling of the LJM2 partnership that was to propel Enron toward the bankruptcy courts. On 16 October 2001 Enron announced that it was taking a $544m after-tax charge against earnings related to transactions with LJM2. It announced a $1.2bn reduction of shareholder's equity related to transactions with the same entity. One month later, the existence of two previous partnerships, LJM1 and Chewco, became public with the decision to restate all financial results from 1997 to 2001. Confidence in the integrity of the Enron business model went into a tailspin. It set in motion the unstoppable journey to humiliating exposure as little more than an upmarket confidence trick and to a questioning of the entire American corporate model. The responsibility spread outward in concentric circles from Enron's morally challenged board, to its auditors, the investment banks and ultimately to the political culture itself.

Following the collapse of the corporation, the board appointed William Powers, Dean of the Law Faculty at the University of Texas to draw up a report into what exactly had happened and why. The report's authors were incredulous that the Enron board could have allowed such a fundamental breach of prudent corporate governance rules. Allowing Fastow to participate on both sides of the same deal was viewed as "fundamentally flawed. A relationship with the most senior financial officer of a public company – particularly one requiring as many controls and as much oversight by others – should

---

[16] *Powers Report*, p. 72.

not have been undertaken in the first place."[17] Nor, in the estimation
of the *Powers Report*, should the company have left itself open to a
scheme in which it was effectively a patsy for the financial alchemy as
practised by Fastow and his other colleagues operating the partnerships. This personal enrichment of Enron employees, however, was
merely one aspect of a deeper and more serious problem. According to
the *Powers Report*, allowing derogation from the regulations governing
the Ethics Committee not once but twice was indicative of a board
unwilling or unable to do its job:

> These partnerships – Chewco, LJM1 and LJM2 – were used by Enron manage-
> ment to enter into transactions that it could not, or would not, do with
> unrelated commercial entities. Many of the most significant transactions ap-
> parently were designed to accomplish favourable financial statement results, not
> to achieve bona fide economic objectives or transfer risk ... They allowed
> Enron to conceal from the market very large losses resulting from Enron's
> merchant investments by creating an appearance that those investments
> were hedged – that is, that a third party was obligated to pay Enron the
> amount of those losses – when in fact that third party was simply an entity
> in which Enron had a substantial economic stake. We believe these transac-
> tions resulted in Enron reported earnings from the third quarter of 2000 through
> the third quarter of 2001 that were almost $1 billion higher than should have
> been reported.[18]

An examination of the compensation paid to Enron's board and the
lucrative consultancy sinecures many held provide further damning
evidence of the conflicts of interest endemic within Enron. Put
simply, there was a corporate failure to invigilate the direction
management was taking the company. In part, this reticence can be
traced back to the fact that the ramping up of share price via the
dispensation from ethics regulations served to enhance their own
compensation.

In the apportionment of blame, the *Powers Report* self-consciously
extended culpability outward from the board to the auditors, who had
failed to even note the conflicts of interests. "In virtually all of the

---

[17] Ibid., p. 9.
[18] Ibid., p. 4.

transactions, Enron's accounting treatment was determined with extensive participation and structuring advice from Anderson, which management reported to the board. Enron's records show that Anderson billed Enron $5.7m for advice in connection with the LJM and Chewco transactions alone, above and beyond its regular audit fees."[19] The investigation into the wider issue of the role of the investment banks was severely handicapped by its lack of power to subpoena witnesses to testify. The full truth behind the incubation of the virus that was to destroy the immunity of Wall Street was to await wider investigation by Congress. Enron's fall from grace and the complex issues it raised about the role of the corporation in modern society made the involvement of Washington simultaneously necessary and further destabilizing.

The hearings raised more questions than they answered. Ken Lay and Andy Fastow refused to testify; pleading the Fifth Amendment. Jeffrey Skilling did fence with the investigators, but claimed ignorance of the machinations involved. "The entire management and board of Enron has been labelled everything from hucksters to criminals with complete disregard for the facts in evidence. These untruths shatter lives and do nothing to advance the public understanding of what happened at Enron," Skilling told congressional senators he accused of presiding over a witch-hunt.[20] The hearings did give the appearance of placing those who had displeased their masters into the modern equivalent of the medieval stocks, allowing for an unctuous display of hypocrisy from an assembly that had consciously lacked oversight during the long years of Enron's ascent. A prime example was the 1996 deregulation of the Californian energy markets. Rather than reducing costs, the result was rolling "brown-out and an increase in energy costs per kmegawatt from $30 to $300"; in some instances that rose to $1,000. When the State governor imposed price caps to restrain the avaricious nature of Enron and the other players in the

---

[19] Ibid., p. 5.
[20] Peter Spiegel, "Ex-Enron chief Skilling lashes out at critics", *Financial Times*, 27 February 2002.

market, who were profiting enormously from power blackouts, Vice-President Dick Cheney condemned the move: "Frankly, California is looked on by many folks as a classic example of the kings of problems that arise when you use price caps ... There's no magic wand that Washington can wave.[21] Attempts by the state to force the issue of price manipulation onto the agenda were ignored by the White House, which endorsed many of the recommendations on energy supply – including opposition to price caps – that Enron had promulgated. Until the firm's bankruptcy ripped off its political cover, the symbiotic relationship was one in which ethics were replaced with self-interest at both the corporate and political level, a failing that encompassed pro-business Democrats.[22]

Much more enlightening was the decision to call on the banks to explain not only their involvement with the Enron management but also the methods through which they attempted to recoup the multi-million dollar exposure, while remaining silent about the impending catastrophe. The evidence adduced by the Senate Permanent Sub-committee on Investigations in three separate hearings into the alleged complicity of some of the most prestigious firms on Wall Street not only exposed a culture of denial but provided damning evidence for the class action now before the Houston court.

Citigroup had provided almost $5bn in loans and JP Morgan and other institutions almost $4bn. In return, not only did the banks receive a major payment in consultancy business and interest charges, more insidiously, as noted above, senior investment

---

[21] Quoted in Woodrow W. Clark and Istemi Demirag, "Enron the failure of corporate governance", *Journal of Corporate Citizenship*, Winter 2002, pp. 107–22.

[22] Woodrow W. Clark and Istemi Demirag, "Enron the failure of corporate governance", *Journal of Corporate Citizenship*, Winter 2002, p. 110. The extent to which the White House slavishly followed the Enron agenda in its determination of overarching policy remains hotly contested. The White House refused the General Audit Office access to its documents, thereby preventing independent adjudication of the executive's claim that Enron was not unfairly advantaged. Clark and Demirag argue that not enough attention has been placed on the politics and economics of the problem of deregulation. "In short, the politicians who supported deregulation from both political parties are as much at fault as the accounting firm" (p. 119).

bankers availed themselves of the corrupted systems designed by Enron's management team. "Just as responsible" was the jaded response of the chief investigator of the congressional subcommittee Robert Roach.[23]

Roach argues that the banks provided the means and the funding for the financial alchemy and are as culpable for the corporate collapse as the managers themselves. "In some cases, the financial institutions were aware that Enron was using questionable accounting. Some financial institutions not only knew, they actively aided Enron in return for fees and favourable consideration in other business dealings. The evidence indicates that Enron would not have been able to engage in the extent of the accounting deceptions it did, involving billions of dollars, were it not for the active participation of major financial institutions willing to go along with and even expand upon Enron's activities. The evidence also indicates that at least in one case these financial institutions knowingly allowed investors to rely on Enron's financial statements that they knew or should have known were misleading."[24]

In his presentation to Congress, Roach argued that the banks had facilitated a number of "prepay" contracts that illegally disguised loans through shell companies as legitimate trading. The company had obtained a staggering "$8bn in financing over approximately 6 years, including $3.7 billion from 12 transactions with Chase and $4.8 billion from 14 transactions with Citigroup."[25] The net result of this fraudulent accounting was a 40% reduction in its total debt and a 50% increase in its fund flows from operations. This deception had a fundamental effect on the company's credit rating and share price and was only achievable with the collusion of the corporate world. In a damning assessment, Roach revealed that "internal communications show that it was common knowledge among Enron, Chase and Citigroup employees that the 'prepays' were designed to achieve

---

[23] Robert Roach, "The banks that robbed the world", *The Money Programme*, BBC, 29 January 2003.

[24] Robert Roach testimony, p. 14.

[25] Ibid., p. 16.

accounting, not business objectives and that Enron was booking the prepay proceeds as trading activity rather than debt. The evidence indicates that Chase and Citigroup not only understood Enron's accounting goal, but designed and implemented the financial structures to help Enron achieve its objectives. Moreover, they accepted and followed Enron's desire to keep the nature of these transactions confidential. By design and intent, the prepays as structured by Enron and the financial institutions made it impossible for investors, analysts, and other financial institutions to uncover the true level of Enron's indebtedness."[26]

Jackie Avery, a former tax manager with Enron, endorses this view of systematic collusion. In an interview with the *Money Programme*, she alleged that investment bankers constantly bombarded her with presentations on how to manipulate or "sidestep the accounting rules or sidestep the tax rules."[27] The *modus operandi* was tax avoidance rather than tax evasion, but the outcome was the same: the institutionalized deception of individual and institutional investors and the evasion of billions of dollars in federal taxes. As the Joint Committee on Taxation noted in its exhaustive survey of Enron's strategy, the use of prepaid contracts were designed to mask rising indebtedness as trading profits. "Because of the way in which the transactions were structured, Enron portrayed its financial condition in a more favourable light – from the viewpoint of its credit rating and market valuation – by reporting the transactions as part of its trading operations rather than as debt for financial accounting purposes."[28]

In February 2003, Merrill Lynch agreed to pay $80m to settle civil charges from the SEC that it had participated in a fraudulent scheme

---

[26] Ibid., p. 17.

[27] The role played by the investment houses in the tax shelters utilized by Enron are fully explored in a 2,700-page report published by Congress in February 2003. See Joint Committee on Taxation, *Report of Investigation of Enron Corporation and Related Entities regarding Federal Tax and Compensation Issues, and Policy Recommendations*, JCS-3-03, February 2003.

[28] Joint Committee on Taxation, *Report of Investigation of Enron Corporation and Related Entities regarding Federal Tax and Compensation Issues, and Policy Recommendations*, JCS-3-03, February 2003, p. 346.

to artificially enhance Enron's earnings. In a press release the company noted "without admitting or denying any wrongdoing, Merrill Lynch would consent to an injunction enjoining the company from violations of the federal securities laws."[29] The non-chalant response deliberately underplays a revelation of staggering proportions. The SEC charges that in December 1999 Merrill had facilitated Enron with a disguised $7m loan that would allow Enron to book $12m in revenue secured from the sale in Nigeria of electric power generated from three barges. In its complaint, filed with the Houston court and accepted by Merrill, the SEC argued that "based on their substantial assistance to Enron, defendants aided and abetted Enron's violations of federal securities law."[30] A separate transaction involved $60m in fictitious oil and gas trades. In both cases, significant evidence was uncovered in both the congressional investigations and the SEC civil charge that pointed to institutionalized collusion, despite the testimony of the company's Senior Vice-President and President of International Private Client Division Kelly Martin that "Merrill Lynch believes that our limited dealings with Enron were appropriate." Martin claimed, somewhat unconvincingly, that the bank had been unwittingly duped:

> Our firm dealt with Enron at an arm's length relationship and made business decisions based on information that was then available. We relied on Enron's accountant's opinions, its board approvals, its lawyer's opinions, its audit committee oversight and other governance processes, and felt justified at the time in believing Enron's financial representations ... At no time did we engage in transactions that we thought improper.[31]

Martin maintained that the deal was secured "largely to build a relationship with Enron" and believed that it was likely, although

---

[29] Merrill Lynch Press Release, 20 February 2003. Available online at http://www.ml.com/about/press_release/02202003-1_enron_issues_pr. htmwww.ml.com. See also Randall Smith, "Merrill Lynch reaches pact with SEC on Enron issues", *Wall Street Journal*, 21 February 2003.

[30] *SEC vs. Merrill Lynch et al.*, Civil Action No. H-03-0946 (Hoyt).

[31] Testimony of Kelly Martin, "The role of the financial institutions in Enron's collapse", *Hearings before the Permanent Subcommittee of Investigations*, 23 July 2002, p. 174.

not certain, that a third party unaffiliated with Enron would ultimately purchase Merrill Lynch's shares in the company. He further noted that it was not Merrill Lynch's role to ascertain whether Enron had accounted for the transaction properly. "In general, when we act as a purchaser or a seller, we are not asked for and do not provide advice on the other party's accounting treatment; rather we expect them and their experts to determine the appropriate accounting treatment onto themselves."

An internal memo produced at the hearings, however, painted a much bleaker picture:

> Jeff McMahon, Enron Vice-President and Treasurer, has asked Merrill Lynch to purchase $7m of equity in a special purpose vehicle that will allow Enron Corporation to book $10m of earnings. The transaction must close by 12-31-99. Enron is viewing this transaction as a bridge to permanent equity, and they believe our hold will be for less than six months. The investment would have a 22.5 percent return.[32]

A further document from Merrill described the deal as "most unusual ... This transaction will allow Enron to move assets of balance sheet and book future cash flows currently as 1999 earnings, approximately $12m. IBK [Investment Banking] was supportive based on Enron relationship, approximately $40m in annual revenues and assurances from Enron management that will be taken out of our $7m investment within the next three to six months."

Merrill executives confirmed to the congressional committee that the negotiations over the barge contract were concluded with Enron agreeing to "repay Merrill Lynch's money plus a 15 per cent rate of interest and an upfront $250,000 fee, making the effective interest rate 22.5 percent."[33] Carl Levin was scathing about Merrill's role in the funding, "It is very clear, overwhelmingly clear, that the risks of owning Ebarge were not transferred to Merrill Lynch and indeed there was never a real sale by any of the accounting standards which have to

---

[32] Ibid., p. 178.
[33] Senator Carl Levin, ibid., p. 179.

be applied before the term 'sale' can be applied to a transaction ...
This was a relationship loan. The accounting rules indicate that it was
not a real sale. Merrill Lynch knew it, Enron knew it, and yet Enron
booked $12m in income from the proposed sale or supposed sale, and
that was a deception in its financial statement, and Merrill Lynch was
a participant in that deception."[34] This despite the fact that a senior
executive within the corporation had flagged up the "reputational
risk" involved in aiding financial engineering. Kelly Martin was left
with only one card to play – herd instinct:

> Enron was a very aggressive client. Enron was recognized by everybody in the
> United States and perhaps globally, from Wall Street to government to con-
> sulting to academia, as the future way that American companies could poten-
> tially be run. It was $40 billion in revenue. It was an aggressive company. Their
> whole thesis, as stated publicly in multiple situations, was physical assets aren't
> needed; financial assets and off-balance sheet assets are the way to go ... So
> clearly, we were focused on working with them as a growth company, as a big
> company, as a seeming industry leader, certainly in their industry and corporate
> America.[35]

The deal, which ends the SEC's investigation of Merrill Lynch's
dealings with Enron, leaves unresolved the wider issue of the
company's involvement in the LJM2 partnership. It served notice,
however, that further protestations of innocence by the banks
would be met with derision by the regulators and legislators. As
Senator Joseph Lieberman pointed out in his cross-examination of
Kelly Martin, "Enron was like a poisonous spider spinning a web for
its own benefit, in which it was engaging and entrapping a whole host
of very reputable financial institutions, including your own, but your
entrapment was not unknowing, or in some sense unwilling ... The
poisonous web that Enron was spinning, nonetheless had some
attractive qualities to it for you. It had a business relationship. It
had fees."[36]

---

[34] Senator Carl Levin, ibid., p. 183.
[35] Testimony of Kelly Martin, ibid., pp. 183–4.
[36] Senator Lieberman, ibid., p. 189.

The corrosive compact between ethically challenged corporate figures and their bankers was magnified precisely because of the deregulation of the American financial services industry and the development of sophisticated financial engineering both in terms of increasing revenue and, crucially, reducing tax exposure.

"Enron and its advisers conspired to mine the tax code for tax schemes," was the desultory response of Senator Max Baucus, the most senior Democrat representative on the Finance Committee. Quoted in the *Wall Street Journal*, Baucus maintained that "they ensured that no one – particularly the IRS – would ever discover what they were up to."[37] Among the firms providing the advice on the tax shelters were the powerhouses of corporate financing: Bankers Trust, Arthur Anderson, JP Morgan, Chase Manhattan, Deutsche Bank and Deloitte & Touche.

In recommending a fundamental reassessment of the tax code, the congressional report into Enron's tax strategies noted "increasing challenges to the rationality of certain tax rules that have been developed on the basis of categorical distinctions that may no longer reflect meaningful economic distinctions. In general the tax rules should endeavour to reduce or eliminate the extent to which the tax consequences of economically similar transactions are impacted by their characterization ... For example, notional principal contracts with significant upfront nonperiodic payments, prepaid forward contracts and secured lending transactions should all have the same or similar tax consequences to the extent that they all yield the same or similar economic results."[38]

The various measures aggressively adopted by Enron proved exceptionally useful in reducing its tax liability and amounted to a calculated attempt to defraud the treasury. Behind the opaque façade, when the complexity of the aggressive accountancy was unravelled, there

---

[37] Deborah Solomon, "Enron report urges penalties for corporate-tax abuse", *Wall Street Journal*, 14 February 2003.

[38] Joint Committee on Taxation, *Report of Investigation of Enron Corporation and Related Entities regarding Federal Tax and Compensation Issues, and Policy Recommendations*, JCS-3-03, February 2003, p. 362.

was an obvious deceit. While Enron was booking revenue of $2bn, it was also posting an operating loss for tax purposes. According to the congressional Enron report, the IRS failed to spot the warning signs:

> A company with significant net operating losses is of less immediate concern to the IRS because the losses will offset any increased taxable income arising from the audit. Thus the IRS has less incentive to investigate and devote resources to such examinations.[39]

Lambasting the "general ineffectiveness of present law in regulating tax shelters" the report concludes that Enron was able to manipulate "the ambiguity of complex provisions of law, lack of administrative guidance, or inconsistent interpretations of the law by courts":

> Tax shelters often involve the juxtaposition of unrelated, incongruous Code provisions in a single transaction or a series of connected transactions. Taxpayers use the complexities of the system to their advantage and perform a clinical assessment of the risks and benefits of an action often concluding that the low risk of effective enforcements (including the low risk of penalties) easily is outweighed by the promised benefits. Until the costs of participating in tax-motivated transactions are substantially increased, corporations such as Enron will continue to engage in transactions that violate the letter or the spirit of the law.[40]

If the IRS lacked the resources to subject the audited accounts to adequate invigilation, the maintenance of the Enron fan club on Wall Street, even as the executive suit began to empty, poses even more fundamental questions. The departure of at least 10 senior Enron executives in the months preceding its collapse is a case in point. No pattern was detected, or if it was it was not publicly disseminated, nor was sufficient doubt generated in the minds of analysts or regulators, who found their computer models incapable

---

[39] Ibid., p. 23.

[40] A further case involving tax shelters created by Ernst & Young for executives of the Sprint Corporation in order to protect bonuses accruing from a major merger, blocked by federal regulators, demonstrates the complexity of ruses used even when the IRS does investigate. See Editorial, "Unbridled greed", *New York Times*, 24 February 2003.

of assessing data from a company involved in a permanent restructuring process. The restructuring generated in turn over $250m in consultancy fees from six major investment banks in 2000 alone.[41] It is estimated that between 1986 and 2001, Enron alone paid Wall Street firms $323m in underwriting fees, powerful incentive then for the minimizing or offsetting the early warning signs that Enron was in trouble.[42] It was a vicious circle that implicated not only the doyens of 1400 Smith Street, the headquarters of Enron in downtown Houston, but also the investment bankers of Wall Street, two thousand miles to the east.

The danger was magnified by the fact that the entire edifice was built on debt. As Kindleberger has pointed out, "an edifice of debt contracted to finance very risky ventures is unstable."[43] Enron's difficulties, masked by the favourable credit rating and high stock price, in part achieved by the dissemination of partial research reports, could essentially be traced to its propensity to use its own stock to hedge against itself, in the hope – and expectation – that the market would continue to rise. It only became vulnerable when the giddiness turned sour and exposed the accounting fraud that underwrote it.

New and radical solutions were necessary to generate new revenue and maintain Enron's share price, which in turn guaranteed exponential increases in consultancy fees. Despite the lack of credible, reliable information, many brokerage houses retained their love affair with a company that constantly rewrote its own rules to ensure it maintained investment-grade rating. One of the few exceptions was a senior gas energy analyst for Merrill Lynch, John Olsen. Working out of the investment bank's Houston office, Olsen was consistent in his refusal to raise the stock recommendation of Enron, despite continued

---

[41] Joshua Chaffin and Sheila McNulty, "A victim of its own greed and ambition", *Financial Times*, 27 November 2002.

[42] John Plender, *Going off the Rails, Global Capital and the Crisis of Legitimacy* (John Wiley & Sons, Chichester, UK, 2003), p. 166.

[43] Charles P. Kindleberger, *Manias, Panics and Crashes, A History of Financial Crises* (John Wiley & Sons, New York, 2000), p. 55.

pressure from his supervisors. In May 1998 Olsen was forced out of his job by refusing to change his analysis. Speaking to the *Washington Post*, Olsen observed that "if you're choice is to walk the plank and get eaten by alligators or retire your job, what are you going to do?"[44] It later transpired that a month prior to the compromise agreement leading to Olsen's departure from the firm, two investment bankers had written to the company president Herbert Allison, complaining that negative stock rating had precluded Merrill from a $750 common stock offering Enron was about to issue.

The memo, discovered during congressional hearings into Enron's collapse, noted that "our [Merrill Lynch] research relationship with Enron has been strained for a long period of time." It complained that Olsen "has not been a real supporter of [Enron]" and had made "snide and embarrassing remarks". They asked Allison to intervene to resolve the dispute. Whatever promises Allison made to his counterpart at Enron, Ken Lay, the results were the same: Merrill's participation in the Enron offering and the showdown with Olsen a month later. Olsen's replacement upgraded the analysis of the stock, and by January 1999 the company found itself with between $45–50m of new investment business. The Chinese walls separating investment and analysis, so lauded by the banks, had in this case served merely to demonstrate how captive the analysts were to the needs of the predatory instincts of the bankers, who ultimately used the research as bait.

Most analysts did not have the scruples of John Olsen. Lacking the information to make rational, informed judgements, Wall Street analysts, like many in the financial press who relied on the brokerage experts to ascertain market sentiment, bought into the hype through ignorance or sold it through wilfulness. Add to this the academic credibility bestowed on Enron by its phalanx of MBA graduates and its widespread use as a case study in innovation, and it was not hard to

---

[44] Quoted by Paula Span and Ben White, "The market scholars' star turn", *Washington Post*, 15 November 2002. The article is the sixth and final part of a landmark series "Bubble: The roots of the 90s boom and bust".

see why the Texan gas-line company was transformed into the seventh largest company in the United States, with aspirations to become the most powerful corporation in the world. Its reputation significantly bolstered by the use of media columnists, who were paid handsomely for providing advice to Enron, and then disseminated its world view without acknowledging their relationship. Among those caught up in this nexus was the *New York Times* columnist Paul Krugman. To the severe embarrassment of both the academic and practitioner communities, these conflicts of interest only became apparent when Enron became the largest bankruptcy seen in American history. Even that was a short-lived dubious distinction. A mere three months later came the similarly unexpected collapse of the telecommunications giant, WorldCom, with total losses of over $9bn.

Malfeasance on such a scale revealed not only the inability of Wall Street to police itself but also the regulatory failure of government, particularly in ensuring basic honesty in the auditing of accounts, the only true way for an outside investor to assess the intrinsic worth of a company. It is a failure acknowledged by the former Chairman of the SEC, Arthur Levitt: "In many ways, Enron's collapse was brought upon by the collision of all the unhealthy attitudes, practices, and conflicts of Wall Street and corporate America."[45] In a devastating critique, the influential political scientist Moises Naim went even further, delivering this damning assessment:

> Aware of the complexity of their operations, rogue managers assumed – often correctly – that even the most probing outsiders would have a hard time detecting the manipulation of financial statements. The pressure to meet or exceed Wall Street earnings expectations, plus the culture of "everybody is getting rich doing it", often made book cooking too tempting to resist. Thus in the 1990s, opportunity, impunity and motive converged in the corporate suites to induce the wave of financial malfeasance.[46]

[45] Arthur Levitt, *Take on the Street* (Pantheon, New York, 2002), p. 13.
[46] Moises Naim, "The roots of corporate scandals", *Financial Times*, 29 September 2002.

The collapse of Enron, one of the most politically savvy corporations in the United States, demonstrated the precarious nature of the overall system. In his exposé of the Enron failure, Robert Bryce notes sardonically that corrupted enterprises "like fish rot at the head."[47] On this reading, Wall Street investment banks, accountants and analysts willingly accede to the publication of suspect company reports to gain business; both corporation and fiduciary provide money to the politicians who in turn create, maintain or change the regulatory framework in which they operate.

It is supremely ironic that the United States has "the most detailed set of ethics regulation and the most extensive network of implementers ever to exist in any country in the history of the world", yet remains powerless to prevent the deleterious effects of the corporate scandal.[48] Those charged with policing the economy lacked the resources or political support to win a game in which the complexity of the new financial offerings made by Wall Street constantly challenged the ability of enforcement departments to understand the implications, let alone ensure adequate policing. In a political, financial and economic system governed by law rather than principle, pragmatism rather than ethics, normative questions ceased to have meaning. The result is that the responsibility for Enron extends beyond even the banking sector and to the corridors of Capital Hill itself.

In noting the increasing power of the corporate sector, the President of the World Bank, James Wolfensohn, has observed that "the governance of the corporation is now as important in the world economy as the government of countries."[49] Equally important, however, is the relationship between the corporate entity and the political system. In an important contribution, Ken Coghill, an

---

[47] Robert Bryce, *Pipe Dreams, Greed, Ego, Jealousy and the Death of Enron* (Public Affairs, New York, 2002), p. 12.

[48] G. Calvin MacKenzie, *Scandal Proof, Do Ethics Laws Make Government Ethical* (Brookings Institution Press, Washington, DC, 2002), p. 83.

[49] Centre for International Private Enterprise, *Corporate Governance: An Antidote to Corruption* (text available online at www.cipe.org).

Australian political scientist, argues that contemporary governance is best described as an interdependent and interconnected compact between state, corporate and civil society. "It is a relationship in constant flux, determined not only by rules and regulations but also relative power and weakness; conditions that vary according to circumstance, both determined and uncertain."[50] The result is a constant battle for advantage within and between each pivotal sector.[51]

While the business scandals owed their emergence to problems within the sector, the conditions that allowed them to flourish can be traced directly to the weakness of either government or wider society to curtail the operation of the capital markets. A number of explanatory factors can be put forward for this structural imbalance: the dependence of politicians on corporate donations to finance ever-increasing election campaigns; the effective lobbying of Congress to change or weaken the regulatory framework in which corporations operate; the ideological retreat from government intervention; and the hubris associated with the self-proclaimed invincibility of the American political and business models that, in turn, can be traced back to the collapse of communism and the failed promise of an Asian dawn.

Central to the untrammelled operation of corporate interests to run roughshod over a weak regulatory structure has been their combined effectiveness in deploying pre-emptive strikes to set the political and economic agenda in legal ways. During the long run of the bull market, donations to charitable causes (particularly the arts and education) were accompanied by astute propagandizing through the placement of favourable – or unquestioning – stories to supplicant sources in the media and intensive lobbying of politicians to prevent regulation, legislation or investigation. In the constant

---

[50] Ken Coghill, "Governance for uncertain times", Research Paper presented at *Judge School of Management, Cambridge University, 18 June 2002.*

[51] This view of a dynamic interchange is central to Robert Dahl's critique of the American fascination with Reagan's doctrine of untrammelled deregulation. See Robert Dahl, *After the Revolution* (Yale University Press, New Haven, CT, 1990), p. 84.

struggle for competitive advantage, already attained power to shape the political agenda was used in a Hobbesian framework to ensure its own dominance:

> I put for a generall inclination of all mankind, a perpetual and restlesse desire of Power after power, that ceaseth only in Death. And the cause of this, is not always that a man hopes for a more intensive delight, than he has already attained to; or that he cannot be content with a moderate power: but because he cannot assure the power and means to live well, which he hath present, without the acquisition of more.[52]

In the context of a booming economy the consequences of the disparity of power in the tri-circular interlocking and interdependent dynamic structure is masked. Following the erosion of three trillion dollars in share value, the pendulum has shifted, with potentially huge consequences in the power structure. What is at issue, therefore, is how to deal with a business culture based on technical compliance with narrowly defined legislation and a working assumption that unless a particular action is declared illegal, it isn't. Precisely because the ethical lapses were allowed to occur through a policy of wilful ignorance, the scandal now afflicting Wall Street is much more serious than the insider-trading investigations that toppled Michael Milken's junk bond operation in the 1980s. Much of Enron's activities had been signed off by accountants and underwritten by investment banks, acting without compunction. Likewise, the conflicts of interest over research analyst independence were endemic and systemic within Wall Street and totally legal. The excesses of past transgression by each sector of the corporate elite were simply forgotten.[53]

It is a fact, now recognized in Wall Street. Gary Lynch, a former head of enforcement at the SEC, made his reputation with the successful prosecution of Milken. Lynch is now Vice-Chairman of Credit

---

[52] Thomas Hobbes, *Leviathan* (Penguin, London, 1985), p. 47.

[53] The memory failing did not only encompass the lesson of the Great Depression or the activities of Milken. Many of the structural failings surrounding the conflicts of interest played by the auditors were central to the collapse of the savings and loans institutions. See for example William Sternberg, "Cooked books", *The Atlantic Monthly*, January 1992.

Suisse First Boston and charged with deflecting further regulation. He believes that the crisis facing the credibility of the market is the most severe he has ever encountered. "It was a case of corrupt individuals encouraged by the times. I don't know how to separate the system from the times from the individuals involved. It was all one piece for me. When you talk about [conflicts of interest over analyst research] that, that was clearly endemic, systemic, whatever, that was true throughout the industry. I have to say it only became viewed as a corrupt problem after the bubble burst."[54]

The problems associated with corporate America in the wake of Enron have also demonstrated clearly that the problem of malfeasance, malefaction and effective governance cannot be solved by reference to the individual firm or even the corporate sector itself, neither in diagnosis nor solution. In large part therefore the traditional debate over effective corporate governance has been irrelevant in tackling the major structural problems or addressing what Plender terms "the crisis of legitimacy facing Anglo-American capitalism." Understanding the causes of the problem is therefore necessary if the cycle of corporate crime is to be broken. Steve Letza is undoubtedly correct in highlighting the need to reformulate the debate to take into account "the fact that corporate governance is a social process, which cannot be isolated from social and non-economic factors such as power, legislation, social partnerships and institutional contexts."[55] In short, it is necessary to construct a political economy of corruption in the United States that gives due cognizance to the operation of the political and economic marketplace. Given that the structural problems incubate the virus of corruption at every level of operation, the need to map its interlocking components becomes pivotal to any understanding of contemporary America.

It is impossible to overestimate the extent of the challenge facing

[54] Interview with Gary Lynch, New York City, 7 February 2003.

[55] Steve Letza, James Kirkbride and Xiuping Sun, "Shareholding versus stakeholding: A critical review of corporate governance", paper presented at *Third International Conference of the British Accounting Association Special Interest Group on Corporate Governance, Queen's University, Belfast, 16 December 2002.*

legislators, regulators and the corporate sector itself arising from the crisis of confidence facing the equities market. "Unless the key people who work in such institutions possess a moral compass, it doesn't matter how many regulations and how many laws you pass – this stuff is still going to go on," is the unambiguous and fatalistic conclusion reached by a senior congressional investigator, a sweeping verdict that indicts corporate America's deceit. Roach's dismay, while understandable, misses a central point: corporate policy does not exist in a vacuum. The lack of transparency in audited accounts and the wider failure of audit and regulatory enforcement functions are the result of political action, or more accurately the lack of it.

Widening the debate involves, however, a fundamental reassessment of the entire political system. This is a crucial element in the Houston challenge, which argues that the ultimate responsibility for the Enron fiasco rests not on Houston or Wall Street but on Capital Hill itself. The evidence to back up this assertion comes from the decision to revoke legislation that precluded the operation of the structured finance deals that had so degraded the integrity of the investment banks. This in turn leads one back to the decision by Congress to repeal Glass–Steagall in 1999, a move that provided the financial services sector with an unparalleled opportunity to enhance profits by engaging in a corruptive compact with major corporations to the detriment of ordinary investors.

For more than 60 years, a fear that conflicts of interest could precipitate a return to the financial implosion of the American securities market had precluded the bundling of commercial and investment banking under one corporate roof. In the four years following the Great Crash of 1929, a third of all banks had failed, 11,000 in total. In the search for scapegoats for the enormous economic and social dislocation, Congress latched onto the banking sector, fuelling the populist but disputed belief that the implosion of the American economy was the result of irresponsible speculation alone. At congressional hearings chaired by Ferdinand Pecora, the banking system was castigated for boosting profits by: manipulating the market through insider-trading; price-fixing and dispensing favoured status to preferred clients. In the mood for retribution at the time, however, the entrepreneurs of the gilded age had no option but to accept meekly the charge that irresponsible lending and speculation had precipitated an economic meltdown that had spawned the Great Depression.

The crisis was an extreme example of how power relationships can change in response to external factors. A degree of intervention unheard of in American politics was ceded and gained widespread popular support. The result was the introduction of the 1934 Securities Exchange Act. A strict probation on banking power over the economy was put in place. There was to be a ban on inter-state operations and separate regulatory supervision for the now decoupled commercial and investment banking sectors. Most importantly, in order to police the system a new federal agency was established: the SEC.

The corporate entities whose manipulations created the need for independent oversight in the first place railed against the restrictive powers of the newly formed Commission, and an ideological battle against regulation has been raging ever since.[56] In an unending war of attrition, the SEC was pitted against the most powerful forces in American society: corporate self-interest was predicated in emasculating the regulators by controlling the political masters. This had led inexorably to the further skewing of the political system, elevating the

---

[56] The debate over regulation was vicious in the extreme and centred on perennial concerns: whether oversight was necessary or an impediment to growth. See, for example, two articles published in *The Atlantic Monthly* in the immediate aftermath of the passage. Bernard Flexner, "The fight on the Securities Act", *The Atlantic Monthly*, February 1934. Flexner argued that attempts to amend the legislation with "ingenious weasel words" were in fact attempts "to confuse the careful interrelations which give the Act its lawyer-proof quality." Eustace Seligman strenuously rebutted Flexner's arguments the following month. He argued "the punishment does not fit the crime. The Act imposes too severe penalties for honest mistakes." Steligman concludes that the main problem associated with the Act is that it makes it "vastly more difficult for even the best companies to raise needed capital." See Eustace Seligman, "Amend the Securities Act", *The Atlantic Monthly*, March 1934. Both articles are available online at http://www.theatlantic.com/

individual at the expense of society and fostering an ideological climate distrustful of governmental intervention in the operation of the market. Needless to say, this distancing of federal responsibility for the operation of the marketplace has been dressed up in the language of greater public good rather than self-interest, but its impact on the structural nature of the crisis is profound and cannot be understated. As Arthur Levitt has recalled in his provocative memoir of a life spent on Wall Street, the subservience of Congress to the increasing power and sophistication of special interest groups, cutting across both parties, is central to the inability of the regulators to police the industry effectively:

> Despite Congress's belated lurch towards reform, only a few lawmakers truly care more about individual investors than about their corporate patrons. The Congress that enacted the landmark investor protection statute – the Securities Act of 1933 – in response to the 1929 stock market crash bears little resemblance to recent legislatures that have short-changed the SEC.[57]

What was acceptable to a chastened banking sector in 1934 became an unacceptable restriction in the deregulated vision championed by Ronald Reagan in the 1980s. Revisionist paradigms positing banking failure as a consequence of inadequate economies of scale and lack of diversification were amplified by the collapse of the savings and loans institutions in the United States and the collapse of the banking sector in Japan, whose regulatory model was introduced by the American occupation after World War Two and remained relatively intact when a real-estate crash exposed the banks to colossal losses. Glass–Steagall was presented as not only an impediment to American financial expansion but as an unacceptable risk to the American economy.

The law was a cash cow for the political class, which received contributions from lobbyists on both sides of the divide. From 1989 until Congress eventually repealed the offending legislation in 1999, a total of $187.2m was spent in lobbying politicians, almost half of it in

---

[57] Arthur Levitt, *Take on the Street* (Pantheon, New York, 2002), p. 14.

unregulated "soft money" contributions.[58] The argument for repeal strengthened significantly with the arrival of Robert Rubin, former CEO of Goldman Sachs at the Treasury Office in 1995. Rubin was at the forefront of arguing that the changing reality of the financial marketplace had made Glass–Steagall unworkable and that banks had already found ways to circumvent the restrictions. The merger of Citicorp and Travellers Group, a corporation that specialized in the delivery of securities and insurance, in April 1998, necessitated a change in the legislation if the merged conglomerate was to be sustainable in law.

Rubin recognized the potential conflicts of interest involved in establishing the new conglomerate, but argued that these could be managed by the creation of Chinese walls, a loophole exploited by lawyers acting for Sandy Weill, who, in forcing through the merger, had broken the spirit if not the letter of the law. His colleague Joseph Stiglitz was Chairman of the Council of Economic Advisors at the time, a think tank within the White House. Stiglitz regarded the approach taken by Rubin as riddled with risk. If the banks had found a way to circumvent the regulations, he argued, then the gaps should be dammed, not allowed to further disintegrate. But the political imperative involved, including the enormous sums made in the legislative process, ensured that such concerns were pushed to one side.[59]

The following month, the Republican-dominated House of Representatives voted by a margin of one to repeal and passed it to the Senate. The powerful Chairman of the Banking Committee Alfonse d'Amato, who was facing election in that September's mid-term election, announced that the issue would be shelved until after the election, a decision that guaranteed further lobbying and contributions by the financial services industry. According to the veteran political correspondent Elizabeth Drew, the decision paid off hand-

---

[58] Elizabeth Drew, *The Corruption of American Politics, What Went Wrong and Why* (Overlook Press, New York, 2000), p. 277.
[59] Joseph Stiglitz, "The roaring nineties", *The Atlantic Monthly*, October 2002.

somely for the senator. In the 1997–98 election cycle he personally received $2.9m in contributions from both sides in the dispute.[60]

Safely back in Washington, the Senate moved quickly to ensure repeal, a move that was broadly welcomed. *The Economist* proclaimed in a leader editorial, "surprising nearly everyone, including itself, Congress has done something right. House and Senate have agreed to dismantle a law that was badly conceived and kept alive out of sheer prejudice."[61] While welcoming the acceptance of corporate reality by the legislature, the newspaper warned that deregulation without a simultaneous overhaul of the regulatory framework risked future calamity. "History is liberally dotted with crises caused by liberalising finance without improving supervision." Regulation in the United States was and remains fragmented, with responsibility shared between the Federal Reserve, the Office of the Comptroller of the Currency, the SEC and the Commodities and Future Trading Commission. Passing control of the markets back to the banking sector itself, in the context of an unreconstructed, weak and divided supervisory framework, was a key failure, masked by the long years of the bull market. According to the Houston complaint, "this recombination contributed to the banks involvement in the scheme to defraud Enron investors."[62]

The consequences of inaction in 1999 were to return to haunt the politicians as they gathered to adjudicate on the role played by the investment banks in artificially boosting the value of Enron prior to its collapse and to analyse why both the regulators and the ratings agencies failed to spot the fraud prior to the collapse of Enron. The rebirth of the American economy in the 1990s, based on deregulation, largely on terms dictated by corporate interest, therefore proved pivotal in storing up the problems now besetting the securities market, making the crisis facing regulators potentially more intractable than in 1934.

---

[60] Elizabeth Drew, *The Corruption of American Politics* (Overlook Press, New York, 2000), p. 82.

[61] Leader, "Killing Glass–Steagall", *The Economist*, 30 October 1999.

[62] *Consolidated Complaint*, p. 341.

Sixty-eight years after its formation, under-resourced and over-loaded with complex derivative-trading investigations relating to 15,000 publicly listed companies, the SEC has been consistently wrong-footed by the sheer scale of the corporate crime now being reported. The inability of the SEC to provide meaningful leadership is a direct consequence of a lack of political will and resources in equal measure. It has a permanent staff of just 3,100 to investigate the world's largest securities market. In 2001 only 16% of all corporate reports received were analysed to assess whether irregularities had taken place.[63] Its technology is outdated, and attempts to deal with corporate fraud have been further hampered by the fact that its New York offices were destroyed in the maelstrom of 9/11. Its most important subsections – enforcement, trial and accountancy regulation – are facing major problems associated with a lack of trained staff and inadequate professional back-up. An investigation by the *New York Times* discovered that 20 of the 75 trial lawyers working for the SEC are engaged in the Enron case alone.[64]

As the crisis of confidence in the probity of the securities market intensified during the summer of 2002, the political class introduced controversial and potentially far-reaching corporate legislation: the Corporate Responsibility Act, more commonly referred to as Sarbanes–Oxley. It passed responsibility for implementing and monitoring the change to the SEC, an agency rendered incapable of dealing with the pressure. To make matters worse, in the midst of the crisis the Chairman of the SEC Harvey Pitt was forced to resign, leaving the regulatory body rudderless at precisely the same time as it was charged with establishing new codes of practice for the operation of the market.

It is through examining the decline and fall of Pitt that another element in the crisis of governance is exposed. The failure of regulators to regulate is linked not merely to personalities at the helm of these agencies, rather to a wider political failure to provide the

[63] Editorial, "Policing Wall Street", *New York Times*, 5 August 2002.

[64] Stephen Labaton, "SEC facing deeper trouble", *New York Times*, 1 December 2002.

resources necessary in pursuit of a wider political goal: the financing of political campaigns. In the weeks immediately prior to mid-term polling day, as speculation intensified about the possibility of war in the Persian Gulf, Pitt plunged the SEC into one of the most serious crises since its formation. It emerged that his preferred candidate for oversight of the accountancy profession William Webster was implicated in a conflict of interest over a suspicious audit. To compound matters, the Chairman of the SEC was aware of the ethical cloud overhanging his preferred candidate, but chose not to disclose this to his fellow commissioners prior to ratifying the appointment.[65]

Pitt eventually bowed to the inevitable, recognizing that his position had become untenable, but not before he performed a final service for the White House. The timing of his resignation had political overtones and raises fundamental issues about the impact of patronage on key oversight positions that extend beyond the management of the SEC. Pitt announced his decision to resign just as the polls closed on 5 November, too late to influence voters. The White House had made a strategic decision to brazen out the crisis and in many ways was playing according to a preconceived game plan. The administration had already made the calculation that the travails facing the SEC would make a negligible impact on the electorate.

As a political issue, its importance had ebbed significantly from the dangerously high levels sensed by the President when he addressed corporate America from within its very citadel during the torpid New York summer. When the wave of accountancy failures reached a crescendo in July, President Bush made a keynote speech at the Regent Wall Street Hotel. The resolve then could not have been clearer:

> I've come to the financial capital of the world to speak of a serious challenge to our financial markets and to the confidence on which they rest. The misdeeds now being uncovered in some quarters of corporate America are threatening

---

[65] Stephen Labaton, "Pitt under fire for not telling all he knew about Webster", *New York Times*, 1 November 2002.

the financial wellbeing of many workers and many investors. At this moment, America's greatest economic need is higher ethical standards – standards enforced by strict laws and upheld by responsible business leaders.[66]

Using the bellicose rhetoric that has transformed his standing in the wake of 9/11, Bush promised the introduction of a corporate fraud SWAT team and the movement of "corporate accounting out of the shadows, so that the investing public will have a true and fair and timely picture of assets and liabilities and income of publicly traded companies. Greater transparency will expose bad companies and, just as importantly, protect the reputations of good ones." The President lauded the SEC and proclaimed:

> Today, I announce my administration is asking Congress for an additional $100m in the coming year to give the SEC the officers and the technology it needs to enforce the law. If more scandals are hiding in corporate America, we must find and expose them now ... I've also called on the SEC to adopt new rules to ensure that audits will be independent and not compromised by conflicts of interest.

This was precisely the charge against William Webster, the former Director of the FBI and Harvey Pitt's nominee for the sensitive post of accountancy board regulator. This pivotal position was established as a consequence of the potentially far-reaching Sarbanes–Oxley legislation on corporate reform. The principal function of the new body was to set new, more stringent rules and review the performance of the profession against them. It represented a major policy change and one that had enraged the accountancy cartels. The legislation, which emerged from congressional hearings into Enron and WorldCom as the crisis unfolded throughout the spring of 2002, had been opposed vociferously by much of corporate America, its legislative allies in Congress as well as the President. He changed tack as the sense of

---

[66] George W. Bush, "President announces tough new enforcement initiatives for reform", Remarks by the President on Corporate Responsibility, Regent Wall Street Hotel, New York, 9 July 2002.

unease about the extent of the problems facing the securities market threatened to destabilize the presidency.

Sarbanes had argued successfully in Congress that "we had to try to break this consultancy–auditing link, because that was obviously placing the auditors in a highly conflicted role, trying to draw up a good strong audit when they were collecting huge fees for the consulting. They were ending up auditing their consulting work."[67] For Sarbanes, relying on the conscience of the auditors was not a feasible option. This was borne out by the fact that, as a percentage of revenue, management consultancy to the firms they were auditing had risen to 51% of total income. The invigilators had become partners, eschewing credibility, if not in all cases honesty.

This fear was in contradistinction to the preferred option of the Chairman of the SEC, who had privately discussed the remit of the new regulatory board with the profession and substantially agreed with its analysis that the rules governing the oversight commission would be drawn up by those being invigilated. It was Pitt who was now charged with finding a suitable candidate. Nominating Webster was therefore a calculated rebuke to the wishes of Congress and an indication of how ineffective the Commission had become in policing the industry, precisely because of the penetration of former players in the securities market. It provoked a political storm within the SEC itself, with two commissioners using an open meeting of the Commission in Washington to lodge formal dissent. Roel Campos, the most recently appointed commissioner, was furious at what he saw as duplicity, shading into self-destruction:

> The truth is that there is a perception that Chairman Pitt and the entire Commission are being influenced by the views of the accounting profession. The existence of this perception is extremely unfortunate . . . As certain as I am that the sun will rise tomorrow, I am that certain Chairman Pitt will not allow himself to be influenced by an outside lobby or politicians . . . However, the American public and American investors do not have the benefit of the personal acquaintance that I have with the Chairman and the other

---

[67] Paul Sarbanes, quoted by Peter Spiegel and Deborah McGregor, "King of corporate reform", *Financial Times*, 27 July 2002.

commissioners. Therefore, the perception of this Commission being influenced by the very industry that we seek to regulate through the Oversight Board is real and rational, based on the events that have occurred.[68]

This intervention brought the simmering disputes within the SEC out into the open and dealt a fatal blow to Pitt's integrity. The accountancy profession argued that the initial choice John Biggs, the head of the country's biggest teachers' pension fund TIAA-CREFF, was too hostile. The basis for this concern was Biggs's appearance at the Senate Banking Committee, where he argued that "accounting firms must know that they cannot refuse to open their books or prevent their staff from co-operating with this new agency. It must have the authority to discipline firms and individuals without the delays of an [industry-run] investigating process."[69]

To a large extent, the issue of audit reform is central to the problem facing investor confidence. Investment reports prepared by merchant banking corporations can be heavily discounted or binned because of perceived or actual concerns over potential conflicts of interest. Indeed, investors can obtain, for a fee, independent research from boutique research firms. One set of numbers, however, is sacrosanct for the credibility of the entire securities market: the audited accounts. If the figures in the corporate accounts are rendered meaningless, then assigning true value is a futile task. If the audit is rendered suspect by the use of off-balance sheet alchemy to inflate earnings, that true value is rendered impossible to tabulate. Audit reform is therefore central to corporate reform.[70] The profession may accept that some form of oversight is necessary, but as its opposition to Biggs's proposed appointment demonstrated, genuine enforcement was not envisaged as part of the solution. Harvey Pitt's

---

[68] Roel Campos, "Statement by SEC commissioner: New Public Company Accounting Oversight Board", SEC Headquarters, Washington, DC, 25 October 2002. Full text available at http://www.sec.gov/news/speech/spch600.htm

[69] Peter Spiegel and Adrian Michaels, "Biggs at centre of political struggle over accounts post", Financial Times, 7 October 2002.

[70] See Sebastian Mallaby, "Accountable accountants", Washington Post, 4 February 2002.

acceptance of this analysis and active collusion in bringing it to bear was a conflict of interest too far.[71]

A damning report issued by the GAO just before the Christmas vacation served witness on how dysfunctional the SEC under Pitt had become. Several politicians mandated the GAO, an investigative unit within Congress, to examine the circumstances surrounding the Webster appointment. The selection process was nothing short of a disaster. "It was neither consistent nor effective" and led "to the eventual breakdown of the SEC's selection and vetting process."[72]

Pitt's own background, as a securities lawyer for Enron and the failed Arthur Anderson partnership and lobbyist for the accountancy profession, provided further cause for the perception, if not the reality. When Arthur Levitt, his predecessor at the SEC, had proposed new regulations preventing auditors from providing consultancy services for the companies whose accounts they were supposed to be invigilating, Pitt was at the forefront of opposition, arguing that consultancy would enhance the New Economy. Levitt, who lost the battle, has written recently that self-regulation by the accountants is a bad joke.[73] So, too, was the short tenure of Pitt, who had to recuse himself from no less than 29 SEC decisions because of his past association with the accountancy profession. Pitt compounded matters significantly by apparently seeing no wrong in meeting former clients in social settings who were now subject to SEC investigation.[74] His credibility never recovered after he remained silent, even as President Bush retracted a key pledge to buttress the investigative capabilities of the financial watchdog.

---

[71] See Sebastian Mallaby, "The chairman joins the lobbyists", *Washington Post*, 28 October 2002.

[72] See Kathleen Day, "Agency faults SEC on handling of audit panel", *Washington Post*, 20 December 2002. Full report, GAO 03-339, "Actions needed to improve Public Company Accounting Oversight Board selection process", 19 December 2002 is available online via www.gao.gov/

[73] See Arthur Levitt, *Take on the Street* (Pantheon, New York, 2002), pp. 105–43.

[74] Senator John McCain, "Speech on corporate governance reform", National Press Club, 11 July 2002. Available online at: http://www.senate.gov/~mccain/corpgovspch.htm

Less than three months after signing legislation that allowed for an increase in the SEC's budget of 77% to $776m, the administration sought to reduce that increase by 47% to $568m on the grounds that the increased appropriations needed to fund the war against terrorism meant that it was impossible to fund the planned increase.[75] The legislation was therefore being gutted before the ink was dry, hardly a reassuring portent of its likely effectiveness in general.

The creation of new legislation is a complex affair based on the need to create and build on disparate coalitions in order to achieve desired objectives. The attempts by President Clinton's choice as chairman to change the framework failed because of the power of corporate America to influence Congress to stymie reform. Levitt was unable to build sufficient consensus to change the law. In contrast, President Bush's appointee self-consciously delimited his scope for action to a strict interpretation of the existing law and moved the SEC away from confrontation with Wall Street by accepting its analysis of the problem. The result was the same: the protection of vested interests at the expense of regular investors.

As the crisis unfolded, Pitt's organization became a willing cipher for an administration unwilling on both ideological and pragmatic grounds to address the systemic failings of unchecked corporate power that had necessitated the creation of the Commission in the first place. Given the scale of the problem, Pitt's tenure, characterized by the elevation of the strict interpretation of the letter of the law as policy goal, amounted in the circumstances to what J. Patrick Dobel terms moral abrogation:

> This model invites an excessively legalistic narrowing of concern. Except for reasons of reputation or self-interest, individuals feel little motivation to

---

[75] Stephen Labaton, "Bush tries to shrink SEC raise intended for corporate cleanup", *New York Times*, 19 October 2002. Bush changed tack again on this issue in January 2003, using his weekly radio address on 11 January to announce that the budgetary increase initially promised would be delivered. He said that he would push Congress to deliver $842m to the SEC, a 77% increase in the 2002 figure of £487m. See Richard Stevenson, "Bush proposes big increase in SEC budget", *New York Times*, 12 January 2003.

identify and correct wrong or harm within the system, and they are discouraged
from feeling responsibility towards precedents that they set or procedures that
they follow. The model strips them of the moral resources they need either to
initiate positive actions or to resist immoral or illegal actions.[76]

Concerted action to stem the flow of confidence was at once revealed
as meaningless. The subservience of the regulators to their political
patrons and to the corporate interests they depended on, rather than
to the need to clean up America's damaged securities industry, writ
large both by Pitt's acceptance of this state of affairs and the dubious
machinations surrounding his attempts to secure the appointment of
Webster. If the regulator was itself compromised, how meaningful in
reality was the President's exhortation for "the urgent work of
enforcement and reform, driven by a new ethic of responsibility"?

There is a distinct if discrete linkage between the level of funding
given by the financial services industry to political parties and the
minimalist approach taken to address the design flaws within contemporary capitalism in its American guise. In certain key respects
there are similarities between the 1929 crash that led to the creation
of the SEC and the current crisis. As with the 1920s, so too in the
1990s, the American securities market was riding a wave of technological revolution that necessitated the inculcation of a laissez-faire
ideology to underpin the pursuit of profits.

Running in tandem with the market fever was a disproportionate
increase in the amount of money going to political parties. What
has been fundamentally transformed is the relative power of the
lobby over the political process and its ability to delineate the
extent of the reform. The exorbitant costs involved in modern
electioneering have served merely to intensify the subservience of
politicians to the interests that fund them, or more seriously to
distort the deliberative process themselves by engaging in political

---

[76] J. Patrick Dobel, *Public Integrity* (Johns Hopkins University Press, Baltimore, 1999),
p. 10.

blackmail, making the risk of endemic and systemic corruption an unavoidable reality.[77]

As Kevin Phillips has observed, "legislators casting votes on business or financial regulation cannot forget the richest 1% of Americans, who make 40% of the individual federal campaign donations over $200. Money is buying policy."[78] And it has been so for a considerable period of time. Phillips' former boss Richard Nixon was a past master at using financial alchemy to destroy his opponents, a tactic that helped win him election in 1968 and again in 1972, when the illegal activities of the Campaign to Re-elect the President culminated in the break-in at the Democratic headquarters at the Watergate Complex, a bungled burglary that eventually led to his forced removal from office. Attempts by the politicians to fix the system proved meaningless. Self-regulation in both politics and economics in the American context has been revealed simply as an assurance devoid of content.

The *Wall Street Journal* infamously editorialized in 1983 that far from being a model of good governance, Washington, DC should be more accurately compared with "the mutants' saloon in *Star Wars* – a place where politicians, PACs [Political Action Committees], lawyers, and lobbyists for unions, business or you-name-it shake each other down full time for political money and political support."[79] In the intervening period, there has been an exponential increase in both cost and effect. As David Magleby has pointed out in his study of the 2000 election cycle "the process is, in short, like an arms race, where no one knows how much money is enough and it's safest to assume you can never have too much

---

[77] For an exposition of a model of rent extraction in action in Congress see Fred McChesney, *Money for Nothing* (Harvard University Press, Cambridge, MA, 1997), pp. 38–41.

[78] Kevin Phillips, "The cycles of financial scandal", *New York Times*, 17 July 2002. The argument is further developed in Kevin Phillips, *Wealth and Democracy, A Political History of the American Rich* (New York, 2002).

[79] "Cleaning up reform", *Wall Street Journal*, 10 November 1983, cited in Larry J. Sabato, *PAC Power: Inside the World of Political Action Committees* (New York, 1990), pp. 185–6.

money."[80] It is not only the content of the message, therefore, but the payment for dissemination that provides a linkage between the issue of corporate malfeasance and political responsibility.

The currency of choice for this secretive trade is accepted across the political spectrum. In exchange for financial support, politicians fail to change laws, threaten with alarming regularity regulators with budget cuts, while proclaiming the decisions reached are the consequence of the need for job creation and the freedom of the market rather than the requirement of interested money. While active lobbying is not unique to the securities industry, its financial muscle, when coupled with professional groups such as accountants and lawyers, means that it exercises enormous political power to shape the agenda. The emphasis on documented corporate abuse risks therefore approaches the problem from the wrong end of the telescope. It is through un-tangling the web that intertwines the world of business and politics that the true extent of the corruption of political and economic life can be measured. And it is where those worlds collide in Washington, DC that the corruption of American democracy by the self-serving and complex interactions of the needs of corporations and politicians intersect. It is a point graphically made by Arthur Levitt, the former Chairman of the SEC:

> During my seven and a half years in Washington, I was constantly amazed by what I saw. And nothing astonished me more than witnessing the powerful special interest groups in full swing when they thought a proposed rule or piece of legislation might hurt them, giving nary a thought to how the proposal might help the investing public. With laser-like precision, groups representing Wall Street firms, mutual fund companies, accounting firms, or corporate managers would quickly set about to defeat even minor threats. Individual investors, with no organised lobby or trade association to represent their views in Washington, never knew what hit them.[81]

The failure to provide ethical leadership has infected the entire gov-

---

[80] David Magleby, *The Other Campaign, Soft Money and Issue Advocacy in the 2000 Congressional Elections* (Rowman & Littlefield, Oxford, UK, 2003), p. 234.

[81] Arthur Levitt, *Take on the Street* (Pantheon, New York, 2002), p. 236.

ernance structure in the United States. Political parties act as a conduit to the powers exerted by the state. As such, the financing of political parties offers a means to gain influence over the direction of state policy, particularly in areas in which the state itself regulates scarce resources or has monopolistic control. As the cost of electioneering increases so too does the need for political parties to gain access to external sources of funding, the provision of which is invariably linked to the possibility of an ideological and/or material *quid pro quo*. Even more likely is the probability that the influence is designed to maintain the status quo. As Tancredi, the ambitious nephew and favourite of the old Sicilian prince, explains in Giuseppe Lampedusa's classic tale of power transfer *The Leopard*, "if you want things to stay the same you have to change."[82]

---

[82] Giuseppe Lampedusa, *The Leopard* (Panther, London, 1996, p. 26).

3

An appalling vista: the rogue of Rhode Island

The threat posed to the credibility of the political system was exemplified by an extraordinary trial in New England, an event overshadowed by the build-up to war and corporate scandal. The trial, involving a popular mayor, marked the first time that legislation designed to root out the malign power of organized crime had been used to retrospectively criminalize an entire administration. The theoretical consequences are so enormous that the trials and tribulations of Vincent A. Cianci have the capacity to fundamentally transform the very nature of American politics.

The former mayor stared morosely into his whiskey at the hotel bar, apparently unable to comprehend the enormity of what had happened to him. After the elation of an hour spent reminiscing with a producer from American television's premier current affairs programme 60 Minutes, came a sudden realization: his role in the transformation of Providence, Rhode Island, from decayed urban squalour to thriving post-industrial powerhouse was totally irrelevant to the shrewd New York-based television professional. She was in town not to cover his rise to power or what he had achieved, but his spectacular fall from grace. The national recognition accorded by his peers for a remarkable achievement in urban regeneration and the access to the citadels of power such a successful programme had occasioned served merely to highlight the extent of the betrayal. It was not for rebuilding his New England hometown that Vincent A. Cianci had attracted the attention of the national media; it was more interested in exposing his role as the architect of a renaissance founded on corruption.

The excess associated with his rule was symbolized by the producer's insistence that Cianci drive around Providence the next morning in an upmarket convertible. The image of the mayor coasting nonchalantly through the glistening steel and mirrored canyons of a cityscape reborn en route to the nearby affluent resort of Cape Cod would provide a perfect visual contrast to the sordid underpinnings of a reign based on graft. The former mayor had not driven an open-top for 30 years, preferring instead the gravitas provided by being seen in a chauffer-driven Lincoln town car with darkened glass. For the documentary team, however, authenticity was to be sacrificed in pursuit of dramatic licence in the telling of a tale that has profound implications for American democracy. Cianci may well hold the distinction of being one of the longest serving and most successful mayors in modern American history, but he also carries a criminal record.

Just six weeks earlier, on Friday 6 September 2002, Vincent Cianci performed his final duty as first citizen. His last journey in the official black limousine, with the number plate 1, was to the imposing courthouse in downtown Providence, where a phalanx of television crews recorded for posterity the mayor, defiant to the last, witness the passing of judgment. Cianci was attending the federal court not as a visiting dignitary, but rather to await sentencing on a racketeering conspiracy charge. Before the sentence was read out, Cianci apologized to both the court and to the people in whose name it had been convened. "My heart will always be with Providence. I never intended to do anything wrong, Your Honour," he opined to a disbelieving audience. If the last-minute apology was designed to sway the presiding judge, Ernest Torres, it was a miscalculation.

Torres reached to the fictional world of Robert Louis Stevenson to find a comparator to the shamed public official. He likened the contradictory personality traits of charisma and venality, displayed in equal measure by Cianci, to that of "Dr Jekyll and Mr Hyde", intoning from the bench that the most skilful charismatic politician in the history of Rhode Island oversaw an administration so bereft of integrity that it represented "an egregious breach of public trust." Despite the jury's decision to clear Cianci of all substantive specific charges involving personal involvement in corruption, Torres ordered that the mayor serve a five-year-and-four month prison term for his responsibility in running a sophisticated criminal enterprise that had corrupted the entire Providence City government. Cianci was also directed to pay a $100,000 fine and perform 150 hours community service upon his release.

Spared the discomfiture of an immediate transfer to federal prison, Cianci was immediately stripped of his post and the $135,000 salary that came with it. The symbolic transfer of authority at the courthouse was mirrored across Kennedy Plaza in City Hall itself, the powerbase of a political machine built up so assiduously over a 25-year period. Workmen changed the nameplate that had hung outside the private office for a generation and stripped the mayoral parlour of any remaining vestiges of the *ancien regime*.

The official limousine pressed into service for a new owner, the disgraced former mayor was forced to take private transport back to the Biltmore Hotel, where he watched the swearing-in ceremony for his successor, John Lombardi, live on television. At a stroke, the formidable political machine he had created, nurtured and developed since 1991 was being obliterated before his eyes. The first action taken by the new mayor was to slash the mayoral budget from $2.4m to $1.3m. The seven speechwriters retained by his predecessor were going to have to find new employment, as were a substantial number of the other 46 people who toiled in the mayor's bloated private office. The cull had begun. Long-term associates, such as his chief of staff and the city solicitor, were divested of their positions and joined Cianci, his lawyers and a growing number of his former staff in the Biltmore bar.

In a gesture of insolence, the former political boss booked a table at an upmarket restaurant opposite the state buildings, where he held court to a much-reduced audience on the outside terrace. Vincent Cianci was not going to let the small matter of a five-year prison sentence for conspiracy to racketeer spoil dinner in the afternoon sun of a New England summer with those who had played a major role in the very enterprise he was accused of directing. It marked the culmination of an incredible day and the dishonourable end to an equally remarkable career in politics. The courts had achieved what his political opponents had singularly failed to do: the forced removal from office of Vincent A. "Buddy" Cianci. The transformation from conviction politician to convict was complete.

Even then, the degradation was not quite complete. Cianci has since been stripped of his licence to practise as an attorney. He no longer has any visible means to support his rental of the Biltmore's presidential suite other than a radio talk show. The conviction has led to the forfeiture of his state pension as well as his reputation and, on 6 December, his liberty. With nothing left to lose and only weeks left before he was scheduled to appear at the gates of a federal prison camp, Cianci gambled on one last throw of the dice. He made the calculated gamble to utilize that most manipulative of mediums – television – to reverse the judicial verdict and present himself to the nation as a victim of a monumental miscarriage of justice.

His agreement to an interview with CBS was designed to provide an opportunity to rail against what he saw as the injustice perpetrated by a politically inspired trial, conducted by overzealous prosecutors on the back of a flawed investigation that achieved its result only because of the unique decision to charge the former mayor under legislation designed to combat the influence of the Mob. It was an audacious strategy, and one overshadowed by the theatre that surrounds the Cianci case.

The strategy required control of the agenda, and control rested not with the disgraced mayor but the New York production team. Vanity, a key component in any politician's psychological make-up, rendered him incapable of assessing the personal danger associated with driving a cabriolet in the blustery autumnal sunshine. It risked dislodging the ill-fitting toupee that he last lost when posing for a mugshot the previous spring, when formally arrested following an extensive FBI sting operation. Any vestige of dignity could disappear along with his reputation, already comprehensively shredded in the corruption trial that had transfixed New England that summer. The deployment of the convertible was a deliberate, if clichéd, vehicle that demonstrated the production team's intent to concentrate on the larger-than-life characters that populate this story. Nevertheless, it is undoubtedly the case that the conviction does raise uncomfortable home truths about the nature of American politics. Furthermore, the precedent now set by the successful use of legislation designed to root out the malign influence of organized crime to try political corruption cases has the potential to open a Pandora's box.

As the 60 Minutes team retired to prepare the cameras for a very public humiliation, a wounded Cianci retreated to the bar. After all the bluster, the arrogant façade was disappearing at a similar rate to the ice in his whiskey. The gnawing prospect of life behind bars diluting the confidence that had once propelled Cianci throughout a tempestuous career and sustained him throughout the high-profile trial.

"They say I should know about the corruption because I was in charge, now that is a hell of a way to end a career," he complained, the audible slur occasioned by an equal measure of alcohol and self-pity. "I don't think the word [to describe the conviction] is bitter, it is disappointment. I gave my life to this city, my heart, my soul, and my blood. I lost my family. I just think I didn't deserve it. I didn't take the bribes, I didn't take nothing. Give me a lie detector test and I'll pass it. Take me to the person you want to give it to me," he averred.

A middle-aged couple shouted over their support, testament to the affection with which the disgraced political boss is still held in his native city. Cianci half-heartedly lifted his glass, drowned it in one gulp and turned, transformed. Another audience, another possibility to convince that he was more sinned against than sinner, another opportunity to hog the limelight. In an instant, Vincent "Buddy" Cianci was back on the campaign stump, or, more accurately, preparing for his greatest role: his impending appeal to the Rhode Island Supreme Court to overturn a conviction, which if upheld, has the potential to transform American politics.

"Now shoot," he hissed, as he sought vainly to overturn a political defeat beyond even his undoubted tactical skills. His eyes once again fired up: the whiskey working its magic. "I can tell you and look at you straight in the eye and say that I didn't know anything about a chief of staff who took two $1,000 payments from an FBI mole that were thrust upon him after he had refused initially. How does that indicate a conspiracy?" Cianci had an answer for everything. Even if his chief of staff was guilty of accepting bribes and it was, after all, "only for $2,000", that didn't mean that he was. He had built this city; he was a victim of a show trial, of high-level political skulduggery designed to stymie his attempt to launch a national career by standing against an unpopular sitting senator.

I was mesmerized by his apparent inability to accept any responsibility for wrongdoing and immediately struck by the similarities with Charles J. Haughey, the subject of a previous book I had written on political corruption in Ireland. Separated by the Atlantic and very different political systems, there were, however, many similar attributes, which saw the political DNA of one replicated in the other. Both shared an instinctive ability to read the popular mood, to engage in innovative economic decision-making in order to generate income and instil a wider sense of identity. Haughey's decision in the 1960s to abolish income tax on artists' royalties was replicated unconsciously by Cianci in his effort to regenerate the waterfront, itself a carbon copy of Haughey's plans for artistic renewal in Dublin's Temple Bar. Like Haughey, Cianci was a charismatic figure. He had defined the political sphere in which he operated and demonstrated an uncanny ability to resurrect his career after revelations of scandal that would have finished lesser practitioners of the black arts of political persuasion.

Like his Irish counterpart, the American politician was now in denial, his predicament internally rationalized as a result of hidden political forces rather than due judicial process. Haughey had famously told a tribunal of inquiry investigating payments to him of more than $10m throughout his career that he saw no wrong in a group of wealthy benefactors distributing largesse to a politician. In sworn evidence, Haughey declared the giving of gifts to politicians controlling governmental contracts for unspecified reasons was admissible precisely "because they are running the country well, because they are engaging in initiatives which are beneficial to everyone, as I think I continually did."[1] Where the fate of the two politicians differed was in the verdict of wider society. Unlike Haughey, whose successful prosecution was hopelessly compromised by a combination of ineptitude and a lack of political will, Cianci was going to jail, the result of the state's decision to use every means at its disposal to force him from office and into the federal penitentiary.

Gesticulating wildly at the bar of the Biltmore Hotel, Vincent Cianci was now in full flow. "The whole thing was politically motivated, you have to be a dumb-bell not to realize that, and *agents provocateurs* were deliberately installed." He remains convinced that he has been made a scapegoat for structural flaws in the entire American political system, where paying money for access has become a necessary, if corrosive rule of the game.

"Let's face it," he proclaimed, "if you have the choice of helping your friends or your enemies, and all other things are equal, which would you do?" The inability to see that influence-peddling was itself corrupt was indicative of the contradictions surrounding not only his entire career but also the political culture in which he operated. The unspoken implication was that, if everyone else was doing it, why shouldn't he? To be fair to Vincent Cianci, it is a fair question.

A brief perusal of Cianci's political biography renders it even more surprising that he had the opportunity to make Providence a byword for the rejuvenation of the machine politics that had so debilitated confidence in the integrity of metropolitan American government in the early part of the 20th century. A century on and Cianci stood accused of creating a "criminal enterprise" whose malign influence rivalled that of the big-time political bosses of Chicago and New York

---

[1] Charles Haughey, evidence to Moriarty Tribunal, cited in Justin O'Brien, *The Modern Prince: Charles J. Haughey and the Quest for Power* (Merlin, Dublin, 2002), p. 152.

at their most venal. Three months after the FBI had signalled its intent to close down the enterprise by launching a high-profile raid on City Hall in April 1999, the sudden retirement of Cianci's long-serving director of administration Frank Corrente ensured it was only a matter of time before the investigation reached its real target, a prey that had proved until then maddeningly elusive. Just how elusive was revealed in a profile in the influential *New York Times*, written as the swirl of rumour and innuendo reached higher and higher levels within the administration. It accurately ascribes to Cianci the attributes of "a political Lazarus, whose capacity to heed the lessons of death seems forever in question . . . He has served longer than any other big-city mayor in the country, and he is the most defiant, if not the very last, of an old school political breed: cheer-leader, bully and lounge singer, all rolled into a fist of a man."[2]

In 1984, it appeared that Cianci was destined for the history books. He had reached the nadir of his career, his ambition foreshortened by allegations of sleaze and personal vengeance. By then Cianci had been mayor for 10 years, a Republican office-bearer in a Democratic heart-land. He may have secured enormous approval ratings, but the rot had already set in. Cianci's position was undermined by the revelation of corrupt practices at every level of City Hall. A total of 30 indictments were issued, 22 people were convicted in the state and federal courts and 16 personnel served prison sentences. As he sought to prevent the floodwaters from rising to the heart of the citadel, a key defence became his personal integrity. That defence was hopelessly compro-mised when the simultaneous implosion of his personal life brought Cianci to the dock to face charges of assault. Cianci's position as mayor, and as leading light in the Rhode Island Republican Party, had become untenable.

The anodyne language of "felony assault" belies the seriousness of the charge: Cianci tortured his wife's lover, a contractor the mayor had invited to his house on the pretext of discussing a lucrative building contract. Cianci used a lit cigarette, an ashtray and a log

---

[2] *New York Times Magazine*, 31 December 2000.

from the fire to extract revenge, and, it has been alleged, a demand for $500,000 in reparation for wounded pride. The contractor told police that the encounter was akin to being confronted by a madman. The truth of what happened that fateful night remains obscure, largely because of the legal strategy deployed by the mayor's defence team. By accepting guilt, Cianci prevented the lurid details of his attempts to restore his dignity by engaging in torture from becoming public knowledge. By reducing court time, he was rewarded with probation. He left court promising to be more discreet in the future, but acknowledging "I am what I am and I guess that is what I will always be." With Cianci forced to relinquish power, the corruption investigation spluttered to an inconclusive halt and the question of the mayor's responsibility for fostering a climate in which it could flourish remained unanswered.

It was not long before Cianci found a new metier, running a combative talk show on a local radio station. His unparalleled knowledge of local politics and access to the airwaves to disseminate that intelligence proved a potent combination. His show rapidly became required listening, as he engaged in an extraordinary propaganda offensive to recall the halcyon days of his administration by rewriting history. Cianci charged the main political machines of an unwillingness or inability to arrest what appeared to be Providence's terminal decline. He used the station as a surrogate platform to suggest policy changes. He created the impression that an alternative was available if only the public could forgive irrelevant personal transgressions, a development he believed was merely a question of timing: personal and citywide redemption became the leitmotif of a show designed to provide a beachhead for a renewed final assault on City Hall.

When the probation for the torture charges ended in 1990, Cianci spotted an opportunity to recapture the initiative. Despite the political capital to be made by concentrating on the linkages between Cianci and the Republican Party, the Democrats, who had a majority in both the city and state legislature, failed to widen their hold on power in the interregnum following the mayor's battered retreat. Electoral parity and an indecisive administration had created legislative gridlock. Disillusion and apathy had set in and with it the possibility that an adroit campaign, focused exclusively on renewal, could propel an independent into the mayor's parlour.

Cianci added to his credibility by finding God, a useful move in the predominantly Catholic society of Rhode Island. Forgiven by Christ in accordance with doctrine by repenting before God, Cianci now turned to the voters for similar absolution. In a three-way split, the former Mayor squeezed a narrow victory in his first campaign as an independent, during which he outmanoeuvred the main political parties with a message based on selling Providence by selling himself. He was determined to rejuvenate his career by standing on a platform based on selling the city – as a tourist destination, as a conference centre and, ultimately, according to his detractors, to the highest bidder.

There is no doubt that Cianci worked tirelessly to promote his city, in the process boosting its quality-of-life ratings to such an extent that *Money* magazine now ranks it the "best place to live in the North East of the United States." He utilized tax breaks to encourage an end to urban flight, exempted artists from income tax to generate loft-living, encouraged Brown University (one of the leading academic institutions in the country) to provide cutting-edge research into real problems facing the city, built a convention centre business that rivalled Atlantic City and promoted the city as a romantic break for the nearby, Bostonian middle classes. A frequent guest at national conferences on regeneration, he was one of five mayors to receive the 1994 Civil Liveability Award, given by the US Conference of Mayors. In 1996, the American Association of Governmental Officials awarded Cianci the ultimate accolade, "America's Most Innovative Mayor".

In an article written for the *Providence Journal* on his last day in office, Cianci listed his not inconsiderable achievements: "The 'Providence Renaissance' has transformed the downtown into an urban showplace; made our neighbourhoods much safer and liveable; raised the stature of our art, entertainment, health and educational institutions; generated billions in public and private investment;

fostered a dramatic increase in residential property values across the city; preserved one of America's greatest concentrations of historic architecture; made Providence a leader in gourmet dining, fashion, retailing, medical research and the reform of public education; and raised the self-esteem of Rhode Island's citizens as their capital rose to national prominence."[3]

There is only a hint of hyperbole in Cianci's account. The problem is what the mayor left out. Cianci's difficulties stem from the fact that all too often innovation strayed into perceived illegality, developments unchecked by the political mainstream, which found itself unable to break the stranglehold the mayor exerted over the city. Such was his success that the main party organizations in Providence further atrophied. Buddy developed a cult of personality and curtailed the development of any nexus of control operating without his knowledge. Every initiative either was presented as the progeny of the ubiquitous mayor or was co-opted to serve his interest.

Faced with an overweening ambition and a work rate designed as much to provide meaning to his life as to impress the electorate of his commitment to Providence, the two main political parties effectively retired from the electoral battlefield, leaving Cianci master of all he surveyed. Neither the Republicans nor the Democrats fielded a candidate in the 1998 election, the last time that Cianci faced his voters. By default, Buddy had become an autocrat, his physiological features adorning everything from billboards to the marketing of a marinara sauce that bore the legend *Mayor's Own Brand*. As Cianci consolidated his hold on power he worked the patronage his office bestowed on him to maximum effect. Fifty-three people worked in his private office alone, including seven scriptwriters. What was good for Cianci was good for Providence and vice versa, another throwback to the self-personification of Haughey with the "Spirit of the Nation".

Although the demographic make-up of the American political machine has changed considerably, its ability to translate promises

---

[3] Vincent A. Cianci, "A mayor's reflections, and farewell", *Providence Journal*, 5 September 2002.

into reality in exchange for continued electoral support remains a defining characteristic. Gone are the days when one ethnic group could dominate a city, as, for example, the infamous Tammany Hall rule of William March "Boss" Tweed in New York in the 19th century or the ward-based patronage that debased Chicago under Mayor Daly. In both cases, the machine, given respectability by its inextricable linkage to the Democrats, successfully gerrymandered wards and used their power of patronage to act as a conduit to local government for large, mainly illiterate populations.

With new waves of migration weakening the power of the Italian and Irish communities, suburban flight and declining voter participation, the modern urban machine has become much more sophisticated in presenting its message. This was particularly the case in Providence, which has seen a dramatic increase in its Hispanic and Asian population. While much has been made of Vincent Cianci's Italian American background, his success lay not in his ethnic allegiance, but on a return to the basic rules of machine politics: the subservience of ideological principle to the pragmatic pursuit at all costs of the achievement and maintenance of power to distribute its fruit to those who ran and worked for the organization.

The authority of the boss was linked directly to his ability to demonstrate that his word was law and there could be no doubting his reach. His entire life was spent working for re-election. No gathering was too small to attend, every vote counted as Cianci adapted to the era of the permanent campaign pioneered at national level by Bill Clinton. From morning to late at night, the mayor attended shop openings, religious, sporting and cultural events. He hosted business breakfasts and brainstorming sessions with senior academics, played an active role in revitalizing the city zoo and developing theme parks. An advance team was deployed to scour the local papers for events to attend, from political dinner dances to opening of Little League baseball tournaments: no member of the population was too young or too ideologically opposed to escape the embrace of Vincent A. Cianci.

Above all, Cianci was a personality-driven practitioner who adapted the precepts of the traditional machine to the modern era.

If it was happening in Providence, Buddy had to be part of the action. The question of who benefited from the mayor's presence – the organizers or the organization – was swept to one side as an irrelevance. He internalized an operation not dissimilar to that typified by one of Tammany Hall's most famous practitioners, George Washington Plunkitt:

> What tells in holdin' your grip on your district is to go right down among the poor families and help them in the different ways they need help. I've got a regular system for this. If there's a fire in Ninth, Tenth, or Eleventh Avenue, for example, any hour of the day or night, I'm usually there with some of my election district captains as soon as the fire engines. If a family is burned out I don't ask whether they are Republicans or Democrats, and I don't refer them to the Charity Organization Society, which would investigate their case in a month or two and decide they were worthy of help about the time they are dead from starvation. I just get quarters for them, buy clothes for them if their clothes were burned up, and fix them up till they get things runnin' again. It's philanthropy, but it's politics, too – mighty good politics. Who can tell how many votes one of these fires bring me? The poor are the most grateful people in the world, and, let me tell you, they have more friends in their neighborhoods than the rich have in theirs.[4]

While other politicians and the media scoffed that Cianci would attend the opening of an envelope, the mayor ensured that the television cameras remained a constant presence at his side. In many ways he was the story. He carried a portable lectern in the boot of the Lincoln in case there was a need for an impromptu speech. Cianci left nothing to chance. Estrangement from his wife led him to sell a converted mansion in the affluent east side to take up residence at the Biltmore, the grandest hotel in the downtown area, rescued from neglect and now a symbol of renewal, based on continuity with the past. For the mayor it had the added bonus of being located next door

---

[4] George Washington Plunkitt, "Plunkitt of Tammany Hall, a series of very plain talks on very practical politics, delivered by ex-Senator George Washington Plunkitt, the Tammany Philosopher, from his rostrum – the New York County Court House Bootblack Stand." Available online at www.digital.library.upenn.edu/webbin/gutbook/lookup?num=2810

to the City Hall. The Biltmore restaurant quickly became a surrogate office for out-of-hours appointments.

"You have to remember that the functions of the mayor changed dramatically in the 1980s," Cianci explained. "In the 1970s we were social workers, in the 1980s he had to become more entrepreneurial and that meant taking more risks." For Cianci, governing Providence effectively meant ensuring that all decisions benefited not only the city but also his own political machine, an organization that was attracting the envy of those excluded from it and the renewed attention of the FBI.

No amount of the *Mayor's Own Brand* marinara that still dominates the shelves in Providence's supermarkets could disguise the unsavoury reality of Cianci's rule. The overt way in which Cianci did business to enhance his credibility with the voters made a mockery of democratic government. It was inevitable then that the stench of corruption would, once again, began to permeate the harbour front, envelop the City Hall and drift inexorably to the penthouse of the Biltmore. Across the street, in the federal building the dust was taken off the stalled corruption investigation. If Buddy Cianci was back in business, so too was the FBI, whose chief field agent saw in the mayor the personification of everything that has gone wrong with local American politics: sharp practice, profiteering, petty corruption and moral atrophy.

It was not his commitment, nor even evidence of plans for self-enrichment, that made Cianci ultimately vulnerable to successful prosecution for abuse of office. Rather it was the loss of political cover. Cianci was susceptible to corruption charges precisely because the pragmatic pursuit of power was not backed by the ideological power of a national political grouping. The redaction from Republican standard-bearer to a self-serving convicted felon, capable of displaying extreme violence in order to protect his pride, made him an easy target, despite his undoubted success in transforming Providence. It may have been a moral compromise that the voters were clearly prepared to endorse, time and time again, but not federal authorities. To the FBI, Cianci was an aberration and his lack of political support at national level made him vulnerable. In a further ironic twist to this remarkable tale, Cianci, a one-time federal prosecutor who first came to prominence for investigating the Mafia in the 1970s, would find that the lower standards of proof required to secure convictions against people involved in organized crime cases would be used to ensnare the first citizen of Providence. In effect, Cianci was charged with being a godfather who, as head of a "criminal enterprise", embezzled over $1.1m in a concerted attempt to loot the city coffers for his own self-aggrandizement. The weapon to bring him down was the Racketeering and Corrupt Organization Act, a draconian piece of legislation known by its acronym RICO.

The need to combat the baleful influence of the Mafia was recognized in the 1960s, as organized crime began subverting legitimate business. President Lyndon Johnson established a commission in 1965 to overhaul a criminal justice system that had been rendered obsolete because of the growing sophistication of organized crime. The commission, headed by the Attorney General Nicholas Kastzenbach, was under no illusion about the nature of the problem confronting America. He demanded that society too due cognizance of the inexorable rise in the sophistication of criminal enterprises:

> The core of organized crime activity is the supplying of illegal goods and services – gambling, loan sharking, narcotics, and other forms of vice – to countless numbers of citizen customers. But organized crime is also extensively and deeply involved in legitimate business and in labor unions. Here it employs illegitimate methods – monopolization, terrorism, extortion, tax evasion – to drive out of control lawful ownership and leadership and to exact illegal profits from the public.[5]

The commission maintained that it was necessary to define illicit business on organizational terms and then make it a criminal offence to engage in any activities that benefited the organization. By refocusing the problem of organized crime as one that needed to be dealt with in structural terms, rather than concentrating on the transgressions of individual defendants, the commission hoped to break the

---

[5] *Commission Report*, p. 187.

power of the godfathers, who invariably benefited from the profits made by entry into legitimate business without actually incriminating themselves. Congress essentially accepted this argument in 1970, by passing intact the recommendations of the commission as the Racketeering and Corrupt Organization Act. A congressional report released with the legislation stated boldly that its aim was to combat the "highly sophisticated, diversified, and widespread activity that annually drains billions of dollars from America's economy by unlawful conduct." The legislation specifically outlawed:

- using income derived from a pattern of racketeering activity to acquire an interest in an enterprise;
- acquiring or maintaining an interest in an enterprise through a pattern of racketeering activity;
- conducting the affairs of an enterprise through a pattern of racketeering activity; and
- conspiring to commit any of these offences.[6]

The passage of RICO marked an important break with the past. The law was used not just to punish individuals of transgressions but to use the criminal code to break the power of complex criminal organizations. Over time, the primary use of emphasis of RICO has expanded well beyond the confines of organized crime, and variations of the federal law have been enacted in many states, including Rhode Island. The RICO statute does not limit an enterprise to an organized crime family, but states categorically that it "includes any individual, partnership, corporation, association or other legal entity, and any union or group of individuals associated in fact although not a legal entity." It has been used to prosecute enterprises as varied as the organizers of an odometer racket in the used car market in Florida, to indict Wall Street firms accused of conflicts of interest and to investigate the operations of the tobacco giants. The expanded use of the statute has been made possible because of the exceptionally broad wording of what constitutes an enterprise. Successive rulings by the Supreme

---

[6] 18 U.S.C. Section 1962 a-d 1982.

Court have endorsed the expansionary dynamic. In essence, if prosecutors can successfully charge that those responsible for breaking the
law can be defined as members of an enterprise and have embarked on
a concerted pattern of lawbreaking, RICO is an available weapon in
the fight against crime.

It was the confluence of interests between a disaffected businessman
and the dogged determination of an FBI field agent who had tracked
Cianci for the best part of 20 years that set up the intricate operation
that was to lead the mayor to the district courthouse rather than the
governor's mansion or the national senate, both offices on which
Cianci had long-term design. The secret plan was code-named Operation Plunder Dome, a deliberate literary play on the abuse of public
office for private gain associated with the mayor.

The key prosecution witness was a local businessman Antonio
Freitas, who first alerted federal agents to corruption in City Hall
and then worked undercover to expose it. Videotape, audio record-
ings, covert photography, all the formidable range of espionage
weapons that were available to the FBI were deployed to provide
evidence that Cianci had not only condoned corruption, he had
actively colluded in it.

Even thinking about the duplicity involved, invoked Cianci's un-
abated rage. "They say that for ten or eleven years we were involved
in an overarching conspiracy when in fact we weren't. The fact is,
whether a government can be involved in a criminal conspiracy is
another interesting legal argument. How can the government be
involved in a conspiracy? It is not possible for a government to be
involved."

But that was precisely the argument put forward by the Rhode
Island Attorney General, when his office accepted the evidence accu-
mulated by the FBI. Cianci was charged with "extortion, mail fraud,
money laundering and witness tampering and through the same means
enriching, promoting, and protecting the power and assets of the
leaders and associates of the enterprise."[7] For the federal authorities,

---

[7] US vs. Cianci, Superseding Indictment, p. 10.

the activities of the Cianci enterprise amounted to racketeering and necessitated a prosecution under the RICO Act.

The 97-page indictment painted a picture of unprecedented corruption within Cianci's City Hall. "Bribes and extortion payments were sometimes euphemistically referred to as 'campaign contributions' when, in fact, they consisted of unreported cash payments."[8] In return, individuals and entities were "rewarded with leases, contracts, employment and promotions, business, and other benefits conferred by the City and its agencies."[9] Cianci was accused of a racketeering conspiracy that involved extorting more than $250,000 from the Tow Truck Association, ostensibly in campaign contributions, and black-mailing an elite club to gain membership. For the lead prosecutor Richard Rose, "the so-called Renaissance City was a city for sale."[10]

As the stakes rose, so too did the mud-slinging. America watched agog at the strange happenings in a city transformed. Cianci immediately went on the offensive, proclaiming that the trial was not only politically inspired but also characterized by an abuse of process. On the morning he arrived in court to answer the indictment, Cianci raised his coat to the waiting media and proclaimed "there's no stains on it", a reference to the infamous incident involving the presence of Bill Clinton's sperm on a White House intern's dress, which had precipitated the attempts to impeach the President of the United States. Despite the growing national prominence of the case, the federal authorities miscalculated in the public relations arena. Their overwhelming confidence played into the hands of Cianci, providing him with leverage in the court of public opinion

Cianci was given further ammunition by the outrageous behaviour of the chief prosecutor Richard Rose, who appeared more interested in impressing his friends than showing respect for the courts. In a clear abuse of process, Rose brought a group to his house to watch edited highlights of the surveillance tapes. Cianci used the nationally

---

[8] Ibid., p. 12.

[9] Ibid., p. 12.

[10] *The New Yorker*, 2 September 2002.

syndicated Don Imus radio show to ensure maximum embarrassment. "I guess Blockbuster's was closed that night," he told Imus, continuing, "I wonder if he sold popcorn?"[11]

Cianci may pour scorn on the manner in which the prosecution conducted its business but there was no doubt that the seriousness of the charges necessitated a judicial hearing. At issue was the way in which key decision-making offices within the City Hall under the control of the Cianci political machine were compromised. The most serious accusation concerned the timing of a payment of $250,000 from the Tow Truck Association in campaign contributions to secure Cianci's re-election. The prosecution alleged that the payment was a direct bribe in order to maintain a presence on the list of approved contractors for the Providence Police Department. The importance of this charge rests on the effective criminalization of an entire political campaign. As such, the potential implications are immense. If the extortion charges could be proven, it would render vulnerable the operation of national party structures.

The trial began on 17 April 2002. His former director of administration Frank Corrente, the Chairman of the Tow Truck Association Richard Autellio and Edward Voccola, a businessman with a criminal record who was accused of paying bribes to the "enterprise" for a lease from the School Department, joined Cianci in the dock. The Voccola charge was dismissed by the judge, who maintained that the government did not prove the case that Voccola was inextricably linked to the enterprise.

As the trial progressed the veneer of sophistication was stripped of the façade, leaving exposed the corrupt reality of local American politics and the enormous power that can be wielded by an elected boss. But the exposure also demonstrated just how difficult it is to prove a direct causal linkage between contributions or benefits and actual favours bestowed in return for the initial investment. Throughout the trial much was made of the curious timing surrounding the

---

[11] Dan Barry, "Colorful mayor of Providence mines indictment for comedy", *New York Times*, 19 April 2002.

mayor's elevation to honorary membership of the city's most exclusive association, the University Club. Cianci had long hankered to be a member, but was effectively blackballed. The Club found itself beholden to City Hall when it applied for permission to reopen after completing major renovations costing more than $1.1m dollars. It failed to convince the planners. When Cianci was made an honorary member, 25 years after first applying, the objections miraculously disappeared. The inference from the prosecution was that Cianci had blackmailed the Club. It may well have been true, but the prosecution failed to prove the case beyond mere plausibility. There was no smoking gun and the jury failed to convict.

In the most damning evidence, videotape showed the mayor's director of administration, Frank Corrente, receive $2,000 in marked bills from Freitas in exchange for help in securing a lease from the City School Department for commercial property at inflated prices. Although the promised lease never materialized, the perception of corruption at the very apex of the Providence City Hall was transformed to proven reality in the grainy images of the senior civil servant handling the proceeds of crime. The incontrovertible evidence gave credence to the prosecutor's charge that Corrente had corrupted the governance of Providence by the abuse of the patronage his office controlled. The fact that Corrente was also the treasurer of the mayor's re-election campaign served to provide evidence of guilt by association, all that was necessary under RICO.

Despite its best efforts throughout the early summer of 2002, no indelible staining could be found to implicate Cianci directly to any of the charges. A former tax official, David Ead, had claimed in sworn evidence that he had collected bribes for the mayor. He charged that these included a $5,000 charge for arranging employment in the planning department and a $10,000 bribe for reducing the tax liability of a prominent member of the still powerful Italian community in Providence. Cianci's lawyers denied the charges and maintained that the former tax official was a liar and a habitual gambler. Ead's credibility, already undermined because of his own involvement in corruption, was undermined still further when the defence provided evidence that he had broken his own bail conditions by crossing state boundaries to gamble.

On 24 June, after nine days of deliberations, the jury cleared the mayor of involvement in the specific charges of extortion for political or self-advancement, while convicting him of the wider charge of conspiracy to commit crime while running a corrupt enterprise. This did not prevent the prosecutors from requesting the presiding judge to sentence Cianci to 10 years in prison and a fine of $100,000. This was far in excess of federal guidelines and would represent a punitive finding, despite the fact that the jury failed to apportion guilt on the substantive charges. For the prosecutorial team this was irrelevant: under RICO, Cianci is held responsible for the crimes of his lieutenants.

In their memorandum to the court, the federal prosecutors stated: "the defendant was the Mayor and chief executive of the City of Providence. He used his power to abuse the taxpayers of the City of Providence. He presided over a corrupt enterprise, which spanned the entire period of his current administration. He used city officials and their offices to accomplish his goals of unjust personal and political enrichment. This was not a shy or humble enterprise. The enterprise never met a hustle it didn't like."[12]

A very different picture emerges from the defence offered by the mayor's lawyers. In a memorandum submitted to the court on 4 September requesting leniency, they wrote that "Cianci has long demonstrated his extraordinary talent, vision and leadership. More importantly, he has long demonstrated his desire and willingness to do whatever it takes to improve the lives of those who live, work or visit in the city he loves."[13]

The judge remarked that he found it ironic that a "skilled, charismatic political figure charged with abusing public trust in elected representatives should use as a mitigating defence the civic improvements he had made to Providence." It was a theme he returned to

---

[12] *Providence Journal*, 29 August 2002.
[13] *Providence Journal*, 5 September 2002.

when passing sentence. "I'm struck between the parallels between this case and the classic story of Dr. Jekyll and Mr. Hyde," Judge Ernest C. Torres of United States District Court said just before sentencing Cianci. "There appear to be two very different Buddy Cianci's. The first is a skilled and charismatic political figure, probably one of the most talented politicians Rhode Island has ever seen, someone with wit, who thinks quickly on his feet and can enthral an audience. The second Buddy Cianci presided over an administration that is rife with corruption at all levels" and "engaged in an egregious breach of public trust by engaging to operate the city that Buddy Cianci was supposed to serve as a criminal enterprise to line his own pockets."[14]

Although Cianci had declared in court prior to sentencing that he had faith in the independence of the judge, the passing of time had dulled his enthusiasm. A key plank of the former mayor's appeal was based on the decision by the trial judge not to permit the inclusion of key parts of the taped interviews that, Cianci claimed, exonerated him of involvement in a conspiracy. Evidence that ran counter to the web of intrigue, so carefully spun by the prosecutors, was ignored or rendered inadmissible by Justice Torres, according to Cianci:

> The FBI shot in a mole, an agent one day to see me. He made an appointment to see me to have lunch. He worked hard to get the appointment. I didn't know he was FBI. They had lunch with me, they said they wanted to put air filters in, conduct a survey and make their profits from any follow up. They said it would not cost the city anything. I said that's fine.

Cianci then explains that the undercover agent asked who he should contact to expedite matters. The mayor told the agent that he should approach the head of building control. Then came a leading question. "They said what if we are going to have to pay him. Remember I'm all on tape. I said you don't have to pay him. You call me and you tell me that he asked you for anything – or anyone asked you for anything – and first I'm going to cut his cock off and then I'm going to have him

---

[14] Pam Belluck, "A sentence for corruption ends an era in Providence", *New York Times*, 7 September 2002.

arrested by the Colonel [the police chief]. That's on tape that they had to give us. But the judge would not let that in. That was in the middle of the overall RICO conspiracy, so it shows my state of mind."

It is the liberal application of the "conspiracy" charge that proved Cianci's undoing. A leading authority on RICO has consistently questioned both the efficacy of the original act and the decision by prosecutors to expand the terms of reference with unforeseen consequences, the implications of which are underscored by the prosecution of Cianci. Gerard Lynch suggested in a seminal article in 1987 that the legislation has mutated from being a failed, if laudable attempt to prosecute organized crime into a blunt weapon with which lawyers seek to create legislation. "Prosecutors have responded by using RICO in a few identifiable patterns, which correspond to what law enforcement officials apparently believe to be substantive and procedural gaps in the federal criminal code ... The history of RICO, moreover, should make us eager to reassess its utility and fairness. If ... the broad consequences of RICO are essentially by-products of a failed legislative effort to address a highly specific problem, it becomes all the more urgent to ask whether those consequences are desirable in their own right."[15] A year later, Lynch testified to a congressional committee on the judiciary that the expansionary dynamic of interpretation rendered it inevitable that sooner or later political activities would come under the microscope:

What makes RICO – both civil and criminal – dangerous to political activists is more or less the same thing that makes it so useful to prosecutors of serious criminals. The very broad and very abstract definitions of the crime make it possible, especially in conspiracy prosecutions, to tie together numerous defendants and very different sorts of predicate acts, committed in different places at different times, into a single prosecution, with the attendant risk that jurors will be confused and overwhelmed by the evidence and convict, by association,

---

[15] Gerard E. Lynch, "Rico – The crime of being a criminal", *Columbia Law Review*, May 1987, p. 663. Available online at http://www.ipsn.org/court_ cases/ rico-crime_of_being_a_criminal.htm

individuals who would never be convicted if they had to be tried for specific, concrete crimes. That is the essence of the problem.[16]

As Buddy Cianci departed the Biltmore bar for bed and prepare for the CBS cameras, he declared his hand with an implicit threat to the entire political establishment. "How can the mayor know what his subordinates were doing, I certainly didn't know and if they were investigating the state administration or any other city they would probably find the same thing. But they selected me because I was popular, I was ethnic and I was independent. If I am to be convicted, then so should President Bush, so should the Democratic National Committee and everybody else."

Three weeks after our meeting, a higher court in Boston rejected his appeal to remain on bail. The final days of freedom were spent remonstrating with anyone that would listen, appearances on the Today show on NBC and a valedictory address on his local radio show. "It's almost like dying without dying," he mused. Checking out of the Biltmore Hotel for the last time he told waiting reporters, "I leave with a heavy heart but with a sense of accomplishment. No one's perfect. I certainly am not."[17]

With New England caught in the middle of a snowstorm, Cianci was driven away to spend the night at an undisclosed location prior to reporting at the Fort Dix prison camp in New Jersey. The falling snow immediately obliterated the tracks made by Cianci on the city he ran with such gusto for over 20 years. Peopled by a collection of larger-than-life characters, the story of Vincent A. Cianci and his eventual downfall at the hands of legislation designed to root out the Mafia, rather than police city hall administration, is symptomatic of what has gone wrong with American politics: the endless pursuit of money and the malign influence it exerts over the democratic process. Given that a number of corruption trials are ongoing across the United States – from Houston to Atlanta, Chicago to New Jersey – the precedent set

---

[16] Gerard E. Lynch, "Testimony on civil RICO, extortion, and public advocacy groups", Committee on the Judiciary, 17 July 1998.
[17] Providence Journal, 6 December 2002.

by the prosecution of Vincent Cianci places all of political America in the judicial cross hairs. The denouement of the Cianci trial occurred at a pivotal time in American politics. The mainstream political parties are attempting to distance themselves from corporate malfeasance while gorging themselves with "soft money" contributions, prior to the enactment of campaign finance reform legislation.

The implications of the Cianci case, particularly the use of RICO legislation to root out corrupt activities, is likely to have a profound impact. There are six ongoing major corruption cases before the courts. In each case the officials are registered members of the major parties. The question is whether RICO could, or should, be used to secure future convictions, and, if so, what will be the likely impact on the organization of American politics? The audience for his appeal is likely to be witnessed by more than a few political staffers.

4

Lynching Merrill

The threat to issue Racketeering and Corrupt Organization (RICO) proceedings is one of the most powerful weapons in the state's armoury. To use it against corporate America in the context of engaging in a criminal conspiracy to defraud investors is the prosecutorial equivalent of a nuclear option. The very threat of a RICO indictment in 1989 was enough to break the resolve of Drexel Burnham Lambert, at that stage one of the most powerful investment banks in the country. The company had already been accused of fraud, stock market manipulation and insider-trading through its Beverly Hills office. In a vicious war of attrition marked by leak and counter-leak, Drexel's powerful public relations machine castigated government lawyers and used pliant media sources to question the deals made with those who were implicating one of the most prestigious firms on Wall Street. Yet even a bank with the substantial economic power of Drexel could not sustain the dramatic loss of confidence in its probity that a RICO indictment would bring. The reputational risk was simply too great even if the corporation could continue paying the legal bills in a forlorn attempt to stave off the resolve of the regulators.

In his seminal account of how the insider-trading fiasco developed, James B. Stewart concluded that "in an era that purported to glorify free-market capitalism, this story shows how the nation's financial markets were in fact corrupted from within, and subverted for criminal

purpose."[1] However, while the Drexel scandal brought down individuals and led to the bankruptcy of the corporation itself, the
"star" system of investment bankers and analysts, which had done
much to incubate the problem, remained intact. When utilized in
1989 to end the insider-trading investigations, those centrally involved developed nationwide political reputations. At the beginning
of the third millennium, their failure to deal with the root cause,
rather than their success, was writ large in banner headlines decrying
corporate greed. With the ending of the technology boom in 2000,
the consequences of an enforcement strategy based on dealing with
corrupt actors rather than a corrupted system was to return to haunt
corporate America when the star culture itself imploded with
devastating effect.

The investigations that led to the fall of Drexel began in 1986, with
the exposure of a complex insider-trading operation, routed through
the Bahamas branch of Bank Leu International, a venerable Swiss
financial institution. Passed the information by the vice-president of
compliance at Merrill Lynch, which had itself received anonymous
information that brokers in its Venezuela office had been engaging in
insider-trading, the Securities and Exchange Commission (SEC)
investigation opened a viper's nest of intrigue, double-dealing and
evasion that was to embroil Wall Street in destabilizing and debilitating scandal.

Orchestrated by Dennis Levine, an investment banker with Drexel,
the initial insider-trading scheme involved the recruitment of a
number of high-profile lawyers and investment bankers. The
network, once formed, grew in strength and sophistication as it recruited like-minded frustrated and greedy executives. As time went on
the former trainees inched up the corporate ladder, picking up frag-
mentary pieces of information and piecing them together to make
certain bets in the mergers and acquisitions playground. As the
SEC and the US Attorney's Office managed to accrue evidence, the
scheme disintegrated. The code of silence on Wall Street collapsed as

---

[1] James B. Stewart, *Den of Thieves* (Touchstone, New York, 1992), p. 22.

self-interest eclipsed loyalty. Bank Leu gave up the name of Levine in exchange for immunity from prosecution, Levine informed on the corporate raider Ivan Boesky, who in turn implicated Drexel, which itself accepted to plead guilty to six felonies and pay record fines of $650m in order to avoid the more damaging RICO indictment. The decision to plead guilty, a forlorn attempt to stave off collapse, made it inevitable that Michael Milken, the corporation's brilliant junk bond strategist, would have to accept guilt. Sentencing Milken to 10 years' imprisonment in 1990, Judge Kimba Wood blamed the investment banker for inculcating a corrupted culture – a crime that necessitated "the discomfort and opprobrium of being removed from society":

> When a man of your power in the financial world, at the head of the most important department of one of the most important investment banking houses in this country, repeatedly conspires to violate, and violates, securities and tax laws in order to achieve more power and wealth for himself and his wealthy clients, and commits financial crimes that are particularly hard to detect, a significant prison term is required in order to deter others.[2]

Twelve years later, two of the lawyers who played pivotal roles in the prosecution of the Drexel case were to find their roles reversed as the stock market began to buckle under the weight of its own contradictions, exposing the corrupted core unaffected by the Milken jailing. As the crisis over analyst compensation deepened, Gary Lynch, the former head of enforcement at the SEC, was appointed by the troubled Credit Suisse First Boston Corporation to bolster its flagging reputation. Harvey Pitt, who was instrumental in securing the immunity deal for Bank Leu and who later represented Boesky, had left lucrative private practice to end his career as Chairman, the SEC, an organization he had joined after qualifying and which he had then spent a career battling. Pitt's main aim was to change the focus of the organization. In order to ensure compliance, Pitt argued that the regulatory authorities needed to refocus the debate. Voluntary compacts in which those being invigilated had a deciding say on what

---

[2] Quoted in James B. Stewart, *Den of Thieves* (Touchstone, New York, 1992), p. 517.

constituted acceptable market practices replaced the credible threat of enforcement. While the decision may have been rational, in the heady mood of the time it demonstrated an outstanding inability to read the political barometer.

With the SEC overburdened and run by a chairman who viewed confrontation with Wall Street as anathema, a window of opportunity existed for another lawyer to make his name investigating the endemic and systemic conflicts of interest within and between the investment houses. Eliot Spitzer, the combative and ambitious Attorney General of New York, grasped the opportunity occasioned by federal and regulatory inaction. In the process he exposed the reality of systemic fraud. He single-handedly cast off the ideological straightjacket of powerlessness when faced with a well-funded and ever-watchful sector determined to safeguard its own independence, no matter the societal cost. The importance of Spitzer's intervention cannot be overestimated, according to one compliance director of a major New York bank:

> States are emboldened and will be more aggressive going forward. To be candid about it while the states have been bringing actions for 60 years the presence and amount of publicity they got was always somewhat contained. They were viewed as having a useful purpose but they never had celebrity status. Spitzer's case has brought glory and publicity and all this attention to the state regulators, not to mention a whole lot of money to the state treasuries. I think state regulators are sitting across all of the United States now saying "Wow! We have real power, we have real authority. We have a way to be very profitable to our states. We need to flex our muscles even more in the future." This tension is going to grow. At some stage something is going to give.[3]

The retreat from federal government – occasioned by the ideological certainty of Ronald Reagan, enhanced by his successor George Bush Senior, maintained by Clinton in the Democratic interregnum from 1992 to 2000 and reinvigorated by George Bush Junior – is based on the belief that a deregulated economic market, combined with devolved power from federal government, offers the path to political

---

[3] Interview, New York City, 7 February 2003.

and economic success. This ideological fervour cut across both major political parties, ensuring that the range of policy options was circumscribed from the beginning. It was indicative of the growing power of the securities industry that any official probe into the workings of Wall Street focused only on actors, not systems. This was the exercise of real power in action: the ability to directly affect the actions of the political establishment.[4]

After the collapse of the technology bubble, Congress did hold hearings into the allegations of endemic conflict of interest in analyst research, but the underlying message was that greater regulation was not the answer. On 14 June 2001, Michael Oxley, Chairman of the House Finance Committee, proclaimed: "We are here today to learn whether the Chinese wall that is long cited as the separation between the research and investment banking arms of securities firms has developed a crack or is completely crumbling. I am encouraged that Wall Street has recognized that this is not a phantom problem, and has proposed industry best practices guidelines to address these conflicts."[5]

When the committee reconvened six weeks later Oxley maintained that self-regulation was the only answer. "As a free-market Republican, I am loathe to legislate in this area. My preference is for industry to clean up this mess. I am encouraged by steps that some companies have taken to address this issue. I will continue to work with the industry to make sure sufficient steps are taken to resolve the problems and to restore confidence in Wall Street research practices."[6]

The congressional hearings served to expose just how corrupted the research analyst model had become. In testimony, Laura Unger,

---

[4] See Stephen Lukes, *Power, A Radical View* (Macmillan, London, 1974).
[5] "Analyzing the analysts", *Hearings before the Sub-Committee on Capital Markets, Insurance and Government Sponsored Enterprises of the Committee on Financial Services*, 14 June 2001, pp. 107–25.
[6] "Analyzing the analysts II: Additional perspectives", *Hearings before the Sub-Committee on Capital Markets, Insurance and Government Sponsored Enterprises of the Committee on Financial Services*, 31 July 2001, p. 125.

acting Chairman of the SEC, outlined four key areas of concern: the
role played by the analyst in the attraction or retention of clients; the
use of research reports to boost trading volume; the linkage of analyst
compensation to investment business; and the personal retention of
stock in companies covered. In an examination of practices, Ms Unger
revealed that three analysts had executed trades on their personal
accounts at variance with their public recommendations that netted
between $100,000 and $3.5m, an abuse she argued was a potential
violation of federal securities law.[7] The SEC, however, delimited its
range of options to ensuring that the issue was adequately publicized:

> Analyst practices are now firmly in the spotlight. That spotlight has exposed
> the conflicts analysts face. This exposure is beneficial for investors. Analysts
> and their employer firms should carefully consider their policies and procedures
> regarding research and, when possible, minimize conflicts of interest that might
> bias their research and recommendations. Where actual and potential conflicts
> do exist, they should be clearly and meaningfully disclosed to investors.[8]

As a result of inaction, the drive to move beyond enforcement and
into addressing the systemic defects originated in the offices of state
prosecutors, most notably Eliot Spitzer in New York, rather than
legislative centres or the federal regulatory bodies, most notably the
SEC. Spitzer's investigation into conflicts of interest within Wall
Street, beginning with Merrill Lynch and extending to indict the
entire investment banking sector, has been pivotal in opening up to
scrutiny the inner workings of corporate finance:

> What makes Spitzer's case a little different is that it is a state regulator who is
> bringing a case against a major Wall Street firm that operates in all 50 states so
> it is a case that has national implications because it is affecting conduct that
> took place in all 50 states. It wasn't just a local action that he brought. It is a
> national action. And that has opened a debate that is only going to continue to

---

[7] Ibid., p. 73.

[8] Written statement by Laura Unger, Acting Chairperson SEC, "Analyzing the
analysts II: Additional perspectives", *Hearings before the Sub-Committee on Capital
Markets, Insurance and Government Sponsored Enterprises of the Committee on Financial
Services*, 31 July 2001, p. 125.

grow. If you are going to pass rules that affect research analysts that operate in all 50, or should we allow a state to tell a firm how to act nationally which is the equivalent of setting rules. It is a debate imposing national standards. Is that proper? That debate will play out at Congress and the SEC.[9]

As Gary Lynch pointed out in an interview, conducted while his corporation was immersed in the fallout associated with its own star analyst–investment hybrid Frank Quattrone, the SEC was simply out-manoeuvred by the Attorney General:

> These issues didn't start with Spitzer. Arthur Levitt and the Commission started talking about them in 1998, basically talking about them as a phenomenon that existed and putting down a marker that something should be done about it, but didn't really take any kind of effective action. They noted it as an issue, commented adversely on it and then didn't do anything. The unfortunate thing that happened is that the SEC got left behind on it when Spitzer started his investigations and focused on Merrill Lynch. He discovered some facts that were clearly very unattractive, at a minimum. That is what really started the whole thing off. But the notion that the regulators want to say now that it was a violation in some way for analysts to get paid on banking deals: fine, but no-one thought it was a [searing] issue back in 1997, 1998, 1999, 2000.[10]

For the New York State Attorney General, a lack of transparency is at the root of the malignancy and "sunlight is the best disinfectant." Within the financial press, Spitzer is regarded with an admixture of awe and suspicion. Derided by critics on Wall Street, sections of the media and their political allies in Washington, DC itself as little more than a common blackmailer prepared to risk thousands of jobs for personal and political aggrandizement, he has nevertheless done more to uncover the true extent – and rationale – of a corrupted system than any previous regulator. As Charles Gasparino put it in the *Wall Street Journal*, the exposure of the inner workings of corporate America was "the result of a collision of Wall Street hubris and the ambition of a political climber who is an outsider to the clubby world of finance."[11] In the process, his investigations have implicated the

---

[9] Interview, New York City, 7 February 2003.

[10] Interview with Gary Lynch, New York City, 7 February 2003.

[11] Charles Gasparino, "NYSE's Grasso led the effort to reach a research settlement", *Wall Street Journal*, 23 December 2002.

entire political and economic elite in a self-serving conspiracy. The investigations also reopened an ideological debate that could have even greater implications.

In Gramscian terms, the circumstances for an ideological entrepreneur, in this case the New York Attorney General, to posit the need for fundamental change had occurred. The contradiction between the reality of the operation of the securities market and the ideological support structures of free market omniscience were fundamentally flawed. For the Italian theorist, in such circumstances the wider legitimacy of the entire structure and the hegemonic conceptions it promotes become devalued:

> Religion, or a particular Church, maintains its community of faithful ... in so far as it nourishes its faith permanently and in an organised fashion, indefatigably repeating its apologetics, struggling at all times and always with the same kind of arguments, and maintaining a hierarchy of intellectuals who give to the faith the appearance at least of the dignity of thought. Whenever the continuity of relations between the Church and the faithful has been violently interrupted for political reasons, as happened during the French revolution, the losses suffered by the Church have been incalculable.[12]

The evidence accrued by Spitzer ensured that the temptation to blame the malaise on corrupted actors could not be sustained. The intellectual deceit was exposed. Given the dissonance between the sordid reality and the theocratic certainty once propounded as justification for its social ordering, corporate America found its value system comprehensively and publicly devalued. A largely sympathetic profile in the *New York Times* captured the wider political significance of the Attorney General's initial intervention in the management of the securities market. "The Merrill Case represents the convergence of a number of forces: the new state-level activism, deregulation at the federal level and Spitzer's own ambitious legal formulations and flair for public relations, a talent common to all successful prosecutors, at least in New York." In evidence to the Senate Subcommittee on

---

[12] See Antonio Gramsci, *Selections from the Prison Notebooks* (Lawrence & Wishart, London, 1998), p. 340.

Consumer Affairs' Hearings on Corporate Governance, Spitzer made it clear that despite the risk of the Balkanization of the securities market, individual state prosecutorial action was not only acceptable but necessary in the absence of federal action:

> It is our job under New York State law to respond to fraud in the marketplace. Further investigations and enforcement proceedings are necessary as is industry-wide reform. Remarkably throughout our investigation, which has now led us to examine the documents of a significant number of companies, there is absolutely no evidence that any compliance department ever took action to stop behaviour that violated internal rules and state and federal law. The failure of the industry's much vaunted compliance structure is appalling.[13]

A graduate from Harvard Law School, Spitzer's first job in the legal profession was acting as an assistant for Alan Dershowitz in his celebrated defence of Claus von Bulow, the aristocrat accused of murdering his wife with a lethal injection of insulin. Oscillating between private practice and the Manhattan District Attorney's Office, Spitzer first came to public prominence for his ingenuous prosecution of the notorious Gambino crime family in New York, while head of the DA's anti-racketeering unit. At the time, the Mafia had a stranglehold over trucking business in the Garment District, forcing legitimate firms to pay exorbitant transportation fees to what amounted to a cartel. Securing a successful prosecution, while a priority for the DA's office, was all but impossible to achieve. Those who were being extorted were terrified about giving evidence against the Mafia.

The lure of a witness protection programme was distinctly unattractive to the mainly family-based businesses, which had worked for generations building up their firms and embedding themselves deep in the social fabric of the city. They were faced with a terrible Hobson's Choice: keep paying and survive, or testify and face a life on the run, constantly looking over their shoulder, terrified about the next knock on the door or the appearance of a strange car idling outside the house. The prospect of life in some obscure mid-Western town,

---

[13] Testimony of New York State Attorney General Eliot Spitzer to Senate Sub-committee on Consumer Affairs, Hearing on Corporate Governance, 26 June 2002.

living under an assumed identity in which all vestiges of the past were obliterated in an uncertain attempt to escape the reach of the Mafia, was a price many were not prepared to pay. Faced with this obdurate reality, Spitzer established a government-owned sweatshop complete with extensive surveillance cameras and hidden microphones.

Although substantial evidence was accrued during the course of the investigation, Spitzer did not run a simple extortion case. Somewhat controversially, he used anti-trust legislation to run the Gambino crime syndicate out of the Garment District entirely. The family pled guilty to the charges, paid a record $12m fine and were forced to relinquish control over the lucrative trucking business for the textile market in return for the avoidance of a custodial sentence. The case marked out not only Spitzer's penchant for utilizing the entire gamut of legislation but also a desire to change the structural nature of the problem. He was not content just to prosecute the symptoms: attempting to deal with the root cause was just as impor-tant. The fact that the approach ensured massive publicity was an added bonus for the ambitious attorney.

In 1994 he ran for Attorney General and failed; in 1998 he suc-ceeded and set to work developing a reputation for protecting con-sumer rights. He successfully sued Midwest industrial polluters for causing the acid rain that fell on New Yorkers. In 2001 he transferred his attention to the operation of Wall Street, then reeling from the collapse of the dotcom market. While the financial market is the meat on which New York feeds (most notably its political class), Spitzer was singularly well placed to take the risk of shaking down the securities industry by unrelentingly attacking its integrity, the currency of last resort in the world of high finance (as in gambling).[14]

Wealthy in his own right as the scion of one of the most powerful real-estate developers in New York, Spitzer utilized little-used state

---

[14] Much of the biographical detail comes in two extended profiles. James Traub, "The Attorney General goes to war", *New York Times*, 16 June 2002 and Adi Ignatius, "Wall Street's top cop", *Time Magazine*, 22 December 2002. *Time Magazine* named him "crusader of the year" for his work in highlighting corporate abuses on Wall Street.

legislation to mount an attack based as much on shrewd political calculation as moral indignation. "It was one of those situations where for years people knew there was a problem but no one had done anything about it. I was less worried about the pension funds and the sophisticated investors who knew enough but the mythical Mr and Mrs Smith who were being misled and it is my job to protect them. We got lucky in the sense that what we came up with brought into very stark reality what many people had believed for many years."[15]

With investors furious over the collapse of the technology bubble and wanting answers, Spitzer turned his attention toward the operation of Wall Street's largest brokerage houses and doubled the size of the securities enforcement office. For a populist lawyer, the fact that the SEC and other regulatory agencies had limited their concern to pious exhortations served merely to enhance the credibility of the probe. It is a fact acutely felt by Gary Lynch, the former head of enforcement at the SEC:

> It is clear that, if it were not for the bursting of the tech bubble here, things may have changed, but would have changed much more slowly. These issues were known to the regulators, they had focused on them. I don't think they would have taken action if it were not for the fact that the bubble burst. They were known well before the bubble burst.[16]

Central to Spitzer's success was the application of the General Business Law of the State of New York, legislation commonly referred to as the Martin Act by the previously untouchable doyens of Wall Street. The Act, passed in 1921, is a landmark enforcement statute that provides prosecutors with a powerful weapon to initiate litigation if brokers knowingly and wilfully promote sales of securities beyond reasonable expectations or unwarranted by existing circumstances. Significantly, for a prosecution to succeed, the Attorney General

---

[15] Quoted by Ben White and Robert O'Harrow, "Wall Street probe puts prosecutor in spotlight", *Washington Post*, 24 April 2002.

[16] Interview with Gary Lynch, New York City, 7 February 2003.

must only prove that there was a failure to disclose information, not intentional fraud, a much more difficult case to bring to court. A further advantage of the Martins Act is that there is no need to prove the purchase or sale of stock as a result of the information released by the brokerage. Spitzer had found the perfect case.

The road to reform began with the tracking of a case involving a wealthy New York paediatrician, Debases Kanjilal, who filed a complaint with the New York Stock Exchange in March 2001 alleging that the recommendations of Henry Blodget, Merrill Lynch's star analyst, were corrupted by conflicts of interest. In an arbitration filing, the doctor alleged: "Blodget's recommendations lacked a reasonable basis in fact and Blodget failed to disclose a serious conflict of interest with the company whose stock he was touting."[17] The claim centred on stock the doctor had bought with InfoSpace within the range of $122–133 a share. When the stock began to decline, the client alleged Merrill maintained a "buy" recommendation and suggested strenuously he should not sell, a judgement call that resulted in a loss of over $500,000. On the day the arbitration was filed the stock was trading at a mere $3.72 a share. Merrill claimed that the claim was without foundation and stated that it would aggressively defend the case. Four months later, the brokerage agreed to pay Dr Kanjilal $400,000 in compensation.

The aggressive marketing of the boom was now returning with a vengeance across Wall Street. The career of Henry Blodget, the media star of the Internet age, who was paid upward of $5m a year by Merrill, was imploding with the same ferocity as the technology boom with which he was synonymous. In a debate on Internet valuations in 2000 he admitted as much: "We've come out of a big-bang period, where investors have been willing to fund anybody with a business plan. The recent pullback in the market is probably going to temper that enthusiasm. [There will be] a pretty brutal shakeout in which valuation is going to become a lot more important. I think you'll see probably

---

[17] Quoted in Charles Gasparino, "All-star analyst faces arbitration after Internet picks hit the skids", *Wall Street Journal*, 2 March 2001.

75% of these companies disappear."[18] Yet, throughout the boom, leading analysts, including Blodget, did not rate accordingly. With the markets in a tailspin and the search for scapegoats a ferocious reminder of the animosity displayed in Salem, Wall Street itself became the crucible for the destruction of false gods. The degradation of language reached its apogee with the analysts' repeated claim that they performed a professional function, utilizing their experience to examine underlying fundamentals, divining the simple truth behind complex documents, offering investors economic salvation through capital transfers. Now they were being decried as false prophets who tempted true believers into avarice, and Merrill, once one of the most respected corporations on Wall Street, appeared to be saying it was true. They were false prophets. The consequences were profound and immediate.

The *Wall Street Journal* speculated openly that "by settling the matter, Merrill could open the door for more legal action by investors who believe they were burned by snapping up shares of once-high-flying technology stocks hyped by, among other things aggressive 'buy' recommendations by analysts. In most cases, Wall Street firms only made minimal disclosures about any potential conflicts, including lucrative investment banking relationships with firms whose stocks they were touting."[19] The clubby nature of the piece, which openly spoke of the conflicts of interest endemic within Wall Street and the way in which forecasts were compromised to attract investment business, provided Spitzer with a prima facie case to move the investigation onto a higher plane.

In June 2001, the Office of the Attorney General had begun investigating the research analysts' reports. In testimony accompanying the claim against Merrill, Eric Dinallo revealed how the scope of the probe had been transformed. Officials from the enforcement office had "reviewed over 30,000 documents, comprising over 100,000 pages,

---

[18] Dan Ackman, "The trial of Henry Blodget", *Forbes Online*, 6 January 2003. Accessible at www.forbes.com

[19] Charles Gasparino, "Merrill settles with former client in wake of analyst's stock call", *Wall Street Journal*, 20 July 2001.

including thousands of e-mails. It has examined close to twenty witnesses under oath, and has consulted with other witnesses, their lawyers and experts." The affidavit conceded that, while the company had been co-operative, "some of the witnesses examined have displayed an implausible lack of recollection of key conversations and documents, even when they authored or received such document and it was placed in front of them. This lack of recollection often related to events and documents that one would be unlikely to forget. The credibility of these witnesses is consequently suspect. Thus further testimony is sought under judicial supervision and with public scrutiny."[20]

The application to the State Supreme Court was evidence that the Office of the Attorney General had decided that only the risk of public opprobrium would ensure compliance about the scale of the deception. A corollary to this was the argument that the primary purpose of the research was not unbiased imparting of analysis, but self-serving propaganda designed to drum up investment banking fees.

Dinallo based the claim on three interlinked charges. First, the public ratings were at variance with privately held views; second, "as a matter of undisclosed, internal policy" Merrill never issued 'reduce' or 'sell' recommendations making its published ratings system a meaningless charade[21]; and, third, "Merrill Lynch failed to disclose to the public that Merrill Lynch's ratings were tarnished by an undisclosed conflict of interest."[22] The claim alleged that the role of the research analyst was not to collate and disseminate independent objective reports, but to act as "quasi-investment bankers for the

---

[20] Affidavit in support of application for an order pursuant to General Business Law Section 354: Eric Dinallo in *Eliot Spitzer vs. Merrill Lynch et al.*, Supreme Court of New York, 8 April 2002, p. 2. Full text available at www.findlaw.com

[21] The five ratings in descending order were "buy" (if growth of more than 20% forecast), "accumulate" (growth of 10–20% expected), "neutral" (stock to oscillate between 10% growth and 10% deficit), "reduce" (10–20% price drop) and "sell" (a drop of more than 20% expected).

[22] Affidavit in support of application for an order pursuant to General Business Law Section 354: Eric Dinallo in *Eliot Spitzer vs. Merrill Lynch et al.*, Supreme Court of New York, 8 April 2002, p. 3. Full text available at www.findlaw.com

companies at issue, often initiating, continuing, and/or manipulating research coverage for the purpose of attracting and keeping investment banking clients."

The efficient operation of the marketplace is determined on trust and integrity, in large part the only security that any investment house can offer. Spitzer's enforcement chief skilfully used the company's own corporate risk management systems against it. He quoted from an internal training document that opined:

> *Objectivity of opinions.* Opinions expressed by Analysts must be objective. Any indication that a research opinion is less than totally objective, or that it may have been influenced by a business relationship of the Firm, could seriously damage the Firm's reputation and lead it to potential legal liability.[23]

The importance of the email discovery cannot be overestimated. Contained within it was the evidence of patterned duplicity, the "smoking gun" of a corrupt enterprise. A research report from 21 December 2000 recommended a new listing by Lifeminders as "an attractive investment". Privately, Blodget noted to a colleague that "I can't believe what a POS [Piece of Shit] that thing is." Publicly the company stock was given a rating of "accumulate", the second highest of the internal ratings system. Blodget used a similar epithet to describe 24/7, an Internet media company that two months earlier his unit had publicly regarded as a "short-term accumulate and long-term accumulate" stock.

Another company with high public ratings was Internet Capital Group. Merrill began tracking the group in August 1999. Initially, the company performed well and reached a high of $212 on 22 December 1999. Like many of the technology stocks its value plummeted in the 2000 crash, trading for as low as $15.69 on 4 October 2000. The following day, with the stock valued at $12.38, the head of the Internet group Henry Blodget predicted that the stock was "going to 5", the lowest rating on Merrill's model and a rating it never gave publicly. The following day he confided to another senior analyst:

---

[23] Ibid., p. 9.

"This has been a disaster . . . there really is no floor to the stock." On 6 October Blodget retained this pessimistic outlook saying that his research unit "see nothing that will turn this around near term." Yet, publicly, Internet Capital was again pushed by Blodget's department as a "short-term accumulate and long-term buy." Even more staggeringly, until a month before, the stock had been touted as one of the top technology picks in the market.[24] On 9 November the stock was eventually downgraded, but only by one investment grade, making unsuspecting investors believe that the company's fortunes could be transformed.[25]

The credibility gap extended beyond the Internet group to impugn the integrity of the entire research market provided by Merrill Lynch. InfoSpace, the company at the heart of the litigation that settled out of court with the New York doctor, was listed among the top 15 companies whose stock was covered by the company in the period August to December 2000. This top rating was in marked contrast to Blodget's private estimation of its value. He had referred to it in an internal communication, written on 7 July 2000, as "a powder keg, given how aggressive we were on it earlier this year and given the 'bad smell' comments that so many institutions are bringing up." By 20 October, Blodget outlined his true feelings by describing it as a "piece of junk".[26] Yet, it still retained its top investment rating.

Even more damagingly, Spitzer's team unearthed a further email that seemed to suggest that the corruption was endemic and systemic within Merrill Lynch. Blodget asked for firm guidance on how to rate stock, otherwise, he wrote, "we are going to start calling the stocks like we see them, no matter what the ancillary consequences are." According to Spitzer, "You had to love it, Blodget made it clear he genuinely didn't believe his own ratings."

[24] Details from emails quoted in Lina Saigol, "Bankers learn that emailing comes with a health warning", *Financial Times*, 28 December 2002.

[25] Affidavit in support of application for an order pursuant to General Business Law Section 354: Eric Dinallo in *Eliot Spitzer vs. Merrill Lynch et al.*, Supreme Court of New York, 8 April 2002, p. 11. Full text available at www.findlaw.com

[26] Ibid., p. 12.

The case brought by the Attorney General raised serious questions about integrity and the viability of self-regulation within a complex financial services firm that offered a full panoply of services under one roof. Suggesting that a company the size of Merrill Lynch was involved in a form of corrupt enterprise was both audacious and compelling. Central to its strategic direction was the argument that ill-conceived deregulation had created a complex business model flawed from the outset, a point conceded by legal and compliance officials. According to a compliance director of a major New York bank, who spent many years as an enforcement attorney with the SEC in Washington, DC, the combination of luck and hard work initiated a process that was to have enormous implications:

> The reason why you hadn't seen many enforcement actions against research analysts by the SEC for putting out research that they didn't actually believe in was there was always the challenge of being able to prove that the analyst didn't believe in the research. You might know that maybe they didn't because these conflicts existed. You might suspect that when this analyst is saying "buy this stock" he cannot mean it because the firm brought that company in as a banking client. But go prove it. I worked at the SEC. To a degree [the rationale for inaction was inbuilt]. How can you bring this case? How can you prove it? It is hard to go into court and prove what was in somebody's mind. Spitzer found the key to this lock. He looked somewhere we never aggressively looked. He found the emails. It was very smart. He drilled and he tapped oil where we never thought to drill. Once he found those emails you just knew we were at the start of something big. Every other firm on Wall Street was going to get investigated for the same thing and you just knew that new laws, regulatory rules and reforms were going to follow.[27]

Merrill Lynch, then, was merely a test case, a forerunner for the indictment of Wall Street. It was important, therefore, for Spitzer and his team to demonstrate that the problems extended well beyond the delusions or greed of the individual members of the Internet research group. Hence, the respondents in the case specifically included not only Blodget and his research colleagues but also

---

[27] Interview, New York City, 7 February 2003.

their direct managerial supervisors, including Deepak Raj, Head of Global Equity Research and the corporation itself. The implication was clear: it was not just Merrill Lynch but the entire operation of Wall Street itself that was in the dock. The mechanism used to buttress the case was the structural failings within Merrill itself; specifically the inability of the risk compliance department to ensure the maintenance of "Chinese walls", designed to keep investment banking apart from research departments.

Following deregulation of the US securities market, financial conglomerates such as Merrill built up formidable industries that were remarkably similar in size and scope to those that existed prior to the Great Crash. The corporations supplied research that was available to both its retail brokerage arm as well as institutional clients. There was, therefore, an imperative to ensure that privileged information on companies Merrill was providing investment advice to or financing for was not disseminated to research analysts, who in turn could pass on the information to the wider market through its subscription service. The system was designed to eradicate the twin evils of insider-trading and the breaking of client confidentiality. By definition, the system was designed to operate in reverse, shielding the research departments from the pressures of acting as cheerleaders for the much more lucrative and voracious investment business. Responsibility for policing the system rested with the company's risk management or compliance department. In the Merrill case the system imploded with devastating consequences for the very credibility of deregulated structures.

The publication of the Attorney General's case represented one of the bleakest days for the standing of the market since the indictment in 1938 of the Chairman of the New York Stock Exchange Richard Whitney, on charges of grand larceny. Throughout the Great Crash and its aftermath, Whitney played a pivotal role in attempting to restore investor confidence. He travelled throughout the country drumming up support for the stock market and attempting to distance its spectacular collapse from the depression that followed it. Speaking to the Chamber of Commerce in September 1932, he told delegates that "brokers must be honest and financially responsible."[28] At precisely the same time as Whitney was preaching moral and fiscal certitude, he was looting money deposited by investors in his brokerage firm to cover his own overextended positions in the deteriorating market. Whitney was not the worst offender, but served a useful function: as what Galbraith describes as a "symbolic evil". In such a prosecution, the hypocrisy is arguably more destabilizing than the larceny itself. And it was precisely this charge that formed the basis of the Spitzer investigation. As it moved from describing what had happened to why – a much more interesting and politically charged contention.

The contagion of weakened investor confidence, shaken by the collapse of the dotcom era and further eroded by the ruination of Enron, was replicating out of control. Congressional investigations into the role played by the investment banks created a tidal wave of revulsion that collided with similar contempt at the revelations in the appellate court of how the arrogance of American corporate capital manifested itself in the bull market. The "perfect storm" analogy, so beloved of the Conference Board, had now changed course and the deluge rained down on the market in a way not seen since the Pecora hearings in the 1930s. Then the banking sector rather than the market itself was deemed responsible. Now, as revelation followed revelation, it was questionable whether adroit public relations or smear tactics that impugned the integrity of the prosecutors could deflect the return of regulation.

Dinallo's affidavit spoke of the "tortured relationship" between investment needs and research imperatives. The synergies of the 1990s were replaced with a focus on the conflicts of interest: "where analysts' compensation is affected directly or indirectly, their contribution to investment banking, objectivity and independence can be seriously eroded."[29]

---

[28] Quoted in J. K. Galbraith, *The Great Crash 1929* (Penguin, London, 1992), p. 181.

[29] Affidavit in support of application for an order pursuant to General Business Law Section 354: Eric Dinallo in *Eliot Spitzer vs. Merrill Lynch et al.*, Supreme Court of New York, 8 April 2002, p. 14. Full text available at www.findlaw.com

A careful examination of the treasure trove of email and confidential correspondence held by the bank demonstrated beyond doubt that the subservience of research to banking needs was a matter of corporate policy. When Blodget joined the firm he compiled a mission statement, which was copied to the head of US Equity Research and senior investment bankers, entitled "Managing the Banking Calendar for Internet Research". Blodget expected that his job would involve an equality of labour between banking and research. For one week, his diary entries demonstrated the true preponderance toward investment activities. His work would involve "85% banking, 15% research."[30] Not only would Blodget provide tailor-made research notes, he would use his high-profile position as a star analyst to move markets. In 1999, Blodget made 77 appearances on television, mainly CNBC and CNN. The company, according to documentation provided to the Spitzer team, logged more than 46 appearances the following year.[31] The company was at pains, however, to present an image to the public in line with its internal staff manual.

One instance cited by the prosecutors involved a scheduled appearance by Blodget on CNN's influential business programme *Moneyline*. The company was accused of deliberately hiding the contradictions inherent in the corporate reporting structure in which "members of the research group routinely acted as quasi-investment bankers." Merrill Lynch pretended there was a clear division, thereby enhancing the analysts' credibility. Thus, prior to the head of the Internet group appearing on television, he was reminded:

> CNN called and wanted to know if we are in AOL deal as an advisor. Head of media relations gave them a no comment. *If you are asked on Moneyline interview about that say something to the effect that you are not in the loop on that as you are in research not banking* [emphasis in original].[32]

In the autumn of 2000, the co-head of Global Equity Research sent an email to all analysts to gather information on the relationship

---

[30] Ibid., p. 15.
[31] Ibid., p. 24.
[32] Ibid., p. 20.

between the two sectors. The aim was not to police it, but to adjudicate how far upward their compensation should be adjusted as a consequence of these flagrant breaches of corporate governance guidelines:

> We are once again surveying your contributions to investment banking during the year ... Please provide complete details on your involvement in the transaction, paying particular attention to the degree that your research coverage played a role in origination, execution and follow-up. Please note, as well, your involvement in advisory work on mergers and acquisitions, *especially where your coverage played a role in securing the assignment* and your follow-up marketing to clients. Please indicate *where your research coverage was pivotal in securing participation in high yield offering* (emphasis in original).[33]

Blodget and his team compiled a detailed response, which was forwarded to management on 2 November 2000. Blodget asserted that he and his team had been centrally involved in more than 52 completed or potential transactions. The company had earned $115m as a result. More would have been accrued, but for the unfortunate fact that the "market window for most Internet companies closed in June." This was code for the spectacular collapse of the dotcom market that Blodget and his team had done much to fuel. Rather than becoming a red flag issue, Blodget found that his salary was increased dramatically. "Overall, Blodget's agreed annual compensation, including guaranteed minimum cash bonus, increased from $3m for 1999 to $12m for 2001."[34]

The flagrant breaching of the Chinese walls without censure as a matter of policy cut across the entire company. Although there is considerable evidence in the document supplied to the court by Dinallo of unease within the Internet research department, there is no indication that the company itself intervened to shore up the gaping hole in the risk management defences. Research was initiated to ingratiate investment deals, rerated to augment those deals, and ordinary investors relying on the allegedly impartial advice from the

---

[33] Ibid., p. 21.
[34] Ibid., p. 21.

titans of research at Merrill Lynch were, quit simply, defrauded. One of the defendants Kirsten Campbell, a senior analyst in Blodget's division, displayed unusual candour in an email to her boss over the decision to upgrade the rating on a company called GoTo, for which the investment bank acted. She complained about pressure to artificially enhance its value and proclaimed that she did not "want to be a whore for f-ing management . . . if . . . we are putting half of Merrill retail into this stock because they are out accumulating it, then I don't think that's the right thing to do. We are losing people money and I don't like it. John and Mary Smith are losing their retirement because we don't want Todd [Tappin, the CFO at GoTo] to be mad with us."[35]

A compromise was reached to lower the rating, as long as Merrill made the decision to lower that of a competitor. The problem was that the analyst covering the rival company Looksmart could see "no reason to do now versus before". Even GoTo senior management saw a potential problem and advised Merrill to prevent any unwarranted attention by not changing the ratings simultaneously. Campbell replied that the rerating would not be "strange". The compliance department certainly did, however, and, when the research note containing the changed rating was sent for clearance on 10 January 2001, the attempt to veto the deal was easily subverted.

This discovery was pivotal. It questioned the entire risk management structures of the company. Dinallo's affidavit points out that, when the final initiation report for GoTo was submitted, a rationally inexplicable downgrade in Looksmart's rating was also attached. This was amended to the previous figure. However, a subsequent report for Looksmart, which independently devalued the rating, was then provided to the compliance team.

There is no evidence that the compliance department even attempted to question why this was done or raise any suspicion about the timing of the change, which could only be justified in terms of GoTo's request to Merrill that it should be.[36] If Merrill's researchers

---

[35] Ibid., p. 26.
[36] Ibid., p. 28.

were prepared to prostitute themselves to boost investment clients, they were also prepared to penalize them if they did not fall for the corporate charm.

When GoTo decided to use arch-rival investment bank Credit Suisse First Boston (CSFB) to underwrite the issuance of new shares, a petty vendatta was planned. On 25 May 2001, a subordinate in the research department decided to sabotage the listing by metaphorically loading "these bullets in a note on my hard drive so that we are ready to pull the trigger quickly." Blodget's response to this act of spite spoke volumes about the true state of corporate culture within Merrill Lynch. Rather than castigate his charge, the managerial response, in writing, was inelegant but brutally frank: "beautiful fuk 'em."[37]

On 6 June, CSFB launched the offering and the research department sent the loaded gun in the form of a revised downward rating to compliance for approval. The last chance to apply the safety catch was squandered. Compliance appeared to acquiesce in the release of vindictive behaviour that damaged not only the corporation but also the integrity of the market of which Merrill was ostensibly such an honourable member. The incident provides no clearer incident of the failure by the investment banks to calibrate the consequences of disregarding reputational risk.

Spitzer's investigation provoked the ire of Merrill Lynch. A senior executive, quoted in the *Wall Street Journal*, complained that the company was being equated to "the Colombian drug cartel."[38] Such a sulphurous response could not hide the bind the company found itself in as a consequence of the electronic record Spitzer had discovered. Merrill was brought to the negotiating table, and when it attempted to settle quietly the Attorney General published the offending emails on 8 April 2002. The impact was dramatic. The editor of *Barron's Online*, a subsidiary of Dow Jones, was almost

---

[37] Ibid., p. 31.
[38] Quoted in Charles Gasparino, "NYSE's Grasso led the effort to seal a research settlement", *Wall Street Journal*, 23 December 2002.

apoplectic with rage: "There's only one word I can use to describe this cynical misrepresentation: corruption."[39]

When the brokerage house baulked at the proposed fine of $100m, Spitzer continued the negotiating process in a round of high-profile television interviews. "Merrill Lynch is going to have to think long and hard about where it wants to go in this investigation," he told CNN. Four days later, Spitzer used an interview with CBS *Evening News* to issue what amounted to an ultimatum. Should the company "maintain that what happened was inappropriate but wasn't illegal, then there will be no settlement. Then there will be much tougher sanctions. There could be criminal charges. And the fate of their company is in their hands." The strategy worked, in part because of the financial havoc the accusations was playing on the company's share price. It lost 20% in value before finally, on 21 May 2002, Merrill bowed to the inevitable and sued for peace. One of the most powerful merchant banks in the country had joined the ranks of the Gambino family on the altar of justice, as defined and put into practice by Eliot Spitzer.

Although much carping was made in the financial press that Spitzer had baulked in the face of intense political pressure, the settlement marked a landmark in securities regulation. Spitzer had secured a position for state officials to mediate federal law. While the settlement was reached without an admission of liability, the public dissemination of its findings revealed the true extent of the humiliation for Merrill. First, Merrill agreed to "comply with the Martin Act", an indication that it had not done so previously. Second, the corporation agreed that in future it "will state on each Merrill Global Equity research report whether Merrill Lynch received or is entitled to receive compensation over the past 12 months, or whether Merrill Lynch is entitled to receive compensation from any publicly announced equity underwriting or merger and acquisition transaction for each company covered by the research report." This represented a

---

[39] Howard R. Gold, "Merrill bombshell shows corruption runs deep", *Barron's Online*, 11 April 2002.

significant addition to disclosure practice and involved the company agreeing to a redrafting of securities regulations in line with the interpretation designed by the New York State Attorney General. This is underscored by the third provision, which amounts to a "buyer beware" clause. "By June 3 2002, Merrill Lynch will include a legend on the first page of each Merrill Lynch Global Equity research report that investors should assume that Merrill Lynch is seeking or will seek investment banking or other business from the Covered Company."[40] Further the company was obliged to include "specific disclosure" of the performance of all companies in the particular sector covered and those "for which, over the prior 12 months, Merrill Lynch performed services."

Under the terms of the agreement, Merrill further agreed to "separate completely the evaluation and determination of compensation for US-based equity research analysts from Merrill Lynch's investment banking business." The company accepted a prohibition on senior managers "soliciting from any analyst or considering, in determining any analyst's compensation, either (i) the amount of investment banking revenue received from clients covered by such analyst, or (ii) the analyst's participation in investment banking transactions." Assessment of performance-related pay could no longer include the contributions of the investment sector in an attempt to rebuild the Chinese walls. A "research recommendations committee" was to be established in order to "monitor performance of and supervise equity research recommendations for objectivity, integrity, and a rigorous analytical framework."

In a move away from compensation tied to the level of the bourse, the application of a bonus would be tied to how the research performed for investors in the stock promoted. Changes in research ratings had to be approved by the Research Recommendations Committee, a further indication that the internal risk management

---

[40] Agreement between the Attorney General of the State of New York and Merrill Lynch, Pierce, Fenner & Smith, Inc., dated 21 May 2002, p. 2. Full text available at www.findlaw.com

and compliance systems were not sufficiently robust to police the system. In order to ensure effectiveness, disclosure of previous relationships over the past 12 months between the research analyst and the investment arm of the business had to be internally disclosed. To ensure that the deal would retain its potency, the agreement called on Merrill to appoint a compliance monitor.

In a staggering indication of the rout faced by the corporation, "the Compliance Officer will be appointed by Merrill Lynch, subject to the acquiescence of the Attorney General, which acquiescence will not be unreasonably withheld." This officer would have a separate reporting structure to the Research Recommendations Committee and offer analysts the opportunity to independently "address issues of actual or perceived undue influence or pressure from investment banking or any other source." Merrill also agreed the payment of a $100m fine, 48% of which would go to New York, 50% to the other states and 2% to the North American Securities Administrators Association. These payments involved those states dropping any separate investigation.

The paradox facing Merrill was that while compliance was the only way to settle the case, its terms provided evidence for class action suits to proceed. It also paved the way for Spitzer to expand his investigation. By settling, Merrill merely ensured that the pain would be spread across Wall Street. Spitzer announced at a news conference that the deal was "a template" for future activities.[41] Caught in the horns of a dilemma, Merrill was left with no choice.

The other reason for Merrill's capitulation was the decision by the SEC Chairman Harvey Pitt that he could no longer ignore the evidence that Spitzer had produced. In the midst of the public stand-off between Merrill and the New York Attorney General Spitzer, Pitt was summoned to Washington for private discussions. Pitt made it clear to reporters that it would be irresponsible for the federal authorities not to intervene. According to the *New York Times*, Pitt "indicated that the commission wanted to take control

---

[41] Howard R. Gold, "Despite Merrill deal, Wall Street's woes ain't over", *Barron's Online*, 23 May 2002.

of the policing of an issue that many on Wall Street think should be left to federal regulators, not sorted out state by state." Quoting a conversation between Pitt and his head of enforcement Stephen Cutler, the *Wall Street Journal* reasoned that Cutler was determined that the SEC could not abdicate responsibility any further.[42] Spitzer welcomed the belated intervention of the SEC and other regulators, but maintained that the investigation would not be trampled underfoot by the addition of the Washington political and regulatory elite. In a pointed response he told the *New York Times*, "I have always believed that the best way to resolve this was to have the regulatory agencies working together. We framed the issue. Now, we need to solve it."[43]

Watching developments from the Vice-Chairman's office at CSFB, Gary Lynch recognized both the importance of Merrill's capitulation and the reality that more fundamental change was a forgone conclusion for all the investment bankers:

> At that point everyone was saying [in the investment banking community] "tell us what you want us to do." What people hoped to avoid, which we didn't avoid, was them saying: "No, we're not going to do that, we don't want to do that, what we want to do is have an investigation and fine you a whole lot of money."[44]

The agreement to hold a joint investigation may have offered a compromise between the New York Attorney General and the most powerful corporations in America, but it also marked the point where the collision course between Spitzer and the federal authorities was set. This was preordained because of profound differences between Pitt and Spitzer on the twin vexed questions of the function of law to shape public policy and whether self-policing models were sustainable. This in turn opened a major fault line with the political establishment in Washington.

---

[42] Charles Gasparino, "NYSE's Grasso led the effort to seal a research settlement", *Wall Street Journal*, 23 December 2002.

[43] All quotations in this paragraph come from Patrick McGeehan, "SEC begins investigation of analysts", *New York Times*, 26 April 2002.

[44] Interview with Gary Lynch, New York City, 7 February 2003.

Spitzer sought to reach a national consensus on the need for regulatory and legislative change. First, he assembled a powerful coalition of state attorney generals, ranging from California to Massachusetts, to investigate the major players on the securities market. This aggressive legal posturing was accompanied by the recognition that a political realignment was also necessary. He attended Senate hearings and advocated the introduction of new legislation that would render illegal the provision of analyst compensation from the profits of investment transactions and make salary levels dependent on an evaluation of the added value of the research, rather than ability to bring in new investment business.

It is perhaps not surprising that the independent spirit manifested by Spitzer is linked to the fact that the state regulators, of which the New York representative is merely the most high profile, face inordinately less pressure from industry lobby groups than either the congressional legislators or the SEC they appoint. For the Chairman of the SEC, by contrast, individual deviancy was the core issue to be addressed. Addressing the National Press Club in Washington, Pitt proclaimed, "I pray every night to the good Lord, hoping for divine guidance and inspiration ... We've got a chance to make a great system better. What more could anyone want?"[45] – an assessment that betrays the timidity toward root and branch reform that is also shared by the political masters who put him there in the first place.

At heart, therefore, the controversy between the regulators centred on differing analyses of the core problem. For Spitzer, the crime was linked to organizational and systemic failure. In a speech entitled "the crisis of accountability", given on 1 May 2002, Spitzer provided a revealing insight into his political philosophy. Spitzer noted that the crisis of accountability stemmed from a more profound crisis of governance that seeped across all major institutions in American society, "whether financial, professional, charitable or religious." He remained convinced that law was the only vehicle

---

[45] Harvey Pitt, "Remarks before the National Press Club", 19 July 2002. Available online at http://www.sec.gov/news/speech/spch577.htm

left to restore the breach of public confidence in the "institutions" of America. It amounted to nothing less than a full-blown political manifesto:

> The mandate of these institutions is to serve their investors and shareholders, their contributors and members, and in many cases, the public. Yet even as they pursue these objectives, we have required them to operate within certain boundaries, delineated by carefully articulated standards of conduct, disclosure and moral responsibility.
>
> Institutions are required to act in accordance with these standards even when they conflict with pure self-interest. Yet recently, abiding by these standards has come to be viewed as an impractical ideal instead of a practiced reality. As a result, these institutions too often have begun to act in a manner that has violated these boundaries and generated public mistrust and cynicism. Our gradual dissipation of expectations for institutional behaviour has now created a crisis of accountability, as the failure of these institutions to abide by proper standards has been exposed to the general public.
>
> Our silence in the face of this decline was perhaps understandable. Because these institutions play such a vital role in our society, the public was hesitant to challenge them. Stories that should have raised concerns of possible misconduct were met not with inquiry and outrage but with a lowering of the standard of what we would consider to be acceptable.
>
> Internally, standards declined incrementally year after year, such that one off-balance-sheet partnership bred exponentially more as the years rolled by. And externally, inquiry and accountability were both avoided and evaded. If conduct seemed inappropriate and demanded an explanation, we simply lowered our standards to redefine that conduct as acceptable. We allowed thin assurances of propriety to serve as a proxy for vigorous accountability guarding against impropriety.
>
> Sadly, the events of this past year have taught us that we have more to lose by lowering our standards than we do from expressing scepticism and demanding accountability. Because after years of downward pressure, the intertwined threads of public trust that give these institutions their true strength have become terribly frayed.
>
> At the heart of this breach of trust is an ever-increasing opaqueness in the operation of these institutions. The lack of transparency and absence of accountability to the constituencies served by these entities only heightened the distrust that developed when inappropriate conduct was finally exposed. Or too long, we allowed these institutions to focus inward, without regard for the effect of their actions on those they were duty-bound to serve. We allowed them to trade on the trust we placed in them by accepting a model of self-policing whose currency was not in accountability but in assurances. Those assurances were too often hollow, and that currency has now been substantially devalued.

Our legal system can serve as a bridge over the chasm of distrust separating the public from these institutions.

The faith that was once reserved for these institutions and their policies of self-policing will be restored by a renewed reliance on our legal system and its insistence on accountability.

For this to work, the law must demand – and these institutions must accept – that standards of behaviour that were being ignored must now be strictly followed. The rigorous enforcement of existing laws and codes of conduct will ensure that these institutions are accountable to the broad public they are meant to serve, and not their own narrow institutional interests. The ideas that I have suggested can signal to a disenchanted public that our system of law can provide – indeed, can itself be – the solution to the crisis created by the betrayal of their trust. Our insistence on a comprehensive system of accountability will announce to a nervous public – to investors and stockholders, to congregants and clergy, to those who contribute to charity as well as those supported by charity, to litigants and lawyers – that our legal system will narrow the breach created by this distrust.[46]

He argued that American society has been guilty of defining deviancy downward, "an increasing tolerance for previously intolerable behaviour." Although the lawyer has been careful to limit his overt criticisms to date on the inadequacies of the structures, implicit in his logic is a powerful critique of the failure of the regulators and, by extension, their political masters, who denied them the framework or the resources to police the largest financial market in the world.

This stance has earned him powerful enemies in Washington, primarily among legislators such as Representative Michael Oxley, a champion of the securities industry.[47] Oxley has complained vociferously about the tactics deployed by Spitzer, "Grandstanding by ambitious and publicity-hungry political officials will not lead to healthy and responsible securities markets" was his estimation of Spitzer's

---

[46] Eliot Spitzer, "The crisis of accountability", address on Law Day, 1 May 2002. Full text available at http://www.oag.state.ny.us/press/statements/law_day-2002.html

[47] Although most press coverage of Spitzer is adulatory, for a scathing assessment see Michael Freedman, "Witch-hunt", *Forbes Online*, 9 December 2002. The profile accuses Spitzer of grandstanding, hypocrisy and cant.

success in forcing Merrill Lynch to pay $100m for breaching securities regulations.[48]

In a letter to the *New York Times* on 31 May 2002, just after the Merrill settlement was reached, Oxley warned that Spitzer's crusade was exceptionally dangerous. For an Attorney General from any other state, such censure, particularly five months before the legal officer faced re-election, could spell the end to a campaign, but New York's central importance to the operation of the American securities industry has given Spitzer incredible clout and, more importantly, protection.

In evidence to the Senate Banking Committee, Spitzer cut an uncompromising figure. For the combative lawyer, it was imperative for the state to act given the failure of the federal regulatory authorities. For Spitzer, it was simply not acceptable to do nothing. It amounted to a comprehensive indictment of Washington, "I believe that the Congress and the federal government cannot have it both ways. If Congress and the Executive Branch decide to curtail federal oversight of areas such as securities, they must recognize it is the responsibilities of state securities regulators such as myself to step in to protect the investing public."

Spitzer used the platform of success against Merrill to launch a broadside against those in Congress who appeared to use spurious ideology to defend the interests of the corporate elite. He condemned the chairman of the banking committee, Michael Oxley, and his deputy Richard Baker: "The Merrill investigation and settlement has spawned another movement that is very dangerous to investors. I am referring here to the behind the scenes effort to pass legislation that would eviscerate the ability of the states to effectively prosecute securities fraud. The threat is very real. Representative Baker – in a letter to all the nation's attorneys general – has threatened that he would 'introduce legislation which would supersede' state efforts in this area." Spitzer complained vociferously about the lack of alterna-

---

[48] Quoted by Gretchen Morgenson, "A friend of Main St., or Wall St.?", *New York Times*, 3 November 2002.

tives put forward by Congress, suggesting that a bill proposed by Baker and his colleague Michael Oxley was little more than pathetic and "requires absolutely no action from anyone. Its sole directive is to the SEC to study and report back to Congress on any final rules a self-regulatory organization may in the future deliver to the SEC. It is difficult to conceive of a more passive – or inadequate response to the problem [of analyst conflicts of interest]." But his most venomous riposte was reserved for Michael Oxley, in a press statement accompanying his evidence to the hearing:

> Mr. Oxley would have us believe that investors derive no protection from the vigilance of state authorities. He fails to recognize that were it not for my office's investigation and court filing, the extent of the conflict at Merrill Lynch would never have come to light.
>
> Mr. Oxley simply does not understand that aggressive action is necessary to restore investor confidence. Instead, he seems intent on undercutting my efforts and those of other state regulators seeking to enforce state laws to protect consumers. His inaction and opposition to those who expose and seek to reform corporate wrongdoing contribute to the spiralling decline in public confidence.[49]

The inherent conflict of interest on Wall Street remains in place precisely because of the decision not to formally request the separation of investment and research. In part the regulators buckled under pressure from the banks that such a move would add to the employment woes on Wall Street. The failure of Congress to introduce the necessary legislation during the summer can be traced to the unwillingness of the industry to tolerate any meddling of substance with the new dispensation arising from the repeal of Glass–Steagall. With congressional elections looming and a presidential contest just two years away, the legislative class backed away from its responsibility for Main Street in favour of the merchants of Lower Manhattan.

---

[49] Statement released by Eliot Spitzer on 27 June 2002 after testifying to Senate Consumer Affairs Subcommittee. Full text available at http://www.oag.state.ny.us/press/2002/jun/jun27a_02.html. The site provides a further link to Spitzer's testimony the previous day.

As Michael Oxley (Spitzer's *bête noire* in Washington) pointed out at a conference organized by PricewaterhouseCooper (one of the four remaining international accountancy firms), even the much-heralded Sarbanes–Oxley legislation, passed in such a hurry during the summer when public dissatisfaction was at its height, may now have to be reviewed. He told a December web-cast that it was a bill "passed in almost a panic sort of situation. Any time that Congress deals with white-hot issues like [those] we dealt with on corporate accountability and accounting misdeeds, there [are] bound to be some issues that probably ought to be revisited."[50]

The future of American politics has been bought at a cut-down price. The unanswered question was whether the maintenance of the policies that allow the defrauding of investors represents criminal collusion on an organized basis. If proven, that could justify a federal investigation under the Racketeering and Corrupt Organization Act (RICO). If so, Vincent Cianci, the former mayor of Providence now languishing in a New Jersey prison, may well be joined by his compatriots, and the task of cleaning up Wall Street left to ambitious politicians whose threats to prosecute have served to create the basis for de facto legislation, bypassing Washington entirely, a development that challenges the credibility of the entire legislative process.

---

[50] Quoted in Andrew Hill, "Has corporate America learned its lesson", *Financial Times*, 30 December 2002.

5

Enforcing the enforcers:
the politics of business

Unbowed by the opposition in Washington, Spitzer pressed ahead. The New York Attorney General took over the investigation of Citigroup and its subsidiary Salomon Smith Barney. His counterpart in Boston steered through the investigation of Credit Suisse First Boston. The revelations from both investigations proved pivotal in discrediting any vestige of support for the model of self-policing on Wall Street. They also heralded the most intrusive regulation of the internal affairs of the securities industry since the Great Depression. The egregious nature of the internal correspondence demonstrated clearly that the risks of allowing the endemic and systemic conflicts of interest to remain intact were unsustainable. If the financial fraud in the company sector was primarily the result of corrupt actors, the entire operation of the securities market – from the provision of stock to preferred clients to the rating of companies on the New York Stock Exchange (NYSE) and NASDAQ – was the result of a corrupted system.

The tenacity displayed by regulators in Manhattan and Boston in securing the evidence was severely embarrassing to the Securities and Exchange Commission (SEC) and to the congressional leaders who had organized such inconclusive hearings into the same issues in the summer of 2000. It also raised fundamental questions about the relationship between state and federal authority. In a year-end profile, the London *Sunday Times* opined that "Eliot Spitzer is that most devastatingly effective of creatures: a lawyer who plays the game like a politician."[1] For the Attorney General "sunlight is the best disinfectant." Extending the metaphor, the quality of the light now seeping through the canyons of Wall Street has bleached away the veneer of sophistication to expose a deeply disturbing moral vacuum.

The poisonous atmosphere at the Senate Hearings in July served notice not only of Spitzer's intent but also the depth of animosity among all the major players in the unfolding drama. In the public relations battle, there was no contest as to who was winning. The ongoing investigations on Capital Hill into the bankruptcy of WorldCom and Enron, the guilty verdict imposed on Anderson for shredding documents and the indictment of individual executives on criminal charges served to exacerbate concerns about a systematic erosion of ethical behaviour in the corporate world.

Throughout the summer high-profile arrests were made in front of the TV cameras, as the political pressure on the US Attorney's Office mounted to secure convictions to mollify public discontent. In an operation not seen since 1987, when the then US Attorney Rudolph Giuliani had ordered armed police onto the trading floor of Goldman Sachs to bring one of its most senior partners, Robert Freeman, in for questioning on insider-trading allegations, once again the excesses of executive compensation shot to the top of the agenda.[2] The parade of compromised executives included some of the most powerful names in corporate America: individuals whose aggressive strategies involved the entrenchment of symbiotic relations with Wall Street.

Among those now paraded in a rogue gallery was Dr Samuel Weiskal, the iconoclastic chief executive of Imclone Systems. His penchant for fine art and the cooking of Martha Stewart were to bring both pursuits into disrepute before the end of the summer. He was accused of using insider knowledge to offload shares immediately before the Food and Drug Administration refused to license a cancer

---

[1] Quoted by Amanda Hall and Dominic Rushe, "Eliot Spitzer – the man who came from nowhere", *Sunday Times*, 29 December 2002.

[2] Freeman was not charged, a development that temporarily deflected Giuliani's rise to national fame.

drug developed by his biotechnology firm. The failure of the clinical trials caused the stock price to nosedive, but not before Dr Weiskal and his friend, the broadcast chef and entrepreneur Martha Stewart, had divested substantial stock in order to significantly reduce her exposure. Stewart, who had spent decades cultivating a wholesome image, saw her credibility crumble overnight. In a further humiliation she was forced to resign her directorship at NYSE representing public investors. In her defence, Stewart says she took advantage of advice provided by her broker, who, coincidentally, also handled Weiskal's trades.

Other figures publicly humiliated by the presence of the cameras included John Rigas, the flamboyant head of Adelphi Communications, and his two sons. The cable network developed by Rigas trumpeted its decision not to show pornographic movies as an attempt to reverse moral decline. In fact, Adelphi's internal accounting demonstrated a much more serious moral torpor. Effectively, the Rigas family had turned the publicly listed company into its own personal savings account to be rifled at will. At least $2.3bn in loans were inappropriately taken from the company in unauthorized loans. Even when the company began to go under in a wave of scandal, the Rigas family displayed sneering contempt for the market. Under pressure from Wall Street to reduce the burgeoning debt, John Rigas announced that the family would invest $400m to stabilize the company's financial footing. What they didn't disclose was that this money was borrowed from Adelphi, thereby adding to the problem.[3] Eventually, the whole house of cards collapsed under the weight of its own internal contradictions. The Rigas family were ousted from control and the company filed for bankruptcy in June 2002. A month later they were charged with grand larceny. As with the other scandals, there was a fundamental breakdown in corporate governance procedures both inside the firm and with external monitors. In retrospect, the failure is all the more damning because the measures used to loot

---

[3] See John Nofsinger and Kenneth Kim, *Infectious Greed, Restoring Confidence in America's Companies* (Prentice Hall, Upper Saddle, NJ, 2003), pp. 60–2.

the company were quite simple. According to John Moscow of the New York District Attorney's office, the problem was that they were not disclosed and none challenged the rosy projections.

These disturbing questions were pushed aside as more scandals emerged. Each prosecution served to highlight charges of hypocrisy and greed, fuelling the "corrupted actor" paradigm and obfuscating the wider issue. In September, the New York District Attorney's office bagged its biggest catch to date, an achievement that simultaneously served to point once again to the systemic flaws. Dennis Kozlowski was arrested and charged with fraudulently obtaining more than $400m without board approval while chief executive of Tyco International.

The disgraced executive had been forced to resign earlier in the summer following grand jury hearings into tax evasion. It was alleged that he and his agents colluded in the evasion of New York state sales tax on works by Monet and Renoir. Empty crates were shipped to company premises in New Jersey. The precious cargo itself was transported the few blocks up Fifth Avenue to his grandiose apartment, another item of expenditure charged to the company.[4] In September, the Tyco board filed a complaint to the SEC that Kozlowski, Mark Schwartz (the CFO) and the firm's general counsel had "engaged in a pattern of improper and illegal conduct by which they enriched themselves at the expense of the company with no colourable benefits to the company and concealed their conduct from the board." A civil suit asked for the repayment of $400m. The District Attorney's Office filed criminal charges on the same charges of egregious conduct. Kozlowski was accused of turning Tyco into "a criminal enterprise",

---

[4] Dr Weiskal had also evaded New York's 8.25% sales tax. He bought $15m of paintings by such luminaries as Francis Bacon and Mark Rothko and evaded tax by shipping them to his pharmaceutical plant in New Jersey, before secretly transporting them to his apartment in the Tribeka neighbourhood of Manhattan. In the process he evaded $1.2m in sales tax. Since the US Attorney's Office began issuing subpoenas to the city's top art dealers, an amnesty arrangement has resulted in tax being collected on $73m of art – a figure that suggests that tax evasion was endemic. See Joshua Chaffin, "New York adopts an artistic approach to taxes", Financial Times, 8 March 2003.

the first indication that organized crime legislation would again be pressed into service to prosecute a fresh outbreak of white-collar crime.[5]

If Ivan Boesky symbolized the "greed is good" generation of the 1980s, Dennis Kozlowski was the epitome of the roaring 1990s. Court documents provide compelling evidence of the lavish lifestyle Kozlowski created to consolidate his reputation as the most aggressive deal-maker on Wall Street. In the process, he had transformed Tyco into an industrial conglomerate that generated enormous fees for Wall Street, which cheered on the acquisitorial strategy. Revenues increased from $3bn to $36bn and market capitalization soared from $1.5bn to $106bn. Corporate headquarters were shifted to a prestigious office building overlooking Central Park in New York, a move that mirrored the public transformation of Dennis Kozlowski himself.

In an attempt to gain corporate acceptability, he began collecting the accoutrements of unbridled wealth. He bought corporate jets and yachts. He endowed a chair at the Judge Business School, a graduate faculty at Cambridge University, to demonstrate his philanthropic credentials. He hired a personal art advisor and an interior designer to ensure his burgeoning real-estate collection passed muster. He became an expert in fine wines and built luxury homes in Nantucket, Florida and Fifth Avenue, all of which he charged to the company under a key employee loan programme, the repayments to which were regularly and inexplicably forgiven. The company yacht was pressed into service for family vacation trips along the East Coast. The corporate jet was used to fly guests to an ostentatious party celebration for his wife in the upmarket Four Seasons resort in Sardinia.

While the market remained buoyant, none questioned the avaricious nature of the personal excess or the enormous debt that the expansionary model created, debt that was impossible to service without engineering the numbers. After the fall of Enron, things changed, and changed dramatically. The aggressive acquisition

---

[5] For an extended profile of the Kozlowski case see James B. Stewart, "Spend! Spend! Spend! Where did Tyco's money go", *New Yorker*, 17 February 2003, pp. 132–47.

model had lulled Tyco's senior management into dangerous compla-
cency. As with Enron, behind the outward veneer of a highly edu-
cated, experienced board of directors, capable of providing strategic
oversight, was a system that inculcated, at best, ethical confusion. At
worst, it was nothing less than gross dereliction of duty. Throughout
the Tyco rollercoaster ride to market dominance none appeared
willing to question the avarice. In the Tyco case study, one finds an
all-too-common failing: a somnambulant board, which was financially
beholden on management. At the same time, such was the moral
ambivalence that, when areas of reputational risk were eventually
exposed, the chief executive was powerless to rectify the situation.
By late summer 2002, the emperor had been denuded of any
semblance of respectability.

One director, Frank Walsh, played a significant role in the acquisition of a financial subsidiary for Tyco. He received a finder's fee of
$20m. The payment represented a blatant example of a conflict of
interest, but the chief executive could not bring himself to force
repayment from his errant colleague. It was to be a combination of
unease at the authorization of the payment to Walsh, the deployment
of a radical change of course to sustain the fiction of sound economic
fundamentals and a subpoena for tax evasion on the paintings in New
York that were to spell the end for Kozlowski's reign as a corporate
superstar.

The aggressive acquisitions strategy appeared to stall as the market
began to collapse. Kozlowski put to the board a radical proposal to
break up the conglomerate based on an analysis that valued the parts
greater than the sum. Goldman Sachs valued the financial subsidiary
at £13–17bn alone. The radical change in direction adopted by Tyco –
in an attempt to ramp up the share price on the basis of investment
advice provided by a bank that stood to gain enormous underwriting
fees – may have been necessary to prevent the truth seeping out about
just how precarious the financial situation actually was. While the
issue of the extent of the corporate malfeasance in Tyco remains
hotly contested, it is undoubtedly the case that the sudden change
in strategic direction rattled already nervous investors.

Suspicions of catastrophic accounting irregularities and wider unease by the board about Kozlowski's integrity, fuelled by the illicit payment to the director of the finder's fee and the tax evasion charge, ensured the vilification of the CEO. It prompted a belated attempt to exert some control over the company's corporate governance. By that stage it was too late. As John Moscow, the Deputy Chief of Investigations at the New York District Attorney's office, explains: the share collapse in Tyco dwarfs even that of Enron:

> In Tyco we have taken a plea from the lead director, we have indicted and are prosecuting the chief executive, the chief financial officer and chief legal counsel and we are looking at the conduct of auditors. In terms of corporate governance that is a pretty clean sweep. Tyco has lost $75bn, which is 25% greater than all of Enron. That is a serious loss, a serious change. The penal consequences are to a certain extent irrelevant. All they really stand for is the proposition that the public is outraged. The corporate governance matter is altogether more serious.[6]

Unanswered, to date, in the investigation into the destruction of the Tyco business model is the justification by Goldman Sachs for its valuation of Tyco's assets. Was the reduction in value the result of a depressed market or were the initial research findings absurdly optimistic, designed to ensure that the sale was followed through, thus generating enormous investment banking fees?[7] In a radically changed investment climate, suspicion about the motives of all those involved in corporate finance is on the rise. It is becoming increasingly clear that the issue of inappropriate behaviour can extend well beyond the attempts by executives like Kozlowski to gain acceptance in high society through the endowment of a university chair and the payment of $6,000 for a designer shower curtain. The problem has deep systemic roots, which need fundamental design modifications if integrity is to be restored.

---

[6] Interview with John Moscow, New York City, 9 April 2003.
[7] For two opposing views see James B. Stewart, "Spend! Spend! Spend! Where did Tyco's money go", *New Yorker*, 17 February 2003, pp. 132–47 and Alex Berenson, *The Number* (Random House, New York, 2003), pp. 206–9.

For those charged with overseeing the operation of the chastened market, cauterizing the problem became an imperative. A pivotal figure was the chairman of the NYSE, Dick Grasso. The NYSE recognized the enormous damage the erosion of confidence in financial statements, occasioned by corporate deceit, was causing. It had introduced corporate governance reforms that dovetailed with the Sarbanes–Oxley legislation in order to deal with particular board-level failings – even though it did not always live up to its own strictures.[8] Behind the scenes, Grasso worked to resolve, or at least neutralize, the much more serious systemic problems highlighted by the conflicts-of-interest investigations. These indicated that the pressure to meet the Wall Street number may have originated within the corporation, but the gaming of the system was facilitated in an institutional manner by the gatekeepers of international finance: the investment banks.[9]

Grasso interceded between the feuding regulators and the banking sector in order to find an agreement.[10] Grasso had played a similar role in the earlier dispute between Merrill and the New York Attorney General. According to a report in the *Wall Street Journal*, Grasso had suggested to Spitzer that a moderation in his initial demand for a fine of $250m would result in the formation of a powerful alliance that had the potential to bankroll any potential future campaign to run for public office. This is not to suggest that Spitzer was effectively paid off, rather a reflection of political realities in the United States. Now,

---

[8] In March 2003 Citigroup's CEO Sandy Weill withdrew his nomination to the board of the NYSE after angry denunciations by Spitzer. The Attorney General argued that it was a disgrace Weill, as chairman of a company investigated for securities fraud, should be considered by the NYSE as a suitable candidate to represent public investors. For full details see Chapter 7.

[9] See Alex Berenson, *The Number* (Random House, New York, 2003).

[10] The fullest account of Grasso's pivotal role can be found in Charles Gasparino and Michael Schroeder, "Pitt and Spitzer butted heads to overhaul Street's research", *Wall Street Journal*, 31 October 2001; Charles Gasparino, "NYSE's Grasso led the effort to seal a research settlement", *Wall Street Journal*, 23 December 2002; and Alex Berenson and Andrew Ross Sarkin, "How Wall St was tamed", *New York Times*, 22 December 2002.

with a wider investigation enhancing the reputational risk to the organization he led and the market incapable of staging a revival in the midst of a high-profile dispute between the SEC and the Office of the Attorney General, Grasso again sought to broker an agreement on the way forward.

The SEC Chairman Harvey Pitt remained privately furious at the way in which Spitzer had elbowed a role for himself as a de facto regulator of the securities market. The disparaging allegations of ineptitude, most notably displayed in Spitzer's inflammatory address to the Senate in July, were personally stinging. Pitt remained wedded to the core strategy adopted since his appointment. For Pitt, the deployment of negotiation and partnership, leading to voluntary compacts rather than confrontation, remained the most effective means of regulating the industry. Under his direction, the SEC re-mained committed to the view that the liberal use of enforcement legislation to solve a systemic problem would not only add to the unease felt by nervous investors but would also, unnecessarily, cost billions of dollars in class action litigation. This emollient stance dovetailed with the views of the securities firms:

> These things existed at every firm on Wall Street. It wasn't that one firm was doing these things and later everyone says, "Oh my God! Can you believe they did it?" This happened everywhere and where conduct happens everywhere, on the four corners of Wall Street that means the chances are pretty darn good that it is not a bad actor problem but you have problems with the structure and the system. If you want to cure it, you need to cure it through rule making or legislation rather than through enforcement actions. Bad actors can be dealt with in an enforcement action level, structural and systemic problems should be dealt with through laws.[11]

However, the fact that a wider investigation had already been ceded ensured that attempting to put the genie back in the bottle amounted to wishful thinking. After the success of the Merrill enforcement action, it had become inevitable that any global settlement would have to include a punitive element. There was, however, room to

---

[11] Interview, New York City, 8 February 2003.

manoeuvre. Grasso gambled that Spitzer's main motivating force was the need to change the structural nature of the problem. Grasso's calculation was correct. Grasso organized a series of dinners at an exclusive Italian American club in Manhattan. The club, complete with a gun range in the basement, is called Tiro a Sengo, or Fire at the Target. It was here that the careful choreography that was to lead to the compromise was worked out.

The first dinner was held on 1 October with the Chairman of the NYSE playing host to Harvey Pitt and the director of enforcement at the SEC Stephen Cutler, along with Spitzer and his chief investigator Eric Dinallo. As director of enforcement at the Attorney General's office, Dinallo had handled the initial Merrill case that had catapulted the state official to national and international prominence. Spitzer joked that the venue looked like a scene from *The Sopranos*; Grasso riposted that the venue and purpose was more akin to *The Godfather*, as, over a dinner of veal and wine, they sought to reach a *modus operandi* for what Grasso termed "the benefit of the markets"[12]:

> Over dinner, the regulators reached a broad understanding about their responsibilities and the goals of the inquiry. Mr. Pitt agreed that the S.E.C. would not try to take over Mr. Spitzer's investigation. In turn, Mr. Spitzer acknowledged that the S.E.C. had the ultimate duty to oversee the structure of the securities industry and that he would not try to usurp that role. And all the regulators agreed that their goal should be reform of the industry, not penalties so punitive that they would permanently damage Wall Street.[13]

With a division of labour established, the regulators set about creating a template that all sides in the dispute could potentially sign off on. Two days later, the agreement on how to proceed became public with a press release from the SEC.

It articulated two distinct purposes: first, "to bring to a speedy and coordinated conclusion the various investigations concerning analyst research and Initial Public Offering allocations. The undertaking is

---

[12] Charles Gasparino and Michael Schroeder, "Pitt and Spitzer butted heads to overhaul Street's research", *Wall Street Journal*, 31 October 2001.

[13] Alex Berenson and Andrew Ross Sarkin, "How Wall St was tamed", *New York Times*, 22 December 2002.

also designed to continue the process of formulating additional rules and regulations in these areas."[14] The SEC Chairman stated that the agreement was a manifestation of a shared vision to find a resolution that "is designed, first and foremost, to protect investors." Spitzer concurred, proclaiming that the joint investigation was "an important step towards bringing closure and resolution to the crucial issues we have been working on." The soothing words masked the scale of the strategic defeat of the SEC's campaign to protect its position as the principal architect of interpreting the rules and regulations of Wall Street.

By accepting that the New York State Attorney General would be intimately involved in the drafting of a global settlement, along with his counterparts in Massachusetts and California, the SEC had mandated the creation of a new economic and political force. The role played by the states in the development of what is, in effect, new federal securities legislation is unprecedented. It represents a pivotal challenge not only to the SEC and the self-regulatory organizations such as the National Association of Securities Dealers (NASD) but also to the legislative class itself.

Pitt himself made the tactical decision to withdraw from the negotiations, in the process neatly cauterizing the dispute with Spitzer, who now held regular meetings with Stephen Cutler. The sticking point surrounded Spitzer's continued insistence on a complete separation between investment banking and research; Cutler maintained that secure firewalls would suffice. A compromise agreement was reached in late October to create a new committee of independent research specialists. They would be charged with overseeing the distribution of independent research and assuring compliance. But announcing the proposed deal in itself then became problematic. Spitzer wanted immediate publication; Cutler asserted that he needed more time to sell the idea to other players,

---

[14] SEC Press Release, "SEC, NY Attorney general, NYSE, NASD, NASAA [North American Securities Administrators Association] reach agreement on reforming Wall Street practices" 3 October 2002. Available online at http://www.sec.gov/news/press/2002-144.htm

including the SEC and other regulators. An early conference call between the vastly expanded ranks of regulators showed the depth of division.

The Chairman of the NASD, Robert Glauber, decried Spitzer's determination to outlaw the controversial issue of "spinning" whereby CEOs of existing or potential investment clients were offered preferential access to IPOs. He suggested that it should not be made a crime to be a CEO, to which Spitzer retorted that he was not there to protect the interests of the CEOs.[15] The confrontations about possible prosecutions over spinning would neither be the first, nor the last, conflict between the two regulators.[16]

As the investigations into conflicts of interest intensified, Spitzer raised the stakes dramatically by indicting Bernie Ebbers, the chief executive of the telecommunication giant WorldCom and four other corporate executives for fraudulently obtaining first-time stock offering from analysts with Salomon Smith Barney. The move was significant for two reasons. Salomon Smith Barney is the securities subsidiary of Citigroup, the financial services conglomerate. It is also the company that the Attorney General's office had undertaken to investigate as part of the wider agreement with the SEC. Second, the Attorney General was serving notice to Washington that a reliance on the corrupted actor model was unsustainable. The actors may indeed have benefited from their illicit trading, but so too did the corporations that facilitated it. The battle for reform was about to reach a higher level. Spitzer's action ensured that regulatory controls would also have to be introduced in order to police yet another deeply flawed area of the market.

Four separate problems emerged. The first involved "spinning" or

[15] Charles Gasparino, "NYSE's Grasso led the effort to seal a research settlement", *Wall Street Journal*, 23 December 2002.

[16] The NASD fundamentally changed its position at the end of the investigation, formally charging Frank Quattrone of Credit Suisse First Boston (CSFB) in March 2003. He was indicted of violating securities legislation by "spinning" IPO allocation to favoured CEOs and CFOs in return for underwriting business. See *NASD vs. Frank Peter Quattrone*, Disciplinary Hearing No. CAF030007, p. 11.

selling the share allocation for immediate profit. This was simply an inducement to clients, with no short-term payback required. Rather it served to deepen the relationship between the investment bank and the executive who received the stock. Despite the illegality, the practice was widespread. The second involved "laddering" the stock, which involved providing executives access to the stock allocation in the certain knowledge that, once the issue appeared on the open market, more stock would be bought, thus driving up value and therefore profits. The third involved illegal "tie-ins" or "kickbacks", a process that involved institutional investors agreeing to pay exorbitant commissions in order to achieve access to scarce IPO allocation. Since 1990, the average rise in the value of 3,900 IPO shares on the first day of trading has been 24%, offering those given the opportunity to invest a remarkable windfall. The issue of IPO allocation had become a cause of major concern on Wall Street because of the collapse of the tech boom and the search for scapegoats. The banks desire to make quick profits enhanced considerably the reputational risk. Confidence was squandered by unacceptable relationships with favoured institutional investors and an alarming number of corporate failures.

When one considers the fact that investment banking houses received more than $2bn in fees from taking technology firms private, one can see an imperative to accept the briefing to securitize tech companies. The problem was that in the rush to secure those fees, due diligence was downgraded or ignored completely. Firms were taken to the market on the basis of ill-defined business plans and strategic and moral bankruptcy.[17] The unease intensified after the crash of the technology sector and the search for scapegoats began. Consider the following statistic. Between 1985 and 1995, the average failure rate of companies given the IPO treatment was 1%. In the two-year period

---

[17] See John Nofsinger and Kenneth Kim, *Infectious Greed, Restoring Confidence in America's Companies* (Prentice Hall, Upper Saddle River, NJ, 2003), pp. 113–21.

1998–2000, at the height of the boom, the failure rate had risen to 12%.[18] A class action filed in the Southern District of New York had alleged that market manipulation, particularly in the technology sector through tie-in agreements, kickbacks to key investors and un-realistic research reports, artificially enhanced the stock price. Ac-cording to the judge hearing the claim, it evidenced a "strong inference that the Defendants [55 securities firms] intended to defraud the investing public."[19] Much of the background for the class action case had been accrued during an 18-month investigation by the SEC into the operation of CSFB's Technology Investment Banking Group. The Tech Group was based in Palo Alto, under the control of Frank Quattrone. Throughout the investigation CSFB maintained its support for its beleaguered star analyst. In January 2002 the corporation had settled the case for $100m, without admitting liability in return for the ending of any criminal investigation. Now, two further official probes seemed to provide the structural basis to the class action. Of particular importance is the manner in which the investment banks used the allocation of shares as a bribe to ensure that corporate executives steered their companies toward using the underwriting facilities of the banks that provided access.

The Spitzer case against Ebbers appeared to provide confirming evidence of this insidious corruption. Although the case did not indict the analyst involved, it served to expose the manner in which investment banks used access to the IPOs as a means to secure access to lucrative corporate accounts. In one trade alone Ebbers bought 5,000 shares in Juniper Networks on 25 June 1999. Three hours later he sold the shares when they reached $100 per share, to reap a $250,000 profit. Further investigation revealed that the tactical and strategic distribution of such largesse was common

---

[18] Ibid., pp. 117–18.

[19] Judge Shira A. Scheindlin, Initial Public Offering Securities Legislation, Opinion and Order 21 MC 92 (SAS), p. 12. The full text of the judicial opinion is available online via http://www.news.findlaw.com/wsj/docs/ipo/ipolit21903opn.pdf

practice on Wall Street. The former Chairman of Qwest Communications Philip Anschutz profited by nearly $5m by the decision by Salomon Smith Barney to give him lucrative access to IPOs. In the same period, the investment bank was involved in brokerage deals with Qwest valued at $37m.

What the investigators wanted to know was whether there was a direct connection.[20] The Boston investigation raised equally problematic concerns. The securities division filed court documents suggesting that CSFB had violated securities law in a systematic manner:

> Research analysts in the Global Technology Group ("Tech Group") at CSFB worked for and were controlled by investment banking personnel of CSFB. This reporting structure and complete control resulted in investment banking exerting undue influence on the research analyst to give favorable ratings to companies for which CSFB had done or hoped to do investment banking work. Analysts disseminated biased, subjective, and compromised research favorable to CSFB investment banking clients, which resulted in the Tech Group producing millions of dollars in investment banking fees for CSFB. CSFB purposely misled investors by disseminating into the marketplace fraudulent material misstatements of fact concerning the companies covered by the analysts.[21]

The complaint alleged that CSFB had purposefully destroyed evidence. The strongly worded complaint alleged that individuals affiliated with investment banking deals were bribed with allocations of shares in hot tech IPOs in exchange for bringing investment banking business to CSFB. This arrangement was explained to those individuals as "something of a 'you scratch my back, I will scratch yours.'"[22]

Two separate sets of relationships were corrupted in this secretive trade. In the first, the executives provided access to the lucrative IPO allocation were chosen primarily on the basis of their ability to procure current or future investment banking business. This, in turn, raises the interesting philosophical question of whether the

---

[20] Editorial, "Average investors unfairly shut out of lucrative deals", USA Today, 17 October 2002.

[21] Commonwealth of Massachusetts vs. Credit Suisse First Boston, No. E-2002-41, pp. 1–2.

[22] Ibid., pp. 14–15.

executives were corrupted by the system or were chosen because they were already morally despoiled. The second set of relationships corroded by the conflicts of interest affected the entire market. In order to generate sufficient profits to entrench the symbiotic relationship inherent in the first trade and to ensure that the aftermarket remained buoyant, thereby improving the underwriting status of the corporation, the manipulation favoured insiders to the detriment of the integrity of the system. Taken together, the betrayal of the principal–agent relationship within the corporation itself and the tacit acceptance of that betrayal by the wider financial system ensured that the spiral down to systemic "competitive corporate corruption" was preordained.[23]

For the securities industry the myopia proved to be exceptionally lucrative and enhanced the shareholder value for the duration of the boom. In the longer term, the ethical shortcoming, based on material misstatements to the market about the true value of the IPOs and the bogus research ratings used to justify those fraudulent conceptions, has served to destroy shareholder value.[24] By November, the three most senior analysts in the star system were totally discredited. The cosmology itself was imploding in real time and with it the reputation of the entire analyst network. If Dennis Kozlowski represented individual greed, the activities authorized by Frank Quattrone at CSFB and Jack Grubman at Salomon, for which they received astronomical salaries, represented institutional corporate greed.[25] When linked to

[23] Moises Naim, "The corruption eruption", *The Brown Journal of World Affairs*, Summer 1995, Vol. II, Issue 2, p. 248.

[24] See Michael Johnston, "The search for definitions: The vitality of politics and the issue of corruption", *International Social Science Journal*, Vol. 149, September, pp. 325–6.

[25] On 6 March 2003, NASD filed two civil charges against Quattrone. The first charge involved enticing clients to use CSFB for underwriting by offering access to "hot IPOs." The strategy, known as "the Friends of Frank" network was deemed fraudulent. According to the complaint, "giving the insider of prospective investment banking clients the opportunity to realize risk-free profits by participating in hot IPOs through discretionary accounts was tantamount to giving them gratuities." *NASD vs. Frank Peter Quattrone*, Disciplinary Hearing No. CAF030007, p. 11.

the ongoing investigation into the wider issue of conflicts of interest in analyst research, it served to produce further evidence of how the entire research process was hopelessly compromised.

Although not indicted in the Spitzer case, the publication of emails from Jack Grubman, head of equity research at Salomon, served to send confidence into a tailspin. When read in conjunction with the earlier Merrill disclosure, and the allegations surfacing in Boston, it suggested a prima facie case that the problems associated with corrupted research spanned the entire industry. Grubman's private emails to colleagues and to his superiors demonstrated not only the research department's subservience to the needs of investment bankers but also the systemic nature of the corruption.

"Most of our banking clients are going to zero and you know I wanted to downgrade them months ago but got huge pushback from banking," he wrote to Kevin McCaffrey, a research executive. "I wonder of what use bankers are if all they can depend on to get business is analysts who recommended their banking clients." Like his competitor at Merrill, Grubman demonstrated his own lack of faith in the research he was disseminating. After one firm Focal Communications questioned his appraisal he warned two Salomon bankers: "If I so much as hear one more fucking peep out of them [Focal] we will put the proper rating on this stock ... We lost credibility ... because we support pigs like Focal."[26]

A sordid arrangement was depicted in which a concerted effort was made to defraud individual investors who were denied access to the true research assessment of the stocks analysed. His case was that successful underwriting was enhanced by the prospect of favourable stock ratings. The result was the corruption of analysts because they were compensated for helping the banking effort, not because of their service to investors, and this moral decay continued once the company was enticed. The complaint cited glowing reports advocating investors to disregard the slide into bankruptcy. At the centre of

---

[26] See Joshua Chaffin, "Lawsuit reveals Grubman's 'pigs'", *Financial Times*, 1 October 2002.

the Spitzer complaint is the depiction of a criminal conspiracy in which investment bankers, research analysts and corporate clients worked together to defraud individual investors of hundreds of millions of dollars.

Each development built on previous cases to present a cogent, coherent argument. The perception of corruption was further enhanced by the decision by Salomon to settle for $5m a separate case involving dubious research that had been filed by the NASD. As usual in such cases, Salomon did not admit liability, but allowed the state of claim to be read into the record and accepted that the findings could not be challenged or denigrated. The complaint centred on overly optimistic research ratings given to Winstar Communications (WCII), a broadband provider and yet another firm for which Salomon acted as chief underwriter. Grubman continued to provide bullish reports urging investors to buy stock even as the company filed for bankruptcy protection, having shed 99% of its highest market capitalization of $3.46bn.

Internal communications from the research department of Salomon demonstrated that it realized there were "pressing liquidity issues ... [and] as the stock continued its downward spiral, its opportunities for sources of funding has diminished and the stock remains speculative." On the following day 4 April 2001 a bullish report on the state of the market was released under the heading *Don't Panic – Emerging Telecom Model Is Still Valid (More Details)*. The report did not mention difficulties associated with WCII, because, regulators concluded, "of Salomon's investment banking activities with Winstar." Instead, WCII retained its "buy" rating from Salomon, a course of action that undoubtedly enticed investors. On 5 April the company announced a major restructuring plan that involved laying off 2,000 employees – 44% of the overall workforce. Salomon put out a global alert changing tack: "Given current market conditions, we believe this is a step in the right direction in addressing WCII's funding gap; however, until the company discloses the details surrounding this plan (i.e., costs savings, effects on growth rates, etc.), we continue to believe that WCII's funding gap remains a risk and the stock remains a speculative investment." It was the first time that Salomon had calculated the extent of the leverage crisis afflicting the firm. A follow-up report, proposed to be published the following day, that would reduce the rating for WCII stock from buy to neutral and reduce the target price in shares trading at $0.44 from $50 to a more realistic $1 was not published.

Again, the NASD held that this decision was a direct consequence of "Salomon's investment banking business with Winstar." On 17 April 2001 Salomon realized that the charade could no longer continue and issued a report downgrading WCII from buy to "under-perform" and withdrew the ridiculously optimistic target price. The report regarded the funding gap as "an insurmountable obstacle that could drive WCII to Chapter 11 [bankruptcy protection]." It took just 24 hours to become a reality.

The WCII debacle demonstrated fundamental flaws in the Chinese walls allegedly separating equity research from equity raising departments that ostensibly had been institutionalized as a consequence of the repeal of the Glass–Steagall legislation. The walls were porous to the point of being non-existent, a fact that Grubman openly admitted in an 18 May 2001 email: "If anything, the record shows we support our banking clients too well and for too long."[27] Under the terms of the settlement reached, Salomon accepted without admitting liability the reading into the record of a damning assessment:

> In contrast to investor losses, Salomon garnered more than $24m in investment banking fees while it helped the company raise more than $5.6billion … Salomon's Winstar reports did not comply with principles of fair dealing and good faith; did not provide a sound basis for evaluating facts; contained exaggerated, unwarranted, unbalanced or misleading statements or claims about Winstar and opinions such as the target price for which there was no reasonable

---

[27] "Salomon Smith Barney's emails reveal private Winstar concerns", *Wall Street Journal*, 25 September 2002. For the full text of the NASD complaint and the acceptance of the fine see Disciplinary Hearing, NASD Office of Hearing Officers, *Department of Enforcement vs. Jack Benjamin Grubman, CRD No. 1505636 and Christine Ruzol Gochuico, CRD No. 2794210*, Case Number CAF020042, available online at www.findlaw.com

basis; and omitted material facts or qualifications which caused the reports to be misleading.[28]

It was beginning to be increasingly clear that Jack Grubman was fast becoming a liability for the firm. Grubman, who was once the highest paid analyst in Wall Street, had been summonsed to congressional hearings into the collapse of WorldCom in July. He mounted a bullish defence of the corporation, based on what he maintained was a proven thesis:

> For the past seventeen years, I have held a consistent thesis that the newer, more nimble and entrepreneurial telecom companies such as WorldCom could successfully compete with and even outperform the entrenched industry giants. More recently, in the mid-1990s, I amplified my thesis to include the notion of global spheres of influence where the most successful companies in the industry would be those that combined entrepreneurial drive with a scale and scope of "end-to-end" network assets and operations. From the late 1990s, until a few months ago, I believed that WorldCom was the company best positioned in terms of assets, earnings and business model to outperform the industry over the long term.[29]

Grubman argued that he, like all of Wall Street, had been hoodwinked by the extensive nature of the fraudulent earnings statements put forward by WorldCom. "It is critical to understand that, but for WorldCom's fraud, I would have seen a more dire picture much earlier." He defended both his relationship with companies he covered and with investment banking in general. "As you would expect, when I form a favourable opinion on a particular company, the investment bankers have found it easier to convince the company to retain our firm for investment banking transactions, and the converse is true as well." Nowhere in his written testimony did Grubman make any mention of the fact that his thesis generated a useful synergy for the aggressive merger and acquisition strategy used by WorldCom to grow, a strategy that required substantial underwriting fees and therefore Grubman's and Salomon's services. Although he did

---

[28] NASD Letter of Acceptance, Waiver and Consent, Case CAF020042, www. findlaw.com, pp. 3–4.

[29] Jack Grubman, Written Testimony on WorldCom, Senate Hearing, 8 July 2002.

concede that the company received $80m in investment banking fees between 1998 and 2001, he maintained there was "no direct tie-in" between the fees and his own astronomical salary.[30] Given Grubman's robust defence of his thesis to Congress, a rerating in 1999 of the telecommunications giant AT&T returned to haunt him. His testimony heightened interest by the regulators as to why, in contrast to his thesis, Mr Grubman radically changed his view on AT&T. The investigation was about to reach an explosive conclusion.

Grubman had told Congress that "the analyst's most valuable asset is his relationship with investors. We are taught that any analyst who squanders that reputation with investors to curry favour with any interested party is pursuing a fool's errand." So why then did Grubman appear to do precisely that immediately prior to AT&T coming to the market with a major equity issue in November 1999? Grubman had raised an issue that was to destroy his reputation and see him barred from the securities market for life.

Under the terms of the Martins Act, the Attorney General did not have to prove an intention to defraud, merely the failure to disclose all relevant information. The result was devastating, not only to the credibility of Grubman, long regarded as a stellar performer on Wall Street, but also to the parent company. Grubman was an acknowledged hostile critic of the telecommunications giant of which his boss Sandy Weill, then co-Chairman of Citigroup, was a director. The desultory performance prompted major concerns in the Citigroup boardroom. On 8 September 2002, the Chairman Sandy Weill convened a meeting of the board. He told his colleagues, "we have to take this crisis very seriously and we have serious choices to make." An internal trawl of the documents relating to Grubman's activities had caused consternation. The corporation's senior attorney Martin Lipton told the board: "The business isn't out of control, the house isn't on fire. But it's clear in the harsh light of hindsight that there have been industry excesses in which the firm participated ... Small

---

[30] Susan Pulliam, Deborah Solomon and Randall Smith, "Top WorldCom executives, analyst feel congressional heat in hearing", *Wall Street Journal*, 9 July 2002.

changes around the margins won't be sufficient."[31] In a press statement announcing a management change, which saw Charles Prince elevated to the role of CEO of Salomon Smith Barney, Citigroup's corporate and investment bank, Weill sounded a contrite note:

> Although we have found nothing illegal, looking back, we can see that certain of our activities do not reflect the way we believe business should be done. That should never be the case, and I am sorry for that.[32]

According to an email uncovered by Spitzer's investigation and leaked to the media, from Grubman to Carol Cutler, a money management analyst with the Singapore Government Investment Fund, the change in rating was designed to further Weill's position in a power struggle with John Reed, co-CEO of Citigroup. In return Weill was alleged to have used his influence to ensure that Grubman's children gained admittance to a prestigious pre-school on the Upper East of Manhattan[33]:

> I used Sandy to get my kids in the 92nd Street Y pre-school (which is harder than Harvard) and Sandy needed Armstrong's vote on our board to nuke Reed in the showdown. Once the coast was clear for both of us I went back to my normal self.[34]

Another email dated the following day 14 January 2001, from Grubman to his colleague in the Singapore Government Investment Fund, made clear that this was not an idle boast, impetuously spluttered out to further his sense of self-importance. He wrote, "I always viewed [AT&T] as a business deal between me and Sandy."[35] Further circumstantial evidence demonstrating an informal linkage between

---

[31] Monica Langley, "Taking a risk to right Citigroup", *Wall Street Journal*, 18 February 2003. The article is an extract taken from Monica Langley, *Tearing Down the Walls, How Sandy Weill Fought His Way to the Top of the Financial World . . . and Then Nearly Lost It All* (Simon & Schuster, New York, 2003).

[32] Ibid.

[33] For a critical exposé of Citigroup's provision for childcare see Rebecca Mead, "Tales out of pre-school", *New Yorker*, 2 December 2002.

[34] Jack Grubman to Carol Cutler email exchange, quoted in Charles Gasparino, "NYSE's Grasso led the effort to seal a research settlement", *Wall Street Journal*, 23 December 2002.

[35] Cited in Charles Gasparino, "New York preschool's Link to Citigroup is investigated", *Wall Street Journal*, 18 November 2002.

the change in rating of AT&T and the machinations surrounding the schooling needs of an anxious employee is contained in a memo written by Grubman to Weill on 5 November 1999, just before the change in rating, entitled "AT&T and the 92nd Street Y". In it he appealed for help in circumventing the "ridiculous but necessary process of preschool applications," and informed him of "very dry, arcane, cost and engineering analysis ... I think all of this will be very productive and frankly, while this process has taken awhile to unfold ... [it] is allowing me to do the type of 'no-nonsense' meetings that, unfortunately, are difficult to schedule with AT&T or at least have been in the past. Anyway, I'll keep you posted on the progress."

According to the text of the email, the focus changes to the matter of providing adequate school care. Then Grubman asks Weill to use his influence with members of the school's board of governors, whose names and corporate positions on Wall Street are usefully detailed, before returning again to the matter of AT&T: "Anyway anything you could do Sandy would be greatly appreciated. As I mentioned, I will keep you posted on the progress with AT&T which I think is going well."

Three weeks later, on 30 November 1999, Grubman upgraded his rating and three months later Salomon was awarded joint management of a $10bn IPO on wireless trading stock. The investigators subpoenaed Carol Cutler, who informed them that "based on her conversations with Mr Grubman over the years, she believed he was under pressure by senior Citigroup officials, including Mr Weill, to change his investment position on AT&T." Further investigation provided evidence that Citigroup had provided a $1m donation to the Upper East Side pre-school at the centre of the controversy and that the donation "was offered by Mr Weill as part of a pitch to help get Mr Grubman's twins into the pre-school." Grubman's children were admitted and the rating was changed, but in a further email two months after the change Grubman was again in contact with Carol Cutler:

> The biggest thing that pisses me off is that [AT&T] did exactly as I knew they would for precisely the reasons I thought ... [In the longer term the stock] would collapse because the core business would fall apart.

The emails presented damning, if circumstantial and contested evidence of a corrupted research design. Weill admitted that he had asked Grubman "to take a fresh look at AT&T in light of the dramatic transformation of the company and the industry. I always believed that Mr Grubman would conduct his own research and reach independent conclusions that were entirely his own." Weill maintained he was "extremely upset" that his philanthropic intervention "on behalf of an important employee who asked for my help" could be "so distorted".[36]

Grubman's lawyer told investigators that his client was prepared to co-operate, adding to the credibility of the probe. He claimed his client was willing to testify that "he was pressured by senior executives at Citigroup to tailor his ratings to win banking deals." The following October, Grubman returned to his earlier rating, causing a further collapse in the level of AT&T's value. Instead, the telecommunications guru noted the positive positions held in the marketplace by his favourite companies. Among these paragons of business virtue were Global Crossing and WorldCom, corporations whose destruction very nearly destroyed the market itself and have made the name Grubman eponymous with the seediness of corporate analysis.

The questions over the ratings change and the institutional benefit that accrued to Citigroup as a result, however, were apparent long before the New York Attorney General decided to lift the lid on the reality of the operation of contemporary American capitalism. As early as October 2000, a negative profile in the *Wall Street Journal* noted the poor performance of WorldCom and other star picks and remarked that Citigroup's track record on bringing lucrative IPOs, which subsequently failed, was the second worst in the market. "But

---

[36] Sandy Weill statement, quoted in Charles Gasparino, "Citigroup probe now leads to an elite nursery school", *Wall Street Journal*, 14 November 2002. Full text of statements released by Jack Grubman, Sandy Weill and Citigroup. When the global announcement was made on 28 April 2003, the New York Attorney General accepted that Weill genuinely believed that AT&T should have been rerated, but argued it was entirely inappropriate for the CEO to attempt to influence an underling, even one as highly paid as Grubman.

make no mistake. Telecom banking is more important to Mr Grubman's firm than many others. The telecom sector, including wireless and other related areas, accounted for 49% of Salomon Smith Barney's stock underwriting in 1999, the most of any major securities firm, according to Thomson Financial Securities Data. By comparison, it represented 28% for Goldman Sachs, 25% for Morgan Stanley and 17% for Merrill.[37]

While the complaint issued by Spitzer of explicit corruption omitted the fact that Citigroup already underwrote a significant part of AT&T's new stock issuance and continued to do so when Grubman reversed his temporary approval in a climate of distrust and suspicion, the potential damage to Wall Street's credibility was enormous. This was bolstered by renewed press attention on an article that appeared in the *Wall Street Journal* on 6 December 1999, which openly speculated that the company was excluded from a $3bn IPO in Laurent Technologies, an AT&T subsidiary, because of negative ratings. "AT&T never said why, but many on Wall Street interpreted the move as retribution against Salomon's star analyst, who had downgraded AT&T's stock in 1995."[38]

Citigroup was forced to release a statement in which it accepted there was a link between the request from Mr Weill's intervention to get the Grubman children admitted to the Y and the $1m donation it provided the school, but not a reverse quid pro quo. "We have never said there is no connection between the donation and Jack Grubman's efforts to get his twins into the 92nd Street Y nursery school. From the

---

[37] The initial decision to rerate AT&T was controversial, even more so was Grubman's decision to rerate after a particularly negative profile in the *Wall Street Journal*. See Randall Smith and Leslie Cauley, "Will upgrade of AT&T stock help Salomon Smith Barney", *Wall Street Journal*, 6 December 1999; Randall Smith, Deborah Solomon and Suzanne McGee, "Missed call on AT&T could affect Salomon analyst", *Wall Street Journal*, 4 October 2000; and Randall Smith, "Grubman downgrades AT&T, reversing controversial position", *Wall Street Journal*, 9 October 2000.

[38] Randall Smith and Leslie Cauley, "Will upgrade of AT&T stock help Salomon Smith Barney", *Wall Street Journal*, 6 December 1999.

outset we have tried to make it clear: Mr Grubman sought Mr Weill's help for the twins in the fall of 1999 and the contribution we ultimately made in the summer of 2000 grew out of that request. However, it is also clear that this request is similar to many we receive from our employees asking for support for the community organizations in which they are involved."[39]

The damage caused by the investigation into Grubman and the shining of the spotlight into the inner workings of Wall Street as a consequence of wider corporate failure was an acute embarrassment to all those who had exercised fiduciary trust as gatekeepers for the system. Not since the 1930s had corporate America faced a more determined foe in the regulation of the marketplace. No amount of suave public relations could assuage the anger of investors who had seen the value of their stock holdings plummet. The imperative to de-escalate a dispute that could not be won trumped any residual hope that Washington could, or would, intervene. Openness and transparency remained secondary considerations to the investment banks, which continued to insist that the Chinese walls separating the analysts and the brokers have substance rather than act as mere marketing tools. This minimal approach is endemic in corporate America. The failure of politicians to deal with catastrophic losses in 2002 made more serious precisely because it failed to back the SEC's attempts to deal with the issue two years previously.[40] The accountancy cartels

[39] Citigroup statement, cited in Charles Gasparino, "New York pre-school's link to Citigroup is investigated", Wall Street Journal, 18 November 2002.

[40] After the loss of $3 trillion dollars in the value of NASDAQ after the collapse of the technology bubble, the issue of partial analysis prompted the SEC to attempt separation. See the account of the former Chairman of the SEC into how he attempted to get the NYSE and NASDAQ to issue rules to disclose conflicts of interest in 2000, but failed because of "a serious failure of self-regulation", in Arthur Levitt, Taking on the Street (Pantheon, New York, 2002), pp. 65–8. Levitt argues this stems from the fact that "the exchanges, whose governing boards are heavily influenced by the heads of the major Wall Street firms, have deep seated conflicts of their own" (p. 67). According to Levitt, the NASDAQ could not reach consensus on what to do and, in the absence of that exchange moving, the NYSE did not want to provide its rival with "any competitive advantage" (p. 68).

had used similar muscle to influence the appointment of the regulator of the accountancy board and nearly succeeded.

The emphasis by corporate America changed from outright denial to a desire to settle without admitting liability. Behind the scenes, agreement was reached; the remaining question was the question of costs. At a meeting at the SEC headquarters in Washington in late October, representatives of the major banks accepted in principle the agreement worked out, paving the way for a careful, choreographed endgame: the corporate admission that arrangements were not what they should have been would morph into the payment of punitive fines and ultimately provide redemption through the introduction of a new regulatory regime. At stake was simply the way in which the issue would be publicly acknowledged. As David Trone, a securities industry specialist for Prudential Financial Inc., put it in an interview with the *Wall Street Journal*, "we do not view the plan as onerous . . . in the grand scheme of things we're talking about [an earnings impact] of a few cents a share."[41]

This insouciance, in turn, is linked to the fact that enforcement fines, no matter how substantial, could be written off against future earnings. Wall Street may be cleaned up, but the cost would be borne primarily by the American taxpayer, the very people who were ripped off by the fraudulence in the first instance.

Displaying cutting disdain of the unsavoury practices that had so debased the operation of Wall Street, Spitzer attended a gala dinner hosted by *Institutional Investor* magazine in November to denigrate those he was there to praise. He began his speech by observing that it was great to be able to put faces to all those emails. He then proceeded to tell the guests that they were celebrating a charade and that none merited the honour of being called the "All America Research Team":

> Tonight's program is devoted to the celebration of individual achievement. At the same time, we must also recognize that there has been industry-wide failure.

---

[41] Randall Smith and Charles Gasparino, "Analysts inquiry may cost Wall Street up to $2 billion", *Wall Street Journal*, 28 October 2002.

For at least the last several years, analysts have labored in a corporate structure that placed undue or improper pressure on them. Too often, they were asked to tailor their investment advice to further investment-banking interests, even if that was in conflict with their obligation to provide honest, objective advice.

The revelations of these past few months have shown how certain analysts succumbed to that pressure. The public's attention has been drawn to several particularly gripping examples of the conflict – of analysts who privately derided as dogs – and worse – stocks that they were touting to the public.

We are now also all aware that the structural problems ran much deeper than that. Because analyst compensation was tied to the ability to assist in or generate investment banking business, there was a strong incentive to act as promoters of the deal and not arbiters of quality.

Some in the industry offer investor greed, wide-eyed optimism and a herd mentality rather than misleading research to explain the losses investors have experienced. These apologists might admit to distortions, but never dishonesty. But to be frank about it, the advice provided to investors was often dishonest.[42]

His barbed comments prompted a walkout, but the banking establishment knew that exiting a dinner would prove easier – and cheaper – than finding an exit strategy to end the fiasco over Wall Street's endemic conflicts of interest. It is a fact acknowledged by senior corporate lawyers:

The problem here is more than a few bad apples. The problems in the analyst area are systemic problems, structural problems, more so than people who are out to be corrupt, and I think that most analysts historically have been very honest, hardworking and accurate in drafting their reports. That doesn't mean there are no problems with research analysts. There are problems and there have been problems, but what it does mean is that those are structural problems. We have a structure that has created and has lent itself to conflicts of interest, and those conflicts of interests have either got to be eliminated or disclosed, and maybe the industry has not been great in recent years in doing that. That has got to change now.[43]

The first indication that a deal was on its way was the announcement in early December that the five largest brokerage companies in the

---

[42] Full text available at www.oag.state.ny.us/press/stements/nov12_inst.html

[43] Interview, New York City, 7 February 2003.

United States were to be fined $1.65m each for failing to preserve internal emails. The total fine $8.25m is the largest ever levied for failing to keep adequate records. An unnamed source, quoted in the *New York Times*, found an alarming attitude prevalent within the securities industry. "What was disturbing here was not that someone made a good faith determination of a rule and was maybe wrong in how they interpreted it. They didn't like the rule and they were talking about changing it and in the meantime they just did not comply."[44]

This corporate insolence could not be sustained after the discovery of the email correspondence. Spitzer's actions had uncovered what he had termed a "treasure trove of evidence that is irrefutable."[45] The investment banks agreed. The corporations did not admit liability, nor was there any suggestion at the time from the regulators that the firms deliberately destroyed the emails to prevent disclosure.[46] The primary focus of the banks was to ensure that the evidence of malpractice unearthed in the investigation could not buttress class action cases under way in the civil class actions taking place both in the Southern District and across the country.

The fear was that any regulatory fine would pail into insignificance if the documentary evidence amassed in the investigation were to be made public. Intensive lobbying was therefore undertaken to ensure that the regulators acquiesced in limiting what was put in the public domain. Releasing the bulk of the information would provide the class action lawyers with the documentary evidence required to move beyond a stay on disclosure. This set in motion a further conflict of interest. For Spitzer, confidence could only be returned to the marketplace if there was full disclosure. For the

---

[44] Gretchen Morgenson, "Brokerage firms fined $1.6m", *New York Times*, 4 December 2002.

[45] Quoted in Lina Saigol, "Bankers learn that emailing comes with a health warning", *Financial Times*, 28 December 2002.

[46] That separate investigation was to produce devastating consequences for CSFB in February 2003, when it placed its chief investment analyst Frank Quattrone on administrative leave for apparently obstructing a criminal investigation.

corporations, disclosure and censure leaves them with multibillion dollar civil liabilities.[47]

There was to be one final attempt to limit the power of the State regulators as the negotiations to put in place the global settlement reached a denouement. The powerful Chairman of the Financial Services Committee, Michael Oxley, with whom Spitzer had publicly locked horns at congressional hearings, wanted to ensure that any settlement would neither enhance the reputation of the states nor cast dispersions on a previous failure of oversight. Oxley was careful to dress the concern in populist language: "Once the global settlement is in place, the acid test of its success will be whether it returns money to the investors who lost money as a result of biased research. It should not be a Christmas gift for state treasuries."[48]

Despite Oxley's protestations, there was little doubt as to who was driving the issue. On 18 December 2002, Spitzer called senior lawyers representing the banks to his office in Broadway. There was to be no more prevarication. "Today's the day," he said. "Sign up or we're going into law-enforcement mode."[49] The threat of enforcement raised the hackles of the Wall Street investment community, even those who accepted that reform had to be initiated. The broad outline of the deal had already been sketched out within weeks of the negotiations starting, but the banks appeared to be stalling for time. According to one of those involved in the negotiations Mary Schapiro, Vice-Chairman of the NASD, pressure needed to be applied to secure movement. "We had really been through these issues many, many times. We felt this wasn't going to get better as

---

[47] It is indicative of the quality of the Spitzer-driven investigation that the figures have raised exponentially as the settlement talks continued. In early December conservative estimates suggested the total cost would be $5bn. See Joshua Chaffin and Gary Silverman, "Wall Street banks fear tide of lawsuits", *Financial Times*, 4 December 2002. By March 2003 that figure had increased to $20bn. See Nicholas Varchaver, "A blow to the Street", *Fortune*, 17 March 2003.

[48] Quoted in Charles Gasparino, "Citigroup's Weill might avoid charges over faulty research", *Wall Street Journal*, 18 December 2002.

[49] Quoted in Alex Berenson and Andrew Ross Sarkin, "How Wall St was tamed", *New York Times*, 22 December 2002.

it got older. We had been very fair in the process of looking at all of the concerns raised by the firms. We were very much down in the weeds, and it was time to bring it to the end."[50]

The threat to move to enforcement and bring criminal charges was typical of the style of the Attorney General, who had used obscure banking regulation to carve out a position for himself to act in the interests of consumers in a way he clearly believed that the SEC had abdicated. Two days later, on the last Friday of trading prior to the holiday period, the investment banks paid a fine of $1.4bn to settle cases alleging that they had misled investors during the bubble by recommending stocks that they had a vested interest in promoting, dwarfing by a factor of 10 the original censure for failure to keep email records earlier in the month[51]:

Bank	Fine (m)	Independent research	Education
Salomon Smith Barney	300	75	25
Credit Suisse First Boston	150	50	0
Merrill Lynch	100	75	25
Morgan Stanley	50	75	0
Goldman Sachs	50	50	10
Bear Stearns	50	25	5
Deutsche Bank	50	25	5
JP Morgan Chase	50	25	5
Lehman Brothers	50	25	5
UBS	50	25	5
Total	900	450	85

Under the terms of the agreement the banks agreed to pay a fine depending on the extent of documented abuse, establish a fund to pay for independent research and engage in a programme of investor education. As with the earlier settlement on email retention, the banks refused to admit liability while accepting a level of reform

---

[50] Ibid.

[51] For full details see Adrian Michaels, "New dawn for Wall St but clouds remain on horizon", Financial Times, 21 December 2002; Patrick McGeehan, "Wall St deal says little on individuals", New York Times, 21 December 2002; Alex Berenson and Andrew Ross Sarkin, "How Wall St was tamed", New York Times, 22 December 2002.

that suggested serious imperfections in the past. The agreement stated that "the insulation of research analysts from investment banking pressure" is central to the deal. While the wording is diplomatic about past failure, the undertones of corruption are to be found in the press release: "Firms will be required to sever the links between research and investment banking, including analyst compensation for equity research and the practice of analysts accompanying investment banking personnel on pitches and road shows. This will help ensure that stock recommendations are not tainted by efforts to obtain investment banking fees."

The regulators stopped short of mandating the companies to formally separate out their investment and research arms, a move that the industry had argued could cause the loss of thousands of jobs. They did, however, mandate the chaperoning of the relationship. It is the most intrusive aspect of the entire settlement, according to Gary Lynch, the Vice-Chairman of CSFB:

> To a certain extent it is overblown. Having said that, there were some abuses and the structural fixes they are talking about are important. The question is could you have done it in a cheaper way, a less intrusive way. Maybe, I don't know. There is going to be a huge infrastructure to set up to deal with this issue of having a research group within an investment banking firm. The notion that you cannot allow a research analyst to talk to an investment banker without having a chaperone present, who then presumably will make a record of the conversation, is really, really intrusive stuff with a huge cost attached to it. Now, ultimately, at the end of the day could you have achieved 90% of what you wanted to achieve just simply by saying that analysts can never be paid out of investment banking deals so there is no economic incentive for them.[52]

The firms also agreed to contract three independent research firms to augment in-house facilities, thus providing greater methodological transparency. In a stinging rebuke to the Chairman of Citigroup, the agreement calls for "the disclosure of analyst recommendations. Each firm will make publicly available its ratings and price target forecasts. This will allow for evaluation and comparison of perform-

---

[52] Interview with Gary Lynch, New York City, 7 February 2003.

ance of analysts."[53] There is to be a complete ban on the practice of "spinning". The manipulation of IPOs by investment banks by curtailing access to favoured executives is to be banned.

Eliot Spitzer, who had done more than any other regulator to force change, proclaimed that the agreement would "permanently change the way Wall Street operates. Our objective throughout the investigation and the negotiations has been to protect the small investor. We are confident that the rules embodied in this agreement will do so." It was a view endorsed by the President of the North American Securities Administrators Association (NASAA) Christine Bruenn. She claimed that the agreement "represents the dawn of a new day on Wall Street."

The delicious ambiguity in Bruenin's assessment encapsulates the problem of irrevocably untangling the conflicts of interest, which remain in spite of the "global settlement". The question of whether it represents a new dawn, or merely a new day of business as usual in a deregulated market that is manifestly flawed, remains unanswered. As Joshua Chaffin pointed out in the *Financial Times*, "the final verdict on the attorney-general's crusade will rest on the success of the new reforms in protecting investors from the conflicts of interest inherent in Wall Street. But no one can deny Mr Spitzer has succeeded in giving ordinary investors a revealing glimpse into the ways of Wall Street."[54]

Rebuffed at every stage by the federal authorities, the strategic brilliance of Spitzer was to play with consummate skill a poor hand in a high-stakes poker game. He was rewarded with the accolade of "crusader of the year" by *Time* magazine.[55] While the agreement represents an overarching settlement agreed between the SEC, the

---

[53] All quotations from the agreement come from a joint press release issued by the SEC, NASD, NASAA, NYAG and NYSE on 20 December 2002. Full text available from www.nyse.com

[54] Joshua Chaffin, "Determination of a crusader brings the banks to heel", *Financial Times*, 21 December 2002.

[55] Adi Ignatius, "Wall Street's top cop", *Time*, 22 December 2002. The accolades crossed the Atlantic with Spitzer named businessperson of the year by the *Sunday Times*. See Amanda Hall and Dominic Rushe, "Eliot Spitzer – the man who came from nowhere", *Sunday Times*, 29 December 2002. For a critical profile see Michael Freedman, "Witch-hunt", *Forbes*, 9 December 2002.

State Attorney-General, the NASD and the NYSE itself with the investment bankers, there is no doubt that even this limited attempt to regulate Wall Street stems from the determination of Spitzer alone, the attempts by Harvey Pitt to claim credit for the SEC notwithstanding. In one of his final comments before retreating back to the embrace of the securities industry, Pitt claimed that the deal was "navigated by the SEC staff". If the SEC had policed the market effectively in the first place, there would have been no need for state intervention, a point that the Attorney General had made forcefully during his testimony to Congress in June.[56]

The NYSE Chairman Dick Grasso was clearly gratified by the resulting agreement. "It is time to close what is perhaps one of the darkest chapters in the history of modern finance. It is time to move on."[57] Citigroup, the parent company of Salomon Smith Barney, announced it too was moving on by announcing a $1.3bn charge on its quarterly profits after tax in order to pay the fines and prepare for future class action litigation, in relation to tainted analysis and its role in masking the true state of Enron's finances in order to enhance its investment business with the failed energy conglomerate and WorldCom. "We all at Citigroup are looking forward to the New Year. The year 2002 has been a very difficult one for our company and our industry."[58]

---

[56] For a scathing assessment of the deal see Roy Smith, "Attacking Wall Street with a blunt instrument", *Financial Times*, 7 January 2003. The writer, a professor of finance at the Stern Business School, New York University, suggests that the settlement is unfair and tantamount to blackmail. "The deal has been extracted by threats of criminal prosecution and by continued public exposure to embarrassing emails and other leaked information. ... Indeed, this global settlement invites the thought of companies being rounded up in the midst of a public scandal because of where they rank and then all lumped together under bright lights for a show trial."

[57] Quoted in Joshua Chaffin, Gary Silverman and Adrian Michaels, "Slow march to the inevitable global deal", *Financial Times*, 23 December 2002.

[58] Quoted in Riva Atlas, "Citigroup tries to move on, takes a charge of $1.5bn", *New York Times*, 24 December 2002. See also Adrian Michaels, "Citigroup to take $1.3bn charge for legal costs", *Financial Times*, 24 December 2002. The discrepancy in the headlines is a result of the *New York Times* adding a further $200m charge that Citigroup announced on anticipated losses in Argentina.

In a press release, Citigroup maintained that it had "substantial defences to the pending private litigations, which are at a very early stage." But it added: "Given the uncertainties of the timing and the outcome of this type of litigation, the large number of cases, the novel issues, the substantial time before the cases will be resolved, and the multiple defendants in many of them, this reserve is difficult to determine and of necessity subject to future revision."[59]

That very difficult year ended with Sandy Weill making a prediction that 2002 figures will demonstrate that the financial services income would be the highest in the world. Even allowing for the $1.3bn charge, it represents less than 10% of 2001 profits of $14.6bn. On 2 January 2003 JP Morgan Chase followed suit with a similar charge of $1.3bn. The cost in terms of future class actions has energized Wall Street, according to Gary Lynch of CSFB:

> Make no mistake. There is no question about it. It is going to cost the investment firms a lot after the publication of all the known facts, of that there is no doubt.[60]

It was precisely for this reason that a new round of delicate negotiations opened up between the investment banks and the regulators. Throughout the investigation regulators had promised to release the information collated. If the release was accompanied by a written determination that the banks had engaged in a deliberate conspiracy to defraud, the financial and reputational damage would increase dramatically. A rearguard action was being fought to ensure that the "statement of claim", detailing the breaches each bank is alleged to have committed does not, in turn, provide sufficient information to allow the filings of multiple multimillion dollar class action lawsuits.

Under American law, those bringing class action suits must prove they have a viable case before a judge will order disclosure, the first

---

[59] Quoted in Katherine Griffiths, "Scandals hit Citigroup for $1.5bn", *The Independent*, 24 December 2002.
[60] Interview with Gary Lynch, New York, 7 February 2003.

stage in the legal process. The legislation for the Private Securities Litigation Reform Act was passed in 1995 to stop frivolous actions by setting the burden of proof exceptionally high. According to one senior compliance officer, the legislation was crucial in protecting companies from effective blackmail: "Plaintiffs can't get discovery, they can't come to your shop and comb through your files, take depositions from key officers, directors and employees. This is the process that is so time-consuming, costly and burdensome that it forces people to settle. They didn't want a squad of enforcement lawyers coming in their door and rummaging through every last filing cabinet, so this action essentially said it had to have enough evidence to get past the motion to dismiss. If the regulators release the detail of their investigations, that crucial initial hurdle will have been passed."[61]

Even more damagingly, the credibility of the allegations were enhanced precisely because they carried federal and state authority, making settlement both necessary and much more expensive. In a statement, the Attorney General's spokesman noted salaciously that "the evidence will show blatant conflicts of interest. It will further embarrass many brokerage firms that swore before Congress that they were not engaging in such behaviour."[62]

Henry Blodget at Merrill Lynch and Jack Grubman at Salomon faced potential criminal prosecution and major fines. Both were served with Wells notices by the NASD and are to be banned from the market for life. Grubman reached an agreement with Spitzer to pay a $15m fine for his role in misleading investors in lieu of the Attorney General prosecuting a case. But the concentration on individual emails disparaging tangential stock risks missing the point of the central value of both men to their respective employers. A critical part of the global settlement reached was the decision by the Attorney General not to proceed with an indictment against

---

[61] Interview, New York City, 7 February 2003.
[62] See Neil Weinberg, "Wall Street braces for damning evidence", *Forbes.com*, 21 February 2003.

those in supervisory roles. Spitzer acceded to the decision to forgo individual prosecutions in order to protect the gains already made. A similar rationale underpinned his initial decision to accept an initial fine of $100m on Merrill the previous April. Drawing a line under the past may, however, serve only to protect those under whose watch the betrayal of trust occurred, a fact belatedly acknowledged by the NASD. Its investigation into Blodget has now implicated the former head of research at Merrill, Andrew Melnick, now head of research at Goldman Sachs.[63]

Another analyst served with an NASD Wells notice was Frank Quattrone, of CSFB. CSFB was the first bank to face investigation over its role in the allocation of IPOs. The SEC and US Attorney's Office had begun to scrutinize the operations of the corporation in December 2000. The investigation centred on allegations that CSFB gave favoured investors larger shares of IPO stocks in exchange for inflated commissions on other stock trades. Although the firm settled the SEC action in January 2002 with the payment of a $100m fine, the criminal investigation petered out due to a lack of evidence. A year later the issue returned centre stage.

On Thursday 30 January 2003, the *Wall Street Journal* reported that senior investment bankers sent out an email on 4 December 2000 calling on staff to implement the company's policy of destroying notes and drafts in line with the company's retention policy. "With the recent tumble in stock prices, and many deals now trading below issue price, the securities litigation bar is expected to [make] an all-out assault on broken tech IPOs. ... In the spirit of the end of the year (and the slow down in corporate finance work), we want to reminding [sic] you of the CSFB document retention policy." Citing the policy, the email added: "no notes, no drafts, no valuation analysis, no copies of the road show, no mark-ups, no selling memos ... no internal memos. Note that if a lawsuit is instituted, our normal document retention policy is suspended and any cleaning of files is prohibited

---

[63] Reuters, "Probe of ex-Merrill analyst now reaches corner office", *Forbes Online*, 6 January 2003.

under the CSFB guidelines (since it constitutes the destruction of evidence)."

Frank Quattrone followed this with another electronic missive in which he endorsed the cull of extraneous material. Citing his experience testifying in a securities trial in Texas, he remarked: "having been a key witness in a securities litigation case in south Texas, I strongly advise you to follow these procedures."[64] Given that Quattrone had been a recipient two days earlier of an email from the corporation's General Counsel for the Americas David Brodsky, which alerted senior staff of impending investigations by the SEC and other regulatory bodies, including a possible federal grand jury, the timing of the warning appears suspicious in the extreme:

> There's been an inquiry going on by both the SEC and NASD into our allocation processes in the IPO market. There have been some recent developments that are of extreme concern that I need to speak with you about as soon as possible.[65]

The firm launched a vigorous denial of the substance of the *Wall Street Journal* story, but started its own internal investigation. To its considerable embarrassment the company was forced to release a press statement on 3 February saying that "information discovered Friday [31 January] raised questions about Mr Quattrone's response to an inquiry last week by the firm about whether he was aware of pending investigation in 2000." Secondly, the firm argued that the "new information raised questions about whether Mr Quattrone acted appropriately in December 2000 when he sent that email and permitted a subordinate to send a similar email to employees."[66]

---

[64] Randall Smith, Susan Pulliam and Charles Gasparino, "CSFB e-mail urged bankers to delete IPO documents", *Wall Street Journal*, 30 January 2003.

[65] David Brodsky to Frank Quattrone, published in Charles Gasparino, "How CSFB's Quattrone got early warning about probe", *Wall Street Journal*, 27 February 2003. The text of the emails was accurate. See *NASD vs. Frank Peter Quattrone*, Disciplinary Hearing No. CAF030007.

[66] CSFB press release, "Firm acted based on new information learned January 31", accessible online via *Wall Street Journal* website http://online.wsj.com/article/0,,PR_CO_20030203_001299,00.html

The press release clearly implied that Quattrone had endorsed the initial email and was therefore guilty of inappropriate behaviour. The firm made clear that the firm's compliance department had superseded the advice to cull material, although the corporation remained reticent about the extent of the information lost. The publication in late February of the email exchange between Quattrone and David Brodsky, then Counsel General for the CSFB marked "PRIVILEGED AND HIGHLY CONFIDENTIAL" served to heighten concerns that a deliberate attempt was made to obstruct the federal investigation:

> Briefly and this should absolutely not be passed on to anyone else, we have received a federal grand jury subpoena asking for testimony and documents about the IPO allocation process from the firm ...
>
> Are the regulators accusing us of criminal activity?
>
> They are not formally accusing us or the individuals yet, but they are investigating because they think something bad happened. They are completely wrong, but merely being investigated and have something leak can be quite harmful, so the idea is to get them to back off their inquiry, we educate them as to the entire IPO process, including [sic] the allovcation [sic] issues and criteria and urge them to back off.[67]

The CSFB case is an exceptionally neat example of the conflicts-of-interest problem on Wall Street. Quattrone was not only one of the most powerful research analysts on Wall Street – and one of the most highly paid – he combined his research function with investment banking. He graduated from the prestigious Wharton Business School and worked as an analyst at Morgan Stanley before enrolling for an MBA at Stanford. Quattrone was enticed to CSFB in 1998 from Deutsche Bank, where as CEO of the Deutsche Bank Technology Group he had developed a model based on exploiting the synergy between underwriting and research in order to maximize revenue. This "amounted to a firm within a firm. Quattrone structured his operation so that the heads of corporate finance, mergers and acquisitions, and research all reported to him."[68]

---

[67] Exchange between Frank Quattrone and David Brodsky, published in Charles Gasparino, "How CSFB's Quattrone got early warning about probe", *Wall Street Journal*, 27 February 2003. The text of this leak is also accurate, see *NASD vs. Frank Peter Quattrone*, Disciplinary Hearing No. CAF030008, p. 6.

[68] *NASD vs. Frank Peter Quattrone*, Disciplinary Hearing No. CAF030008, p. 5.

When appointed to CSFB he insisted that his new employers replicate the business model, a fateful decision that allowed for a similar destruction of the Chinese walls that guaranteed the integrity of the market. What was more surprising was that, in agreeing to the demands by Quattrone for unprecedented autonomy, the corporation's own internal guidelines were effectively torn up. Quattrone developed a loyal band of retinues by ensuring that many of those who worked under him at Deutsche migrated with their boss to CSFB. The difficulties for effective corporate governance were magnified because Quattrone based his operations on the West Coast, allowing him substantial autonomy.[69] The potential to distort the research function was therefore built into the model from the very beginning.

The machination surrounding the case also provides a telling insight toward how carefully managed the corporate response to the egregious nature of the deception has become. While the corporation publicly dismissed the importance of the *Wall Street Journal* revelations, it was also clear that the failure to discover the email exchange between Brodsky and Quattrone prior to the initial leak to the *Wall Street Journal* put the company in an impossible position. It also indicated a crucial corporate governance failure. The fact that the discovery of the emails came from within the firm itself, following a request for the bank to lift attorney–client privilege to investigate correspondence between Quattrone and Brodsky, suggests ineffective control mechanisms.[70] In an attempt to introduce damage limitation, Gary Lynch has initiated far-reaching change, including ensuring that research analysts report directly to his office[71]:

> We've already implemented 90% of the reforms that we are going to have to implement in the terms of the agreement. We don't allow analysts to pitch

---

[69] This problem of supervision was also central to the destruction of Drexel in 1990. Michael Milken's junk bond operation was based in Beverly Hills, Los Angeles. See James B. Stewart, *Den of Thieves* (Touchstone, New York, 1992).

[70] See Charles Gasparino, "How a string of emails came to haunt CSFB star banker", *Wall Street Journal*, 28 February 2003.

[71] Cheryl Winkur Munk, "CSFB alters research protocol amid criticism over conflicts", *Wall Street Journal*, 9 December 2002.

business. We don't allow analysts to talk to bankers about ideas unless it's funnelled through and approved by research management. After the agreement is approved they will have to be chaperoned. Right now we are just insisting on sign off by research management before the discussions occur. Some of them are being phased in but for the most part it's a wholesale adoption. Right now we are taking steps to make it clear that research analysts will not be paid in any way by investment banking deals. We are stopping them from being part of the investment banking team. Effectively we are already moving down that pike.[72]

On 4 May 2003, Quattrone resigned from CSFB, two days before the NASD filed two civil charges against the banker. The court documents demonstrate clearly the risks inherent in a business model accepted for too long by his employers. In highlighting the structural flaws in the organization of the Tech Group and the inadequacy of supervision, they amount to an indictment of the entire corporation. Quattrone was personally indicted for failing to testify to the NASD inquiry. The NASD Department of Enforcement was adamant that the fallen banker star had a case to answer. It castigated the banker for providing advice to clean up the files "when he knew about the pending NASD, SEC and Federal Grand Jury investigations, and shortly after he had contacted independent legal counsel to represent him personally."[73] To make matters worse for Quattrone's protestations of innocence, the NASD filing provides evidence that the Tech Group executive was informed by the Legal and Compliance Department (LCD) that the document retention policy was suspended:

> That email to Quattrone ended with the following statements: "They are aware that this leaves us exposed on the securities litigation front. I will stay on top of this." Notwithstanding the statements in that email, Quattrone did nothing to withdraw the email he had just sent encouraging others to "clean up [their files". CSFB's LCD did not countermand the two emails concerning the destruction of documents until after the close of business on December 6, 2000 at 9.04 p.m.[74]

---

[72] Interview with Gary Lynch, New York City, 7 February 2003.
[73] NASD vs. Frank Peter Quattrone, Disciplinary Hearing No. CAF030008, p. 8.
[74] Ibid., pp. 8–9.

There is recognition on Wall Street that a cultural change is now emerging. Even more substantial than the monetary loss is the acceptance that self-regulation has failed and failed totally. In this context, the global settlement will entail the most intrusive regulation of Wall Street since the creation of the SEC in 1934 in the aftermath of the Great Crash and a vast increase in the power and prestige of compliance. Given the high costs involved in reaching the settlement, it is unlikely that compliance, so lacking in authority during the long years of the bull market, will be relegated in the future to the second tier of corporate decision-making. For John Moscow at the District Attorney's Office in Manhattan, overwhelmed by the sheer scale of the investigations still outstanding, the cost of gaming the system has finally been brought home with a vengeance:

> Chief executives don't want to see their names in the paper with regard to corporate fraud. My guess is that corporate America is going to be straightening out its act. Fashions have changed. I think that to the extent that there are always corporate executives who are going to steal, that is always going to happen. To the extent that there was a fashion as to how much you could loot from your company, I think that right now there is now a fairly serious disinclination to get into that contest. The allure, the glamour of gaming the system has gone.[75]

Calibrating reputational risk has now become one of the most important factors governing the investment banking system. Goldman Sachs has established a Global Business Intelligence Unit, which functions outside the legal and compliance field. Its primary purpose is to ensure that apparently lucrative deals are vetted to ensure that greater losses are avoided if the deal turns sour. Across town, at CSFB, the research component of the investment bank reports directly to Gary Lynch, Vice-Chairman and former head of enforcement at the SEC:

> Compliance is never going to have the ability to second-guess research in terms of their views of a company. There are many changes made to a research report

---

[75] Interview with John Moscow, New York City, 9 April, 2003.

before it goes out: Do we have a basis for saying this? Is it reasonable? And you certainly saw this before Spitzer and after it as well. But to go back to the broader question I think certainly the role of legal and compliance has increased in importance over the past ten to fifteen years. It is going to continue to increase in importance. When you go through an error like this you recognize just the cost of not devoting enough attention to compliance or of compliance not having enough importance within the firm.[76]

Previous attempts to clean up unsavoury practice in Wall Street dealt with corrupted actors rather than a corrupted system. Successful criminal prosecutions resulted, but the "star" system of investment bankers and analysts, which had done much to incubate the problem, remained intact. It was the star culture itself that was to implode with devastating effect on the entire structure of Wall Street with the ending of the technology boom:

> Analysts are not going to get paid on banking deals in any respect. They are not going to get paid for work on them, they are not going to get paid for bringing deals to the firm and they are not going to be able to talk to bankers really about investment ideas. There really is a fundamental change and a dramatic change. You ask research analysts how dramatic it is going to be, it is a different way of doing business. Having said that, I think everyone is going to adjust to it in a year or two. To a certain extent it is going back to the way it was in the 1970s and 1980s where you didn't have the star analysts, where analysts were the green eye shade-types who crunched numbers and weren't that important to investment banking clients.[77]

The irony for Gary Lynch is that the organization that ensured the change was delivered was not his beloved SEC, but an Attorney General whose populist interpretation of the law circumvented the political compromises that had so stymied the regulator since its formation. The deal may not sterilize Wall Street, but it has served notice that the inexorable drift away from regulation can be stopped.

Corporations pay to retain already created wealth as much as to provide new sources of income. The corporate response to the con-flicts-of-interest investigations carried out by Eliot Spitzer and the

---

[76] Interview with Gary Lynch, New York City, 7 February 2003.
[77] Ibid.

SEC provides confirming evidence of this character trait. According to filings provided by the Securities Industry Association, annual pre-tax profits in 1999 reached $16.9bn. In 2000 that figure rose to $21bn before dipping as a result of the bear market to $10.4bn in 2001 and an expected $8.1bn in 2002.[78] Paying the price for the egregious breach of trust is one that the industry as a whole can well afford, class actions notwithstanding.

Spitzer may now find that the offer of friendship extended by cor-porate America to finance future electoral campaigns may well be withheld in favour of more pliant candidates. It is therefore necessary to examine the nature of the financing of the American political system and how the system itself reacted to the investigations on Wall Street in order to ascertain whether the change proposed is a temporary blip or the precursor for major ideological change.

---

[78] Randall Smith and Charles Gasparino, "Analysts inquiry may cost Wall Street up to $2 billion", *Wall Street Journal*, 28 October 2002.

6

Corporate politics: the buying of power

The political operative was showing the unmistakable signs of stress. His fingernails were chewed to the quick. His tie discarded, his shirt showing the crumpled imprint along the shoulder where he had cradled the telephone during a morning spent in the endless pursuit of money. Each call necessitated subtle ideological gymnastics; changes in the spin cycle to target the myriad interest groups, corporate and trades union benefactors. From a ground floor office at the Democrats headquarters in Washington, his job was to co-ordinate the disparate campaigns waged across America. He had to ensure that the party retained at least the semblance of a national strategy while not staking a position that scared off potential donors. Castigating corporate interests may play well in solid blue-collar states, but its financial muscle is instrumental in providing a presence in key congressional races, the so-called "swing states" that would determine control of Congress and therefore the springboard for the presidential contest in 2004. Promises to one interest group could invalidate those made to another. Squaring the circle was proving an almost insurmountable task. Four weeks off polling day for the November 2002 mid-term elections and the pressure was mounting.

Over the course of an hour the incessant ring of the telephone punctuated his narrative account of how money had corrupted the ideals of his party, each interruption confirming the essential truth of how corrupted the Democrats actually were. The contrasting dialectic of idealism and pragmatism as well as the pursuit of the moral high ground and granting access for cash, creating a synthesis in the tortured logic of a back office operative. The soiled realities of American politics exposed in the calls. "Listen, this election represents the only legitimate way of unseating an illegitimate presidency," he tells me after securing $3m from a donor on the understanding that access to a strategically important Senator would be delivered. "I'll arrange the meeting with the Senator, but the money has to come through this account, this afternoon, prior to the meeting." It was a Machiavellian tour de force: the ends justifying the means in the apparent pursuit of a noble objective. The fundamental flaw in the game plan was evidenced in a battle unfolding five hundred miles to the north, with the derailment of the Democrats' campaign in New Jersey over the allegations of corruption.

The senate race in New Jersey had turned into one of the dirtiest and most expensive races in the November election. In a bombshell announcement, Senator Robert Torricelli, one of the most successful fund-raisers in modern American politics, had announced his retirement from the race on 30 September: "I will not be responsible for the loss of the Democratic majority in the United States Senate. I will not allow it to happen."[1] The decision to resign was based on the calculated estimation that even with all the benefits associated with incumbency, even in a state as solidly Democratic as New Jersey, allegations surrounding Torricelli's personal ethics made him a liability. The Democrats' problem was that the closing date for nominations had already passed. The delay in announcing his enforced retirement meant that the State Supreme Court had to adjudicate on whether a replacement name could be put forward. As we met, the political operator was deciding on whether to inject more money into a race he was unsure the party even had a candidate for.

Across town, the Executive Director of the National Republican Senatorial Committee Mitch Bainwol spotted an opportunity: "You can put somebody else on the ballot when somebody else has died, but political death does not qualify. He still has a pulse, which means he's

---

[1] "Torricelli quits N.J. Senate race", *Washington Post*, 1 October 2002.

still on the ballot."[2] Bainwol's caustic analysis, while self-serving, was accurate. Torricelli's initial decision to brazen out the crisis over his censure by the Senate for violating campaign finance regulations in 1996 indicated two essential and interlinked truths about the nature of American politics. It underscored the weakness of political parties to censure candidates and underlined the cavalier approach of the entire political system to allegations of campaign finance irregularities. The case of Robert Torricelli therefore raises serious questions about the nature of political corruption that extend from individual transgression, through party political tolerance based on the comparative weakness of central apparatus to systemic failure.

Robert Torricelli was widely regarded in Washington as a sophisticated political operator. First elected to the House of Representatives in 1982 representing North Jersey, Torricelli transferred to the Senate in 1996. In the process he amassed a personal war chest of $9m, a staggering amount for a first-time candidate, even when judged by the standards of the time. From the beginning he attracted the attention of the moneymen in Congress. "On the day that I was elected to the United States Senate, Senator Bob Kerrey of Nebraska came and met me at an airport hotel in Newark. And Senator Daschle was on the phone. He said to me, 'Bob, we know this is unusual; you haven't even joined the institution. We'd like you to be part of the effort to regain Democratic control of the United States Senate'."[3] He was immediately appointed Vice-Chairman of the Democratic Senatorial Campaign Committee (DSCC) and became chairman of the 2000 campaign. It was an indication of the esteem in which the party leadership held him. Torricelli was the political equivalent of a Wall Street "rainmaker", a man with an uncanny ability to tap into corporate wealth. Torricelli repaid the trust by breaking all records in the financing of that contest and enabled the Democrats to draw level with the Republicans. Central to his success was his recruitment of multimillionaires who were prepared to finance their own campaign,

---

[2] Ibid.
[3] Full text of Torricelli's announcement, *New York Times*, 30 September 2002.

most notably his Senate running mate in New Jersey John Corzine, who spent a staggering $60m of his own money in gaining the seat.[4] John Corzine's previous job was chief executive of Goldman Sachs.

One of the most successful fund-raisers ever to have held the post, Torricelli brought in millions of dollars in contributions to the national party organization that were then farmed out across the country to influence pivotal races. Torricelli's fund-raising wizardry did not only draw the attention of the Democratic leadership, it also prompted a three-year investigation by the federal authorities over payments to his campaign made by David Chang, a flamboyant Chinese American with extensive business interests in Korea.

Chang had made his fortune as a commodities broker in New Jersey, exporting grain to East Asia. He was adroit in using political connections to the Republicans in order to gain a licence to export grain to North Korea in 1991. Central to his success was his employment of Retired Admiral Daniel Murphy, a former Deputy Director of the CIA and Chief of Staff for George Bush Senior when he served as Vice-President under Ronald Reagan. In the early 1990s Murphy had become a lobbyist in Washington, and it was his political connections that were central to the awarding of the licence. When the Republicans lost power in 1992, Chang transferred his allegiance to the Democrats and began supporting Torricelli, then a member of the House of Representatives.

Chang's North Korea venture was a profitable but risky operation, and by the summer of 1995 his business was owed $71m by the North Korean government. Chang went to his local representative for help in pressurizing Pyongyang to pay up. Torricelli wrote to the North Korean ambassador to the United Nations on 22 September 1999 warning that failure to repay Chang could imperil relations between the two countries. This marked a deepening of the relations between the two men. Chang, who had been providing political contributions

---

[4] Paul S. Herrnson and Kelly D. Patterson, "Financing the 2000 congressional elections", in David Magleby (ed.), *Financing the 2000 Election* (Brookings Institution Press, Washington, DC, 2002), p. 108.

to Torricelli since 1992, decided to step up his involvement in domestic politics, a move that coincided with his political mentor's decision to move into the high-money stakes of the Senate.

Chang held a fund-raiser in December and was named a member of the Torricelli Campaign Finance Committee in January 1996. Chang showered Torricelli with luxury gifts including a Rolex, Italian suits and a widescreen television. He even put a deposit on a Mercedes the putative Senator fancied. As the campaign developed, the company he controlled chartered a plane for Torricelli's use in criss-crossing New Jersey. The campaign was a success and Torricelli entered the Senate.

Although only in the Senate for a number of days, Torricelli had become a very powerful individual given his elevation to Vice-Chairman of the DSCC. When combined with his membership of the Finance and Foreign Relations Committee, the network power expanded exponentially. This gave him an unusual degree of access to the senatorial leadership, the ability to forge coalitions and get things done. It also gave him a profile and made him exceptionally useful to Chang and the business interests with North Korea he wanted to pursue. In Christmas 1996, Chang claimed he visited Torricelli in his house in Inglewood, New Jersey with a $25,000 present and the following month one of his assistants claims she provided the Senator with a further $10,000.

Three weeks after Torricelli was sworn in, prosecutors investigating campaign finance irregularities first knocked on David Chang's door with a subpoena. Rather than distance himself from his former benefactor, Torricelli deepened his links with Chang, who in turn becomes a major contributor to the Democratic National Committee (DNC) and DSCC, contributing $100,000 in June 1998. In total Chang provided $235,000 to the Democrats. Running parallel to this deepening political access was an FBI investigation into the bizarre world of David Chang. In June 1999, the FBI arrived at his house to question him about the extent of his campaign contributions. Chang claimed he was merely the gardener in an attempt to avoid answering questions. He then asked why the FBI was harassing him given that he had been given personal assurances that the investigation was about to be wound up by the Attorney General Janet Reno.

At the same time as the FBI was investigating Chang for illegal activity, Torricelli was attempting to use another branch of government to enhance his client's business portfolio. Torricelli convinced the Chairman of the Democrats Terence McAuliffe to take a position as a private consultant to provide backing for Chang's plan to buy the troubled South Korean insurance company Korea Life. McAuliffe's remit was to persuade American insurance companies to invest in the corporation if Chang secured ownership.

It was the first indication that Torricelli was providing a tangible return in the investment. The next step was to persuade the South Korean government that Chang's bid for the auction was politically as well as economically expedient. He asked the State Department to help arrange a meeting between Torricelli and the South Korean Prime Minister Jong Pil and the Finance Minister Kang Bong Kyun, ostensibly "to discuss political, economic and humanitarian developments in North Korea." The initial approach was rebuffed, but Torricelli was not easily dissuaded. In July 1999, an email was sent from Torricelli's office directly to the US embassy in Seoul. "It is IMPERATIVE that the Senator meet the Prime Minister. PLEASE TRY AGAIN with the foreign ministry."[5] A further email from a staffer in Torricelli's office told the US embassy that a separate approach had been made to the South Korean embassy in Washington. Sent on Independence Day, 4 July 1999, in a debasement of the American creed of equality, the staff member Maria Pica wrote: "I told him [the Korean diplomat] that since Senator Torricelli is going to the north and has a 20-year relationship with the ROK government it was critical that he see the PM for 15–20 minutes."

The pressure worked and Torricelli gained access to the South Korean premier, but the only humanitarian discussion he was interested in was the help required to enhance the business interests of

[5] Quoted in Susan Schmidt and James V. Grimaldi, "Torricelli and the money man", *Washington Post*, 13 May 2001.

David Chang. The entire episode was a source of acute embarrassment for the US ambassador in Seoul Stephen Bosworth, who later apologized to the Korean minister of finance, saying that neither he nor his staff had knowledge of Torricelli's true intentions.

For David Chang, the political connections were paying off. Soon after the meeting, Torricelli publicly endorsed his bid to buy the $1.5bn insurance business in South Korea. Chang then sought to provide the Koreans with further evidence of his clout by flying Terence McAuliffe to Seoul the following month. McAuliffe resigned his consultancy when it appeared in Seoul that Chang did not actually have the money to proceed with the deal. It was purely a business calculation, rather than questions surrounding the wisdom of the Chairman of the Democrats engaging in outside political consultancy for a contract that had involved the deliberate hoodwinking of the State Department, that prompted McAuliffe's departure. Chang alleges that McAuliffe was paid $175,000; McAuliffe's office confirms that the sum was $100,000, a substantial profit for a consultancy that never materialized. The collapse of the deal did not prevent further attempts by members of the Senate to intervene on Chang's behalf, presumably at Torricelli's urging. The problems with the North Korean government over non-payment of the grain shipments were still outstanding, and in October and November 1999 Chang received letters of support from several senators.

Then, on 10 December 1999, Chang's world collapsed with his arrest by the FBI for violating campaign finance rules in his attempts to get Torricelli elected to the Senate in 1996. He pleaded guilty to charges of obstruction and making a total of $53,000 in illegal payments. The court hearing was limited to Chang's responsibility in reimbursing four associates for money paid directly to the campaign, a so-called "straw donation". The issue of the gifts and the Korean ventures were not adjudicated on. Given a three-year sentence, Chang pledged to co-operate with the federal investigators in the ongoing investigation into Torricelli.

The Senator angrily denounced the investigation and claimed that his only crime was trusting Chang, who had deceived him. On 3

January 2002 the United States Attorney's office in Manhattan announced that the investigation into Torricelli was to be wound up because of the lack of sufficient evidence to proceed to court. Democrats responded with delight. The reaction of the former Chairman of the Senate Ethics Committee Richard Bryan was typical. "All the fanfare and publicity that an indictment was imminent, and then for the New York US Attorney to close the file, that is pretty much equivalent to a complete vindication."[6] But the Justice Department was determined that the matter should not become a mere footnote. It took the unusual step of handing over the evidence to the Senate Ethics Committee for political, if not judicial, adjudication.

In July 2002, the Senate Ethics Committee lambasted Torricelli for violating campaign finance legislation by accepting inappropriate gifts including a television, CD player and the loan of bronze eagle statues. While the Senate Committee accepted there were credibility problems with Chang's evidence, Torricelli had brought the august chamber into disrepute by acting as an advocate for his concerns:

> Continuance of a personal and official relationship with Mr Chang under circumstances where you knew that he was attempting to ingratiate himself, in part through a pattern of attempts to provide you and those around you with gifts over a period of several years when you and your Senate Office were taking official actions of benefit to Mr Chang (contacting United States Government officials, writing letters to foreign government officials and involving Mr Chang or his representatives in situations where you were meeting with officials of foreign governments) evidenced poor judgement ...
>
> After evaluating the extensive body of evidence before it and your testimony, the committee is troubled by incongruities, inconsistencies and conflicts, particularly concerning actions taken by you, which were or could have been of potential benefit to Mr Chang. Therefore, the committee ... expresses its determination that your actions and failure to act led to violations of Senate rules (and related statutes) and created at least the appearance of impropriety, and you are hereby severely admonished.[7]

---

[6] Quoted in Thomas B. Edsall, "Post-probe future brightens for ambitious Sen. Torricelli", *Washington Post*, 5 January 2002.

[7] Text of Senate Ethics Committee Hearing, published as "Admonishment on ethics by committee", *New York Times*, 31 July 2002.

Torricelli's response was a classic example of masterful evasion. "I want my colleagues in the Senate to know that I agree with the committee's conclusions, fully accept their findings and take full personal responsibility. It has always been my contention that I believe that at no time did I accept any gifts or violate any Senate rules. The committee has concluded otherwise in several circumstances and directed me to make immediate payment in several instances to ensure full compliance with the rules of the Senate. I will comply immediately." In effect, Torricelli was suggesting that he would comply with the rules of the game, but his infraction, for which he rejected responsibility even while accepting the judgment of the Ethics Committee, was merely a technical breach of the code of conduct. The message was clear. The clarion call for tough action against alleged malefactors within corporate America would not be translated into a political form.

This non-apology of an apology was accompanied by an appeal to the people of New Jersey to accept an implausible explanation for a momentary lapse of judgement that lasted several years. "The day that I was elected to the United States Senate remains among the most cherished of my life. During recent weeks I have spent long nights tormented by the question of how I could have allowed such lapses of judgement to compromise all that I have fought to build."[8]

The decision by the Senate Ethics Committee not to expel Torricelli gave him a renewed political lease of life, encapsulated by a TV commercial entitled "fighter". Torricelli was presented in chastened light, sitting behind a desk with the American flag, his hands clasped together as he sought forgiveness for not breaking the law: "Although I broke no laws, it's clear to me that I did exercise poor judgement in my associations and actions ... A United States Senator should hold himself to a higher standard. Ultimately, you, my neighbours, will decide whether the battle I fought and won for the people of New Jersey outweigh these lapses in judgement."[9]

[8] Statement by Senator Robert Torricelli, *Washington Post*, 31 July 2002.
[9] Transcript quoted in "The ad campaign; solemnly seeking forgiveness", *New York Times*, 2 August 2002.

His non-denial denial served merely to stoke up the political tension and deflect attention from contemporary political linkages to the corporate crisis unfolding across the Hudson river on Wall Street. The embattled fighter rebuffed demands that his testimony to the Senate Ethics Committee be released on the spurious grounds that such a decision was beyond his control. A race, which earlier in the year had appeared hopelessly lost, now appeared wide open. The National Republican Senatorial Committee announced that it was making the maximum possible donation allowed under federal rules and added to the credibility of the threat by passing its "soft-money" list of contributors to its local candidate Doug Forrester. Forrester defined his candidacy by what he was not rather than what he stood for. Put simply, his campaign centred on the fact that he was not Bob Torricelli. Forrester had stunned local observers by admitting in a radio interview that he had raised a paltry $100,000 from contributors.

Although the millionaire had released $6m of his own money, the election of Democrat Jon Corzine, a former Goldman Sachs investment banker, in 2000 had cost 10 times that amount. Opinion poll data suggested that the Ethics Committee admonishment in itself was not enough to torpedo Torricelli's candidacy. What was clear was that money had now become an issue. The former Democratic Senator Frank Lautenberg, who retired from active politics in 2000 because of the constant demands for fund-raising, commented sardonically: "This race just got a lot more expensive."[10]

The issue of Torricelli's credibility became the touchstone for the entire race. Forrester printed hundreds of thousands of "Get out of Jail Free ... Until November 5" cards to remind voters of the question marks over Torricelli's questionable ethical record. Torricelli campaigned relentlessly on his record and attempted to undermine Forrester's credibility by concentrating on the fact that his Republican opponent's fortune had come from the pharmaceutical industry, the

---

[10] Quoted in David Kocieniewski, "Ethics ruling puts Torricelli in a tight spot", *New York Times*, 1 August 2002.

bête noire of Democratic politics. As a strategy this was undermined by a particularly effective counter-attack that highlighted Torricelli's own connections with the industry. Forrester combed through Torricelli's voting record and discovered that the standard-bearer for the increase in the availability of generic medicine had introduced legislation in 1999 to extend the patent for the allergy drug Claritin. To make matters worse for Torricelli, the measure was introduced one day after the drug's manufacturer, New Jersey-based Schering-Plough Corporation, donated a $50,000 contribution to the DSCC, which Torricelli had then headed.[11]

The presence of President Bush and Tom Daschle of the Democrats in New Jersey to provide high-level backing for their respective charges on 23 September underscored the importance of the race. Torricelli's attempts to separate the admonishment from the Senate and the impending election were fatally damaged by a question of timing. When Chang was convicted the trial judge had ordered sealed a memo from federal prosecutors. In it they asked the judge to take into consideration when sentencing the co-operation given by Chang to the investigation. Four news organizations appealed the decision to a three-judge panel of the US Court of Appeals in neighbouring Philadelphia. On 20 September 2002, the panel noted that Torricelli "has already made public statements attempting to refute the very material he wants to suppress from public view." This, in the court's view, was unacceptable. It ruled that although the document might contain "statements that are perhaps painful to Torricelli ... [this, in itself is insufficient ground to] overcome the presumption of openness."[12]

It spelt the end of Torricelli's faltering campaign. The Justice Department document described as "credible" the allegations that Torricelli had accepted tens of thousands of dollars in cash and gifts. The decision not to proceed was linked to wider credibility

---

[11] Dale Russakoff, "N.J. voters unfazed by Torricelli's troubles", *Washington Post*, 1 August 2002.
[12] Melanie Burney, "Memo in Torricelli probe to be opened", *Philadelphia Inquirer*, 21 September 2002.

problems with David Chang. The document noted there were "serious credibility problems that would have completely undermined Chang's testimony before the jury."[13] A senior source within the US Attorney's Office refused to be drawn further on the failure to proceed with the investigation when reached by the author. However, when asked if the decision not to bring the matter to court exonerated the Democratic senator for New Jersey, the source suggested pointedly that he would strongly recommend reading the filing with the federal court to discover the validity of Chang's account and its usefulness.

The airing of a television interview with Chang to coincide with the release of the Justice Department memo exacerbated the damage. Speaking from his jail cell to the New Jersey affiliate of NBC, Chang claimed that he had provided $150,000 in return for official favours. The 38-minute segment, broadcast without a commercial break, was politically explosive. Torricelli's appeals for forgiveness fell on deaf ears. He accused NBC of partisan reporting in broadcasting a "rehash solely for the purpose of inflicting political damage."[14] In his valedictory address he asked plaintively: "when did we become such an unforgiving people? How did we become a society where a person can build credibility their entire life and have it questioned by someone who has none? When did we stop believing in and trusting in each other . . . there's a point at which every man reaches his limit. I've reached mine."[15]

It sparked a court battle to replace Torricelli on the ballot, a ploy that sparked derision in large parts of the right-wing press. Typical was a commentary by Fred Barnes, editor of *The Weekly Standard*:

Candidates announce, stand for election in a primary, and if nominated by voters run in the general election. This is the democratic process, orderly,

[13] "Allegations against Torricelli called 'Credible'", *Washington Post*, 27 September 2002.
[14] Ibid.
[15] Full text of Robert Torricelli's announcement, *New York Times*, 30 September 2002, available online at www.nytimes.com/metro; "In his own eulogy, a senator unbowed", *Washington Post*, 1 October 2002.

time tested and based on the popular will. It should be upset only in the most unusual of circumstances. There's nothing unusual about the Torricelli case. He's merely a candidate who's trailing badly and might lose . . . Democrats, who angrily insisted that the court should not have decided the 2000 presidential election, are going to court, seeking to have Torricelli's name erased from the ballot and another name substituted. In its own way, this is as sleazy as the conduct that got Torricelli in trouble in the first place.[16]

Following a divisive court hearing the New Jersey court allowed the insertion of Frank Lautenberg's name as a candidate to replace Torricelli. The combative former senator, who openly despised Torricelli when they served together from 1996 to 2000, mounted a campaign based primarily on the need to ensure the Democrats retained control of the Senate. In solid New Jersey, the strategy worked. Nationally, the party fared considerably worse, losing control of the Senate and the House of Representatives. The scale of the loss is all the more remarkable when one considers the inauspicious circumstances that George Bush and his associates found themselves in during the summer of 2002. It is through examining how the election was framed that another key facet of the political–economic nexus comes into view.

It is in the United States, the powerhouse of the global economy, that the calamity occasioned by the confluence of corporate crime and terrorist threat is most marked. The tabulated drop in market value in the United States bourse alone, since the fall of Enron, represents a decline of 90% of Gross Domestic Product, the bulk of which has been lost by institutional investors, such as mutual and pension funds, and the proprietary department of the major banks. The implications, however, trickle down much further, directly into the pockets of the middle class whose entry into the market was predicated on deregulation in the 1990s.

Despite the lowest interest rates in a generation, confidence remains deflated and manufacturing incapable of staging a renaissance. Unemployment has returned to 1994 levels. In October it reached 6%, despite the $1,345bn tax cut ordered by President

---

[16] Fred Barnes, "The old switcheroo", *The Weekly Standard*, 1 October 2002.

Bush in an attempt to stimulate the economy. It is symptomatic that the major sectors involved in lay-offs were manufacturing and retail sales.[17] In the vernacular, so beloved of middle class America, all the cards are maxed out. Consumer spending outside the auto sector remains buoyant, but is funded not by higher wages, nor increased job security, but by the middle class remortgaging property to sustain lifestyle levels. In 2002, the rate of refinancing increased dramatically, doubling from \$750bn in 1998 to \$1,500bn in four years.[18] Zero per cent financing was not enough to tempt enough consumers into luxury items to promote a manufacturing renaissance. More alarmingly, despite halving the interest rate to a 50-year low of 1.75%, the repossession rate is rising inexorably.

The consequences of the promises made to the technology boom, underwritten by aggressive marketing and agreed to by purchasers with unrealistic expectations are now beginning to bite across the board. At the height of the boom, easy access to credit and irresponsible lending led to a substantial increase in home ownership, a development exacerbated by the introduction of new highly leveraged financial products.[19] Now, as the *New York Times* has reported, "the merchants of the dream have become its morticians." As the banks and mortgage lenders seek to improve their own market position by reducing the level of bad debt on the books, foreclosure is replacing refinancing as the preferred option. A survey by the Mortgage Bankers of America shows that 134,885 home mortgages were foreclosed in the second quarter of 2002, the highest figure in 30 years. The majority of those affected were homeowners with imperfect credit

---

[17] Peronet Despeignes, "Jobless data add to the pressure", *Financial Times*, 7 December 2002.

[18] David Hale, "The resilience of corporate America", *Financial Times*, 2 December 2002.

[19] This behaviour is not unique, rather it informs a repetitive cycle that starts with speculation distorting fundamental corporate values, which extends to mania, before "financial distress" turns a panic to a crash. See Charles P. Kindleberger, *Manias, Panics and Crashes, A History of Financial Crises* (John Wiley & Sons, New York, 2000), pp. 14–15. As Kindleberger points out "details proliferate; structure abides" (p. 19).

rating who were charged a premium for joining the dream. With consumer credit debt at all time highs, servicing the financial commitments becomes increasingly problematic.

More and more people have been defaulting, and not just those with poor credit ratings. As a result, the government itself has taken on the role of lender as last resort, with 72,000 now utilizing a federal repayment package, a threefold increase in as many years.[20] The general economic situation is rendered even more acute because the integrity of the stock market, as a safe investment and as the engine room for funding corporate expansion plans, is now under sustained assault. In such circumstances the Democrats should have been able to deflect attention from the undoubted breaches of trust associated with Torricelli, particularly after the senator was forced to resign. It is therefore necessary to dissect exactly why the issue of malfeasance within corporate America did not become the defining issue for the Democrats in 2002. The answer lies in strategic failure and moral bankruptcy.

The success of any election campaign depends on the ability to "frame the debate" and there was to be no doubting the White House's determination to set the agenda. How it was done is an example of life imitating art. In June 2002, a CD-ROM containing a PowerPoint presentation given by President Bush's most important political counsellor Karl Rove was discovered in Lafayette Park, just across from the White House. Burnt onto the compact disc was a document so breathtakingly cynical that the strategist played by Robert de Niro in the hit movie *Wag the Dog* could have authored it. In the movie, a fictitious war is fomented in Albania to shore up the approval ratings of a president facing a debilitating sex scandal just weeks before an election. For the de Niro character, the only way to rescue the presidency is, with the help of a Hollywood producer and a pliant news media, to "change the story, change the lead." The choice of Albania as the venue for conflict is predicated on the fact

---

[20] Peter T. Kilborn, "Easy credit and hard times bring a flood of foreclosures", *New York Times*, 24 November 2002.

that it sounds faintly sinister and the American people know little about it.

On the CD-ROM, the real-life political tacticians detail how a crisis with Iraq should be managed to ensure maximum political advantage. The President is encouraged to "maintain a positive image environment, identify issue synergies, provide campaign resources and help earn media." Rove notes that the Republicans are poised to make history, in large part because of the high approval ratings and "the increased importance of national security issues." He suggests that the President should focus on "the war and the economy" in that order. He also implies that strenuous efforts should be made to distance the President and his CEO acolytes in business and politics from the suspicion that the stream of corporate scandal owes its existence, if not to the policies enunciated by the administration, then to the *laissez-faire* deregulation ideology that underpins it.

For Democratic strategists, by contrast, the message was deceptively simple: focus on the linkages between George W. Bush and other prominent members of the administration with the gargantuan business collapses of Enron, WorldCom and the accountancy scandals their spectacular fall have exposed. In the dying days of July, James Carville, the Svengali behind Bill Clinton's first assault on the White House in 1992, outlined the strategy the Democrats would use to recapture Congress and serve as a bridgehead for the presidential battle in 2004. Carville, a former marine, pioneered the slogan "It's the economy, stupid" in 1992 in an attempt to focus the attention of his campaign strategists on the wider goal of his candidate. This time the message was even blunter. "We want to focus on how Democrats stay on the offensive, keep evolving and defining the issue terrain, and always keep the Republicans off balance. In short, do not stand still, keep taking Democratic issues to the next step, and refuse to accept the site of battle chosen by the White House."[21]

---

[21] James Carville, Stanley Greenberg and Robert Shrum, "Staying on the offensive", 31 July 2002, p. 1 (carried in *Washington Post*, 1 August 2002).

For Carville four key battlefronts needed to be focused in on, developed and exploited. A critique based on Bush's alleged corporate favouritism should be broadened into "the even larger issue of their handling of the economy." This in turn seamlessly segued into the impact a decline in stock market values would have on pension funds. The final element in the strategy centred on social security. For Carville, "this is the most important extension of the current corporate irresponsibility issue and likely the reason why Democrats will make major gains in November. Privatization of Social Security and the draining of the Social Security trust funds are gigantic issues – and they are directly linked in people's minds to the practices that have already engendered people's savings and pensions."[22] Significantly, however, the Democrats did not suggest far-reaching reform beyond that countenanced by the White House, leaving the party open to charges that its concern over the issue amounted to little more than cheap political point-scoring.

The Republican riposte was devastating. A senior senatorial campaign manager complained that "the Democrats have turned the economy of the United States into their own personal political playing field … they are doing everything possible to drive down the economy in a desperate attempt to win elections in November. What they are doing is no game. What they are doing is very dangerous. The National Democrats are willing to jeopardize the retirement funds, college accounts, and lifelong investments of millions of Americans just so they might be able to gain more political power."[23]

The memo, written by the Executive Director of the National Republican Senatorial Committee Mitch Bainwol, was designed to neutralize the contagion rather than offer a positive route out of the morass that has occurred as a result of corporate malfeasance. The

---

[22] Ibid., p. 5.

[23] Mitch Bainwol, "Democrats and corporate responsibility", *Washington Post*, 1 August 2001. For an assessment of the competing memos see Terry M. Neal, "Duelling memos get party members revved up", *Washington Post*, 1 August 2002. Accessible at www.washingtonpost.com/wp-srv/nation/transcripts/GOPresponse_memo.htm

strategic brilliance of the Republican approach was to provide damning evidence that the Democrats received more that $22m in payments from the companies now under investigation, weakening considerably the power of the corruption charges.

Throughout the summer the game plan outlined by the Rove briefing went into operation, relatively unchallenged by a media distracted by an obsession with the prospect of war and incapable of cracking open a skilful and reticent White House operation that refuses to be drawn on the business background of its chief protagonists. The Vice-President had initially come under sustained assault over suspicions about decisions taken when he was CEO of oil services company Halliburton. The allegations centred on the implementation of new accounting methods to value turnover and the divesting of stock at the height of the company's valuation. In his defence, the change in bookkeeping corresponded to industry norms at the time and the decision to cash in his shares coincided with a decision to run on the Bush ticket for the White House.[24]

While there is no suggestion that Cheney did anything illegal in authorizing the change in accountancy standards in order for the firm to remain competitive, questions remain as to why the company did not report this change for 14 months. At issue is the effect the accounting mechanism had on the stock valuation of the company, with some estimates suggesting that it inflated profits by $234m over a four-year period.[25] There is, as yet, no credible explanation emanating from either Halliburton or from Cheney as to why the company did not report the change in order for analysts to assess the true value of the 1998–1999 accounts.

When it came to offering a rationale for the malaise, the administration worked on the principle that the crisis centred on criminal wrongdoing by a few corrupt executives rather than a corrupted system. On the day that two executives from WorldCom arrived in

---

[24] Charles Krautmammer, "Cheney and the CEOs", *Washington Post*, 9 August 2002.
[25] Mike McNamee and Stephanie Anderson Forrest, "The Cheney Question", *Business Week*, 22 July 2002.

court to face accountancy fraud charges, the Attorney General John
Ashcroft used a news conference to suggest, if convicted, they "could
receive up to 65 years in prison", a figure far in excess of all sentencing
guidelines.[26] President Bush also intervened when three executives
from a failed cable television company Adelphi Communications
were paraded in handcuffs in front of the media. "This government
will investigate, will arrest and will prosecute corporate executives
who break the law," he suggested with administration aides presenting
the arrests – erroneously – as the first fruits of the corporate crime task
force.[27] The comments served a very real purpose. They heightened
the perception that the administration was serious in its dogged
determination to clean up corporate America. They also served to
bring into sharp relief Cheney's silence about his alleged culpability
in not alerting the NYSE and the SEC to the accountancy changes
introduced by him when CEO of Halliburton, a clear breach of the
rules.

This lack of transparency is at the core of the problems besetting
corporate America and the response to the crisis by politicians, hopelessly in hock to the financial services industry that underwrite them.
The more the media probed Cheney's background the more reticent
the Vice-President became, prompting the venerable commentator
Maureen Dowd to opine acerbically, "Republicans are most grateful
to Mr. Cheney. With the time he saved by not explaining administration policy to the president and the country, and the time he saved
refusing to answer reporters' nitpicking questions about his past business schemes, he has been able to fly around raising more than $12
million for Republican candidates."[28]

The crisis of confidence facing the stock market, rising unemployment and the deterioration of pensions were presented by Republican
strategists as mere cyclical moves, the outworking of the "irrational

---

[26] Stephen Labaton, "Handcuffs make strange politics? Not in Washington", *New York Times*, 2 August 2002.

[27] David E. Sanger and David E. Rosenbaum, "Corporate conduct: Washington memo", *New York Times*, 25 July 2002.

[28] Maureen Dowd, "Cheney stays in the picture", *New York Times*, 11 August 2002.

exuberance" that characterized the bull market of the late 1990s. The further charging of corrupt business executives and the maximum punishment handed out to Arthur Anderson for its role in shredding documents relating to the bankruptcy of Enron were relegated further down the television news running orders or jettisoned altogether as the media salivated over potential conflict in the Middle East. Until the arrival of the Washington sniper, the mainstream media had concentrated on little else but the crisis with Iraq. Then, terror on the streets of the nation's capital segued seamlessly into impending war in the Gulf, the inevitability of war made manifest by media outlets' subtitles for coverage, such as "Countdown Iraq" on the normally restrained MSNBC or "Showdown Iraq" on the more bombastic CNN. If the stakes were not so high, the producers of *Wag the Dog* could sue for breach of intellectual copyright.

To a large extent the Democrats were architects of their own misfortune. Principled opposition to the risks of unilateral action in the Gulf was marked by its absence. The Democratic leadership in Congress reasoned that providing the administration with a blank cheque on Iraq would allow for a return to domestic focus. As a strategy it failed totally. The Democrats response to the bombshell from North Korea in October that it was secretly developing weapons of mass destruction in contravention to bilateral agreements with the United States is a case in point. Temporarily caught in the headlights, the administration played for time and initially refused to comment on the opening up a potential new theatre in the Far East or the credibility problems it posed to the Iraqi doctrine.[29] The fact that the Senate Majority Leader Tom Daschle was aware of the North Korea breach, *before* Congress provided President Bush with a

---

[29] That contradiction still exists, and further revelations that North Korea has exported Scud missiles to Yemen have served to exacerbate the problem facing policy-makers. See Quentin Peel, "The world's other dictatorship", *Financial Times*, 20 November 2002 and Andrew Ward, "After Kim: Nuclear tension, economic slowdown, anti-US protests", *Financial Times*, 17 December 2002. As this book went to press (May 2003), talks in Beijing between the United States and North Korea, brokered by the Chinese government, ended inconclusively.

mandate for war, and chose to remain silent reinforces just how out-manoeuvred the Democrats have been. As the disquiet over the Democrats' own subservience to interested money in the Torricelli case demonstrated, the ability to offer radical solutions to corporate reform was severely circumscribed.

While the Democrats were keen to stress the linkages between the Bush administration and individual transgressors within corporate America, the reality of party funding ensured that neither side was prepared to bite the hand that fed it by introducing radical thinking. In political science terminology, this is a "valence issue" – there is only one side to be on: the preservation of self-interest by blaming the excess on corrupted individuals rather than a corrupted system. In that context the die was cast.

While many commentators were reluctant to call the election in advance, there was no mistaking the confidence of the Republican strategists in the lead up to the poll. The influential *New York Times* economics columnist Paul Krugman quoted the mood of Republican political operatives as one of "optimism, bordering on giddiness." Krugman reported that business lobbyists "have their wish lists ready." In a telling comment for future policy directions, one strategist was quoted as saying that "it's the domestic equivalent of planning for post-war Iraq." Such confidence was well founded.

The combination of a strong message from a war-time president and a hopelessly divided opposition incapable of launching a coherent policy alternative meant that the Republicans effectively choreographed the entire election campaign. The central issue of systemic failure was passed over, replaced by a political, wilful ignorance vouchsafed by corporate donations. Taken together, the studied inaction suggested remarkable insouciance. That certainly was the estimation of Christopher Dodd, Chairman of the Senate Banking Subcommittee on Securities and Investment. Commenting in the *New York Times*, Dodd argued: "My sense is this is a White House that is sensing some political relief that this is no longer the issue on the table so they can take a political pass on this. They touched the critical issues last summer and now it's gone. Now the issue is Iraq all the time."[30] Given the dominant role played by Republican pollsters in mapping out the electoral stratagem to be adopted for the mid-term elections, such tactical arrogance was inextricably linked to the recognition that the responsibility for corporate malfeasance could not be pinned on the Republican White House. Central to this evaluation was the assessment that physical security had displaced financial uncertainty as the major voting issue in the November election.

Pivotal to the success of the campaign was the strategic brilliance of Karl Rove, the most powerful advisor to an American president since Henry Kissinger. Rove steered the campaign away from the treacherous rocks of economic reality and toward impending conflict in Iraq under the nebulous "war on terrorism." The move to a tangible enemy gave credible goals, against which the administration could be judged and ensured the centrality of the President to the emerging political discourse.

The slim margin of victory belies the true significance of the Republican electoral advance. For only the third time since the American Civil War – and the first time since 1934 – has a party in control of the White House managed to increase its representation in the House of Representatives. That the Republicans also wrested back control of the Senate, on the foot of a campaign directed by a president who, only two years ago, gained office despite losing the popular vote and has presided ever since over a faltering economy, only adds to the dramatic effect.[31]

The Democrats sought to put a brave face on events. The former Senate Majority Leader Tom Daschle argued plaintively that his party's failure to reap the benefits of corporate malfeasance and a deteriorating economy could be traced to an inability to dislodge Iraq from the media agenda. Like other Democratic strategists, he pointed to the fact that despite record levels of expenditure Repub-

---

[30] Stephen Labaton, "Bush tries to shrink SEC raise intended for corporate cleanup", *New York Times*, 19 October 2002.

[31] Gerard Baker, "Bush's bond with the people elevates him to a new level of political power", *Financial Times*, 9 November 2002.

lican success could be measured in single digit figures. For the Democrats the only benefit of this self-serving analysis is that it hides the
enormity of the sea change that has, in fact, occurred. Neither the
Kennedy name nor its geographical powerbase was enough to save
the Democrats from humiliating defeats. Kathleen Townsend
Kennedy lost her campaign to represent Maryland in the House,
and control of the governor's mansion in Massachusetts moved to
the GOP.[32] High-profile visits to the deeply symbolic state of
Florida by both Bill Clinton and Al Gore failed to rescue a flounder-
ing Democratic campaign for the governorship. The question marks
over the legitimacy of the President, spawned by the flawed election
in Florida in 2000 and endorsed by a dubious judgment by the
Supreme Court that prevented the recount from taking place, were
put to rest by the Republican victory.[33]

In the final analysis, the Republicans were much more successful in
tapping into the public mood of vulnerability and insecurity; core
factors that significantly downgraded the importance of economic
concerns.[34] The black and white world of good and evil so graphically
depicted by George Bush in whistle stop tours across the country,
raising in the process over $140m in electoral contributions, paid
massive dividends at the polls. The resolute action of the President
in the aftermath of the attacks, first in Afghanistan then in Iraq,
provided meaning to a confused nation scarred by the reality of
terrorism appearing within its once-impregnable façade.

---

[32] GOP, the Grand Old Party (the Republican Party).

[33] For an illuminating compendium of essays on the Florida debacle and its
implications see Arthur J. Jacobson and Michael Rosenfield (eds), *The Longest
Night, Polemics and Perspectives on Election 2000* (University of California Press,
London, 2002). For a scathing account of the machinations surrounding the Florida
count in 2000 see Michael Moore, "A very American coup", in *Stupid White Men*
(Penguin, London, 2002), pp. 1–28.

[34] The transfer of power to the Republicans, even by a narrow margin, represents a
realignment of critical importance and was achieved largely as a result of utilizing
national issues. For a theoretical rationale see David W. Brady, *Critical Elections
and Congressional Policy Making* (California University Press, Stanford, CA, 1988),
p. 18.

Such was the power of the rhetoric that in Georgia, one of the key seats for the 2004 election, the Republicans swept away the sitting Democratic senator by waging a campaign suggesting that its candidate, a highly decorated and mutilated serviceman, was soft on terrorism.[35] By appealing directly to the American people, George Bush offered the impression that an offensive policy would secure once again American borders and restore a semblance of order to a chaotic world. It may well do neither, but for now the Republican Party is the repository of popular trust.

What gave the Republican strategy added malign potency was the way in which the Democrats were branded as unpatriotic in the crucial run-up to polling day on 5 November 2002. The administration recognized the importance of forcing the Democrats to accept a bipartisan approach, prior to Washington emptying for the campaign season. Bush had previously stalled on the introduction of a department of Homeland Security, changing his position only when public unease at the intelligence failures by the disparate agencies charged with defending the United States threatened his power base. The volte-face was accompanied with recognition that skilful manipulation of the issue could provide a potent campaign issue.[36]

As the campaign entered its final and most acrimonious stage, the political discourse soured dramatically. George Bush used a campaign speech in Minnesota to call on the American people to punish Democrats for failing to give him a free hand in the establishment of a department of Homeland Security, a device that was being used to force through changes in the federal bureaucracy and as such vigorously opposed by labour unions, who bankroll the Democrats. Senior Republican figures, like the departing senior senator Phil Gramm, decried without a trace of irony the opposition for being in the pockets of special interests. A similar argument could be advanced to castigate those Republicans who introduced into the Homeland

---

[35] David von Drahle, "Bush bets his popularity and scores a big victory", *Washington Post*, 6 November 2002.

[36] E. J. Dionne, "Brilliant politics, at a price", *Washington Post*, 22 November 2002.

Security Bill an extraneous provision shielding one of the country's leading pharmaceutical companies from class actions involving autistic children given an infant vaccine that included mercury.

The introduction of the measure, hidden in a bill that has nothing to do with the substantive issue, is a classic example of the morally suspect nature of lobbying and its malign influence in American politics. According to the Centre for Responsive Politics, Lilly contributed $1.6m during the latest election cycle, with 79% going to the Republicans. The questions surrounding the inclusion of the provision keep on rising because Lilly's Chairman Sidney Taurel serves on the advisory board of the Homeland Security Agency.[37] While there is no suggestion that Taurel was involved in the lobbying, there are close links between the company and the White House. George Bush's father served on the board in the 1970s and the White House Budget Director Mitchell Daniels is a former executive with the pharmaceutical giant. The fact that no one was prepared to claim credit for the introduction of the clause only serves to underscore its impropriety.[38]

It is indicative of how badly the President's domestic agenda has fared that, in the space of a week, the three most important economic policy officials in the country packed their bags. Pitt announced his resignation on the day of the polls; five days later came the terse announcement that the Treasury Secretary Paul O'Neill and the chief White House Economics Advisor had departed. Consummate Wall Street professionals were proposed for all three positions. Synergy, not conflicts of interest, had become the new mantra on both the Street and DC, as the administration began preparations for an assault on Iraq and a presidential contest in 2004.

In a telling comment, Richard Medley, a political consultant, told the *Financial Times* it was immaterial who was appointed to the Treasury. "For all intents and purposes, Karl Rove is the next Treasury

---

[37] Bob Herbert, "Whose hands are dirty", *New York Times*, 25 November 2002. For further information see the pressure group's website, www.safeminds.org.
[38] Sheryl Gay Stolberg, "A Capital Hill mystery: Who aided drug maker", *New York Times*, 29 November 2002.

secretary."[39] This subservience of policy to politics is central to the operation of the Bush administration.[40]

"Karl [Rove] is enormously powerful, maybe the single most powerful person in the modern, post-Hoover era ever to occupy a political advisor post near the Oval Office," is the view of the former chief of domestic policy at the White House. "There is no precedent in any modern White House for what is going on in this one: a complete lack of a policy apparatus," John DiIulio told *Esquire*. "What you've got is everything – I mean everything – being run by the political arm. It's the reign of the Mayberry Machiavellis."[41]

Machiavelli understood more than most the reality of political behaviour. In a key statement in *The Prince*, his primer on politics, he noted sardonically: "There's such a difference between the way we really live and the way we ought to live that the man who neglects the real to study the ideal will learn how to accomplish his ruin, not his salvation."[42] Understanding the politics of Karl Rove necessitates internalizing the lessons from the Florentine political consultant. Rapprochement with Cuba was vetoed because it risked alienating the pivotal Cuban American vote in Florida, a trade war with Europe over steel tariffs was countenanced to protect the key industrial swing states, and O'Neill's scepticism over the advisability or utility of further fiscal stimuli – the only approximation to policy left – made it inevitable that he would fall foul of the White House's chief political strategist, as would Lindsay's injudicious comments about the cost of a war in Iraq.[43] Rove's primary goal is to ensure the re-election of the President, and that requires the marshal-

[39] Gerard Baker, "An amusing economic chat show falls victim to Washington reality", *Financial Times*, 7 December 2002. For a profile of Rove see James Carney, "General Karl Rove, reporting for duty" *Time*, 29 September 2002. Available online at http://www.time.com/time/nation/article/0,8599,356034,00.html

[40] See Gerard Baker, "A devalued discipline", *Financial Times*, 12 December 2002.

[41] Ron Suskind, "Why are these men laughing?", *Esquire*, January 2003. Advance news release available at www.esquire.com [accessed 9 December 2002].

[42] Niccolò Machiavelli, *The Prince* (Penguin, London, 1999).

[43] Editorial, "Dangerous departure, why the sacking of Paul O'Neill matters", the *Guardian*, 9 December 2002.

ling of an enormous war chest. For corporate America, this elevation of politics over policy ensures that its leverage over the range of legislative or regulatory change is enhanced dramatically.

The stakes have increased dramatically because of changes to the campaign finance legislation that would ban "soft money" – or unregulated contributions controlled by the national party and dispersed to pivotal races immediately after the polls closed. The paradox for the Democrats is that the explosion in the use of "soft money", pioneered by the Bill Clinton administration in 1992 and finessed for the 1996 re-election campaign, had made a mockery of federal campaign spending limits. Clinton's move to the centre made the party acceptable to business and allowed it to compete on a level playing field with the Republicans. It also created the circumstances for an exponential rise in the leverage "interested money" has over the legislative process and rendered the party susceptible to charges that it was equally in the pockets of its benefactors.

The resulting public disquiet over documented electoral finance abuse by the DNC in 1996, fuelled scepticism about the probity of politics. When this cynicism was combined with the corporate scandals affecting the United States following the collapse of Enron, it created a crisis of confidence that necessitated concerted action, or at least the appearance of it. The result was the passing of the McCain–Feingold legislation, the most sweeping change to electoral financing in the United States for a generation. Curtailing the corrosive effect of "interested money" may, on the surface, allow for a cleaner electoral system, but inherent dangers lurk in the subterranean depths surrounding the financing of elections in the United States.

War did much to obfuscate these core issues. The Massachusetts Democratic Senator John Forbes Kerry, a decorated Vietnam War veteran who came to prominence by his outspoken criticism of the conflict in Indochina, recognized the point in a profile for the *New Yorker* to accompany his bid for the presidency in 2004: "The Administration mistakes tough rhetoric for tough policy. They may gain short-term domestic gain as a result, but they are damaging the long-term security of the country. This is a far more complicated world than the ideologues of the administration care about or understand."[44] Kerry had endorsed the Bush strategy in the congressional vote, but argues that the unilateral impulses of the White House under George Bush serve only to add to threats to the vital national security interests of the state. Central to his bid for 2004 is a readjustment of Democratic concerns toward a potential paradigmatic change in the nature of American politics. In terms of rhetoric, it offers a throwback to the idealism of the 1960 contest that propelled Kennedy to power. "I think that asking people to be part of something larger than themselves, asking the country to do something better and more important – those are aspects of the Kennedy legacy that are applicable now."[45]

The problem for the Democrats is that the American political arena is a qualitatively different place to that which evinced the passionate mood of the 1960s. The political atmosphere is poisoned by cynicism, and changes to the campaign finance system are likely to intensify that trend. More than ever, it is an arena in which the power of the message is determined by access to the airwaves to propagate it. The passage of legislation designed to reduce the power of interest groups may in fact entrench their position still further. That risk has increased dramatically with the decision by a panel of the federal court on 2 May 2003 to deem unconstitutional a ban on the corporate funding of television advertisements within 60 days of a federal election. In a confused judgment, which split along partisan lines, the judges rolled back a key provision of the McCain–Feingold Act. A final decision on the role played by soft money will be made when the case returns to the Supreme Court in October. Power rests not with knowledge, but with the power to disseminate it. The message being propagated is that the market will prevail, no matter how imperfect, no matter how loud the dissonance between ideal and reality.

---

[44] Quoted in Joe Klein, "The long war of John Kerry, can a Massachusetts brahmin become president?", *New Yorker*, 2 December 2002, p. 74.
[45] Ibid, p. 83.

7

From Chicago to Washington via New York and Baghdad

The aggressive resolve of the United States toward confronting Saddam Hussein has thrown the international community into chaos. The resulting maelstrom demonstrates not only a gulf in understanding that separates Washington from grass roots, if not elite opinion in the Arab world but the fracturing of the Cold War alliance that sustained NATO. With insults freely traded across the Atlantic, objections to the casual disregard of international law are dismissed as yet another manifestation of the dying pains of Old Europe. The charge is made more sinister because opposition to the Manichean world is regarded as latent anti-Semitism.[1] The New World Order, so confidently expressed in the aftermath of the demise of the Soviet Union has in fact transmogrified into a deeply divided and insecure arena, characterized by schism and disorder. It was a point underscored by President Bush in his weekly address to the American people as coalition troops encircled Baghdad. In a conscious act of

---

[1] See Robert Kagan, "The power divide", *Prospect*, August 2002. For a robust response centred on the way in which Kagan has allowed his argument to be simplified for contemporary political purposes see Timothy Garton Ash, "The great divide", *Prospect*, March 2003. Kaplan himself sees Iraq as offering an opportunity to reposition America's strategic interests in the Middle East. "We should forswear any evangelical lust to implement democracy overnight in a country with no tradition of it. Our goal in Iraq should be a transitional secular dictatorship that unites the merchant classes across sectarian lines and may in time, after the rebuilding of institutions and the economy, lead to a democratic alternative." See Robert Kaplan, "A Post Saddam scenario", *The Atlantic Monthly*, November 2002.

dissemblance, the rationale for the war was placed in a domestic context:

> By our actions in this war, we serve a great and just cause. Free nations will not sit and wait, leaving enemies free to plot another September the 11th – this time, perhaps, with chemical, biological, or nuclear terror. We'll remove weapons of mass destruction from the hands of mass murderers. And by defending our own security, we are ridding the people of Iraq from one of the cruellest regimes on earth. The United States and our allies pledged to act if the dictator did not disarm. The regime in Iraq is now learning that we keep our word.[2]

Whether Anglo-American activism represents renewed invigoration and moral clarity or hubris is too early to tell. One thing, however, is certain. Confrontation with Baghdad has the capacity to offer more destabilization, not less. Further attacks against American interests at home and abroad, rather than respite from the threat emanating from the ideological mirror image of a moral crusade, are an unpalatable consequence. Unless significant resources are provided for nation-building in post-conflict Iraq, fear and loathing will lead inexorably to an erosion of the democratic imperative in favour of a security response whose effectiveness cannot be vouchsafed as a consequence. The final enjoining of battle will have long-lasting implications that no amount of war-gaming at the Pentagon or budgetary increase at the new Homeland Security Department can tabulate with certainty.

The external threat is accompanied by a sustained economic downturn. The warped operation of the securities market from the late 1990s onward is a textbook example of what the eminent political scientist Samuel Huntington refers to as the "disharmonic" impulses that underwrite American society. For Huntington, the "gap between promise and performance creates an inherent disharmony, at times latent, at times manifest, in American society."[3] Given the consensual basis of American politics, the key motor of change is moral

---

[2] George Bush Weekly Radio Address, 5 April 2003.
[3] Samuel Huntington, *American Politics, The Promise of Disharmony* (Harvard University Press, London, 1981), p. 12.

outrage at the gap between reality and idealism, or what Huntington refers to as "creedal passion":

> American national identity is in a sense very fragile, threatened not by ethnic separatism but by disillusionment with its political ideals or with the effectiveness of its political institutions. Destroy the political system and you destroy the basis of community, eliminating the nation and, in effect, returning its members – in accordance with the theory on which the nation was founded – back to a state of nature. In other countries, one can abrogate the constitution without abrogating the nation. The United States does not have that choice.[4]

As such, the corporate scandal – centred on an imperfect market that was manifestly unequal – created the circumstances for the Republicans, as guardians of the White House, to be punished for presiding over a dilution of a central element of the American creed:

> Whether or not a consensus on political values contributes to political stability depends on the nature of those values and the relation between them and the political institutions and practices in society ... [T]he core ideals and values of the consensus may provide the basis for challenging the legitimacy of the dominant political institutions and practices. This is precisely the case in the United States, and it is a phenomenon that is a characteristic of politics in the United States as that of no other major society.[5]

Yet, this is precisely what did not happen in the mid-term elections, which saw the Republicans return to power with an increased mandate. The key question is why? First, the President turned the poll into a confidence motion in his own stewardship of the country since the September 11 attacks. Second, the Democrats lacked a unifying national message or credible policy alternative in either domestic or foreign affairs. Third, and most importantly, with both parties contesting the middle ground, neither was prepared to countenance far-reaching policy changes that have the potential to rewrite the rules of political participation in America. Put simply, no

---

[4] Samuel Huntington, *American Politics, The Promise of Disharmony* (Harvard University Press, London, 1981), p. 30.

[5] Ibid., p. 32.

alternative was forthcoming. In the circumstances of war – threat-ened, manufactured or real – the public gave allegiance to a president who promised resolute action in tracking down Osama bin Laden and in jailing those who brought into disrepute American business while maintaining that malfeasance was the exception rather than the norm. Bush may have gained political control, but the threat posed by economic reality has far from passed. Unemployment has out-stripped job creation every month of the Bush administration to date.[6] The societal cost of the tax cut is a yawning budget deficit that can only be meaningfully addressed by further curtailing federal and state programmes. For a third year in a row, the stock market reported losses. In 2002 the major index posted the biggest decline in earnings since 1974. In the same period, a total of $7 trillion has been wiped off the value of the overall market, more than half of it in the capitalization of buoyant technology firms like Cisco Systems and Microsoft. Yet, paradoxically, the underlying system remains surpris-ingly unaffected.

Unlike previous financial meltdowns, the investment banking system has not itself suffered from contagion. This has less to do with increased economies of scale providing a buttress against a run on the banks and more with the fact that sophisticated financial instruments were deployed to successfully pass risk across the entire banking, insurance and pension sectors. The cost of corporate collapse is one that can easily be borne by the investment and commercial banks. Those whose pensions are determined by the value of the stock market have felt the real pain. With the total trade in derivatives now greater than the market capitalization of the entire manufacturing base, the system has taken on the attributes of an enormous hedge fund, with incalculable levels of risk.[7]

---

[6] Unemployment rose by 357,000 in February 2003 and 108,000 in March 2003 according to figures released by the US Labor Department. See Peronet Despeignes, "US economy sheds 108,000 jobs in March", *Financial Times*, 5 April 2003.

[7] Warren Buffet, "Avoiding a mega-catastrophe", *Fortune*, 17 March 2003. The full text of Warren Buffet's annual newsletter is available online at http://www.berkshirehathaway.com/letters/2002.html

The only growth area in the securities market is short-selling, a strategy that has the potential to hasten corporate failure. The manufacturing and telecommunications industries remain bloated by over-investment and overcapacity, highly leveraged and incapable of stimulating demand from an increasingly nervous consumer market. The confluence of personal insecurity, redundancy fears, high levels of repossession and record levels of personal debt that weakens considerably the capacity to survive losing one's job is in fact a more fitting description of the perfect storm metaphor used by corporate America to minimize its own responsibility for the crisis. Across the entire market, price-to-earnings ratios remains stubbornly high, suggesting that American equities are still overly priced. Retrenchment rather than expansion remains the dominant mood on Wall Street.

The technological tool of greatest utility has exposed the hubris of the boom: email. Indiscreet instant communication, stored on hard drives, allowed regulators unparalleled access to the corporate mindset and circumvented the defence taunt to provide the proof. It was the entry point needed by the New York Attorney General's office to build its case. According to the chief investigator Eric Dinallo, "Emails are casual, but intimate. People tend to say what they mean without much consideration or artifice. It is like a water cooler conversation caught on the record. Plus, the context is right there – the back and forth, the attachments, everything."[8] When the evidence was provided in all its dyslexic glory, revealing first major conflicts of interest in Merrill Lynch and spreading outward to the entire analytical framework, the stage was set for a fall from grace of staggering proportions. Spitzer himself shrugs off criticism that the cost of agreeing settlement is the preclusion of jail terms. He argues that a greater victory has been won: the fundamental corporate model has been comprehensively discredited:

> Where were we a year ago? We were in a world where nobody accepted the fundamental premise of our argument – that Wall Street's business model was

---

[8] Quoted in John Cassidy, "The investigation", *The New Yorker*, 7 April, 2003.

rotten. We needed to persuade the policymakers and the investment banks that
the fundamental notion we were articulating was right. We've done that.[9]

With demand sluggish for its services, Wall Street is disgorging the
legions of foot soldiers with a characteristic lack of sentimentality.
Research teams are being decimated by redundancy as the reality of
rising costs and lower utility hit home. As a consequence of the global
settlement, the inability of analysts to act as rainmakers for investment banking and the centrality of their role in the conflicts-of-
interest scandal have made the entire sector an expensive liability
for the financial conglomerates. Even those at the highest echelons,
who have not been implicated in fraudulent activity, are retreating
from the fray. The former head of research at UBS Warburg Dianne
Glossman captured the sense of *fin de siècle* in a resignation letter to
her employers of 25 years. Noting that she wished to fulfil her ambition of an Olympic gold medal for showjumping, Glossman opined,
"it's way more fun when the market is going up, no."[10]

It is not just the analysts who have reasoned that the game has
become much more serious. With merger-and-acquisitions activity
markedly reduced, even those with the aspiration and expectation
to reach the office of CEO are taking stock. The heir apparent of
Goldman Sachs, John Thornton, stunned the market in March by
announcing that he was leaving Wall Street to take up an unpaid
professorial position at Tsinghua University in Beijing.[11] As he
departs for the sweeping willow trees and lawns of China's most
prestigious academic institution, the corporate landscape he leaves
behind is unremittingly bleak.

The pervasive sense of financial gloom is mirrored at state government level, where fiscal meltdown has led to further erosion of an
already frayed safety net. In an ironic twist, the state regulators who
combined to secure a punitive settlement against Philip Morris for

---

[9] Ibid.

[10] Kate Kelly, "Some analysts leave industry in search of 'new adventures'", *Wall
Street Journal*, 28 February 2003. See also Special Report, "The changing world of
analysts", *Financial Times*, 2 April 2003.

[11] Editorial, "Global positioning", *Financial Times*, 26 March 2003.

fraudulently misrepresenting the tar rating of Marlboro Light cigarettes are now seeking to overturn a multibillion dollar bond handed out by a judge in a class action in Illinois. Budgetary restraints have necessitated that the largest company indicted for fraud is kept in operation in order to provide a monetary fix.[12]

The challenge facing George Bush as the nation edged nervously toward the precipice of global insecurity was therefore substantial. How he would use his mandate was a matter of profound importance. Three interlinked conundrums informed policy. Was war with Iraq necessary and, if so, were the risks manageable? Could the United States afford the luxury of sweeping tax cuts when the military demanded substantial, unbudgeted increases to its war chest in order to prosecute a war with questionable international legitimacy and no definable exit strategy? And, third, what strategy should be adopted to ensure economic growth?

How the White House answered those questions provided a route map to the 2004 election. The journey began deep in the American heartland. On 7 January 2003, as the 108th Congress was being sworn in, George W. Bush travelled to Chicago to deliver the first major campaign speech of that campaign. The speech was an attempt to justify twin ideological pursuits that have informed his presidency, confrontation with Saddam Hussein and further retraction of federal oversight. Neither war nor scandal on Wall Street would deflect a born-again president on an evangelical mission to sell preordained truth:

> Government spends a lot of money, but it doesn't build factories. It doesn't invest in companies or do the work that makes the economy go. The role of government is not to manage or control the economy from Washington, D.C., but to remove obstacles standing in the way for faster economic growth. That's our role. And those obstacles are clear. Many jobs are lost in America because government imposes unreasonable regulations, and many jobs are lost because the lawsuit culture of this country imposes unreasonable cost. I will continue to press for legal and regulatory reform.

---

[12] Editorial, "Addicted to tobacco", *Wall Street Journal*, 4 April 2003. For the Illinois ruling see Vanessa O'Connell, "Illinois judge orders Philip Morris to pay $10.1 billion in damages", *Wall Street Journal*, 24 March 2003.

Having established the political battleground, the President then announced the details of a further $674bn economic stimulus plan – designed to accelerate the introduction of already agreed income tax reductions. At its centre is a politically controversial, and economically suspect, plan to end double taxation on stock dividends. According to Bush, "Americans carry a heavy burden of taxes and debt that could slow consumer spending. I'm troubled by that. I'm also troubled by the fact that our tax system unfairly penalizes some productive investments."

As political theatre, designed to target key constituencies in the impending election cycle, the package announced and the rhetorical flourishes used demonstrated the acuity of the presidential barometer. The President noted that half of adult Americans now own stock. The importance of this constituency is heightened by the fact that two-thirds of those who actually vote come from within its ranks and the pivotal subgroup within it is the retired.

Bush told his audience, "double taxation is bad for our economy. Double taxation is wrong. Double taxation falls especially hard on retired people. About half of all dividend income goes to America's seniors, and they often rely on those checks for a steady source of income in their retirement. It's fair to tax a company's profits. It's not fair to double tax by taxing the shareholder on the same profits. So, today, for the good of our senior citizens and to support capital formation across the land, I'm asking the United States Congress to abolish the double taxation of dividends."

The debate was framed the following day by the twin pillars of American journalism, the diametric opposition symptomatic of the incommensurability between new finance theory and its critics. As a package to kick-start the economy, the *New York Times* was scathing about the presidential programme, describing it as "a cynical grab bag [lucky dip] of unrelated and mislabelled policies that would disproportionately benefit the wealthiest."[13] By way of contrast the *Wall Street Journal* was positively ecstatic, if a little bombastic:

---

[13] Editorial, "The wrong stimulant", *New York Times*, 8 January 2003.

We were hoping for a big and bold tax cut from President Bush and, by George, we got one. Yesterday Mr. Bush drew a bead on [took aim at] the twin shibboleths of bad tax policy – the fear of budget deficits and of benefiting middle- and upper-income workers – and pulled the trigger. ... Mr. Bush is offering, on balance, an excellent program to prevent the economy from weakening amid the short-term uncertainties of war and expensive oil. And by wringing out some of the tax barriers to economic efficiency, he is also creating the conditions for better long-term growth. A bull's-eye, for sure.[14]

Economists remain divided as to whether the change would directly impact on either job creation or enhanced payments to the retired community. First, enhanced dividend payments tend to come from mature companies on the bourse – particularly utilities, telecommunications and the banking sector – none of which has a track record in investing in new jobs, a core stated rationale. Nor, after binging on cheap credit during the boom and faced with oversupply and suppressed demand that even interest-free credit cannot shift, are they in a position to do so.[15]

At the other end of the spectrum, 30% of companies on the Standard & Poor 500 index do not pay dividends, preferring instead to reinvest surplus cash in the business, pushing up the stock price and adding substantially to the agency problems that have informed corporate governance debates. Most of these are the technology companies like Microsoft and Oracle, who have substantial cash reserves, but no incentive to turn wealth over to shareholders because of a fear that it could curtail investment opportunities or weaken managerial control.

The debate over the dividend encapsulates some of the arguments that centre on how companies are actually valued. Precisely because earnings per share rather than dividend yield is the main determinant of stock value in the United States market, companies tend to use

---

[14] Editorial, "Bush's big bang", *Wall Street Journal*, 8 January 2003. For a critique see William Gale and Peter Orszag, "America cannot afford a huge deficit", *Financial Times*, 5 February 2003.

[15] See Joseph Stiglitz, "Bush's tax plan – the dangers", *New York Review of Books*, 13 March 2003.

spare capital to buy back stock to buttress the earnings value of the remaining reduced number of shares available to the market.[16]

The planned reduction in dividend tax would have no impact on the majority of small investors, who already are excused the federal levy on dividend payments through their preponderant use of the stock market to fund individual retirement schemes. Large parts of the institutional market are also excused owing to charitable status. Likewise foreign institutional investors will not benefit from any low-ering of the tax liability, as any gains will have to be balanced against tax liability in their domicile. The conservative writer Christopher Caldwell noted the irony of the proposal when he wrote, "Mr Bush has offered the tiniest side dish of middle class aid alongside a Lucullan feast of upper bracket tax relief, and the public is saying: Yum."[17] Initial estimates by the Tax Policy Center in Washington, DC suggest that "54.8% of the new proposed tax cuts would go to the 10% of US taxpayers with incomes over $100,000."[18]

Behind the tax measures, one industry and one industry alone stood to benefit the most: those involved in the trading of equities. By providing the illusion, but not the substance, of equitable tax benefits, the proposal could also be read as a somewhat crude attempt to lure investors back to the market. Stocks rallied on the news of the plan, but quickly slipped back, as the likely impact of the stimulus plan in real terms weakened. Retreating to the argument that the aim of the plan was to help provide retirement income was classic dissembling.

---

[16] See Richard Waters and Gary Silverman, "Shareholders 'unlikely to benefit quickly' from dividend tax move", *Financial Times*, 8 January 2003. For analysis of the wider impact of the stimulus plan see Peronet Despeignes, "Bush plan fuels debate on impact of stimulus", *Financial Times*, 8 January 2003; Jonathan Fuerbringer, "Wall Street finds it likes much of Bush proposal", *New York Times*, 8 January 2003; Bob Davis and Greg Ip, "Bush stimulus package needs many assumptions to pan out", *Wall Street Journal*, 8 January 2003. For a more considered treatment see Joseph Stiglitz, "Bush's tax plan – the dangers", *New York Review of Books*, 13 March 2003.

[17] Christopher Caldwell, "Bush's tax cut is unconservative", *Financial Times*, 8 January 2003.

[18] Cited in Bob Davis and Greg Ip, "Bush stimulus package needs many assumptions to pan out", *Wall Street Journal*, 8 January 2003.

As Gerard Baker, one of the best informed British commentators on America, fumed in the *Financial Times*, "Looking at the condition of the US economy today, there is no way on earth you could honestly argue that, with fiscal resources already dwindling, the priority is to eliminate a tax paid disproportionately by the wealthiest Americans on their long-term investments. And, knowing that this is the case, administration officials are twisting themselves into verbal knots to avoid telling the truth about the proposal. They have resorted to the splendid claim that this is all about helping poor pensioners."[19]

The decision by Congress on 11 April 2003 to reduce the size of the planned reduction to $350m has rendered it unlikely that the plan will be introduced in this fiscal year unless the President exercises his veto. Four days later, with the Pentagon claiming the war was over and key administration officials warning Syria that it was exhibiting rogue state tendencies, George Bush appeared to link domestic and economic arguments for the foreseeable future. He demanded at least $550m in tax cuts and emphasized the need for the United States to keep up its guard. The row over the plan's utility will doubtless continue, but what has been exceptionally enlightening, however, is the light shone on the nature of governance in the United States. In particular, it afforded an acute insight into the extraordinary lengths to which the administration has cosseted the financial services industry – both in terms of providing a stimulus and offering a critique against the voracious appetite of the tort lawyers who, in the light of the global settlement on Wall Street, see rich pickings in the exposed carcass of corporate America.

Throughout the crisis in the financial markets, the constant refrain was that greater regulation would stultify growth and place unnecessary burdens on growth creation, contrasting the heavy hand of regulation with the dynamic and flexible approach offered by self-policing models. Yet, such an emphasis relies on the operation of trust, a commodity that remains in short supply. Colin Scott has

---

[19] Gerard Baker, "The White House strays from the truth", *Financial Times*, 9 January 2003.

argued persuasively that "trust in mechanisms of accountability is a central precondition for the legitimate delegation of authority."[20]

Quantifying the risk of continued subservience to an unreformed systemic problem, in political terms, is exceptionally difficult. Major policy concerns the efficacy of the trading model in providing the foundations for economic growth.[21] This is a far-from-academic conundrum, not least in terms of tax revenue forfeited, because of tax avoidance schemes that all too regularly segue into tax evasion with the complicity of the major actors in corporate America, who have taken advantage of tax shelters and foreign domiciles with a degree of verve only matched by their public displays of patriotism. While it is natural for corporations to do everything in their power to ensure that tax liability is minimized, the societal cost of defending that right in terms of lost revenue is enormous.

The investigation by the New York District Attorney Robert Morgenthau into Tyco has been instrumental in placing the issue of corporate domicile onto the political agenda. It is a development that has been a long time coming, according to the 83-year-old veteran white-collar crime prosecutor. "One of the things I've been concerned about for years is the use of offshore domains, not only to avoid taxes but also to avoid regulation. A lot of people, including the SEC [Securities and Exchange Commission] and IRS [Internal Revenue Service], have looked the other way. If I've only accomplished one thing in the Tyco case, I've gotten the press to say, 'nominally head-quartered in Bermuda' instead of 'headquartered in Bermuda'."[22]

The decision to further reduce taxation to promote growth when evasion on such a scale is commonplace in corporate America represents a stunning conceit. As John Plender concludes, "the most subversive threat to the power of the nation state appears to come from

[20] Colin Scott, "Accountability in the regulatory state", *Journal of Law and Society*, Vol. 27, No. 1, March 2000, p. 39.

[21] John Plender, *Going off the Rails* (John Wiley & Sons, Chichester, UK, 2003), p. 174.

[22] *BusinessWeek*, 23 December 2002. Full text available at http://www.businessweek.com/magazine/content/02_51/b3813011.htm

the financial community ... Financial engineering with derivatives can be thoroughly subversive without being illegal. Because of its opacity, we have no means of assessing the extent of the subversion."[23]

Squaring the circle between ensuring the conditions for responsible entrepreneurial risk taking, while ensuring that the market is conducted within ethical and equitable constraints, is the primary function of regulation. The central issue is how that regulation is achieved. While much of the academic literature focuses on the effectiveness of governance as a means to expand the influence of civil society over policy development, it is also the case that the power of various nodes in the network to effect policy change can have disproportionate influence, leading to fundamental distortion of the deliberative process. The complex nature of contemporary society and the power of contingency to shape outcomes necessitate the development of equally sophisticated models to assess what is actually entailed when one speaks of governance.[24]

In this context, Morison is undoubtedly correct to argue that governance involves the "complex relationships at regional, national and global levels and across political institutions, agencies, networks and associations in the economy and in civil society at each level."[25]

---

[23] John Plender, *Going off the Rails* (Wiley, Chichester, UK, 2003), p. 179.

[24] See Rod Rhodes, "The new governance: Governing without government", *Political Studies*, No. XLIV, pp. 652–67. Rhodes argues that governance signifies a change in the meaning of government, referring to a new process of governing, or a changed condition of ordered rule, or the new method by which society is governed (pp. 652–3).

[25] John Morison, "The government–voluntary sector compacts: Governance, governmentality and civil society", *Journal of Law and Society*, Vol. 27, No. 1, March 2000, p. 99. Citing the French theorist Michel Foucault, Morison argues that power is essentially transmitted through the active subjection of citizens through a socialization process. Thus "governmentality" for Morison centres on Foucault's definition: "the ensemble formed by the institutions, procedures, analyses and reflections, the calculations and tactics that allow the exercise of this very specific albeit complex form of power, which has its target population, as its principle form of knowledge political economy, and as its essential technical means apparatuses of security" (p. 120). This socialization delineates the realms of acceptable debate and obfuscates the core problem. In this model, choice is not free choice but the availability of options based on myriad constraints.

The crucial point to consider is that the shift to governance does not, necessarily, in itself lead to a normative improvement in the quality of policy-making. An increase in partnership, co-operation and participation in development of policy on grounds of ensuring the development of appropriate rules and regulations may, in fact, disguise special-interest-group pleading. Given the ability of corporations to exercise capital flight should the heavy hand of regulation occur – both in changing corporate domicile and ending or curtailing legislative spending – government action is reduced to developing a voluntary compact that, in turn, is centred on narrow definitions of what corporate governance actually entails.[26]

If, as Meehan argues, "governance turns the state from being the central, dominating source of society within a defined territory to being an activator or coordinator in the negotiation of positions which suit a multitude of actors on specific topics over a territory where borders are less obviously fixed," the global implications in the aftermath of the American corporate scandal are enormous.[27] This is particularly the case in circumstances were there is a weak party structure, a distrust of government in the first place and a revolving door between public office and private industry.[28] It is precisely because the connections between the legislative, regulatory and business elites are interchangeable and long-standing that makes the issue of directing and controlling corporate America so intractable

---

[26] See Gary Wilson, "Business, state, and community: Responsible risk takers, New Labour and the governance of corporate business", *Journal of Law and Society*, Vol. 27, No. 1, March 2000, p. 163.

[27] Elizabeth Meehan, "From government to governance: Civic participation and 'new politics'; the context of potential opportunities for the better representation of women", *European Consortium for Political Research Joint Sessions of Workshops*, *Edinburgh 2003*.

[28] See "The Clinton top 100: Where are they now?", Center for Public Integrity, Washington, DC. Full text available online at http://www.statesecrets.org/ More than 50% of senior Clinton officials went on to work for corporations and sectors they were responsible for regulating while in office – most notably, Robert Rubin who moved to Citigroup and was briefly embroiled in the Enron scandal.

a problem to resolve.[29] Special interests have already framed the debate both in terms of economic, military and foreign policy. The price paid is the soul of the republic.

For the newly appointed Chairman of the Securities and Exchange Commission (SEC) William Donaldson, "inattention to good corporate governance structures over the past decade or so is at the heart of what has gone so terribly wrong in corporate America in the past few years."[30] Donaldson cites a predictable litany of complaints: excessive executive compensation, an inordinate short-term emphasis on meeting market expectations to justify those salaries and the crowning of the CEO as "monarch rather than a manager" as key contributing factors in the capital markets crisis. He argued that the crisis has demonstrated the need to place "primary responsibility for the guardianship of corporate governance practices with the board of directors and must not be diluted by the power of the chief executive." This checklist of corporate failure also informs the analysis provided by the Conference Board Commission on Public Trust and Private Enterprise.

The Conference Board argued that long-term strategies for promoting growth rather than tactical playing of the stock market were vital, the responsibility for which it places on the board of directors. This can only be achieved by major structural reform. "Only a strong, diligent board, with a substantial majority of independent directors, that both understands the key issues and asks management the tough questions is capable of ensuring that shareowner interests are properly served."[31] Board failure has magnified the Commission's view that "managing for short-term earnings and stock price results has led to

---

[29] See Amanda Sloat, "Governance: Contested perceptions of civic participation", *Scottish Affairs*, Spring 2002, p. 39.

[30] See William Donaldson, "Remarks at the 2003 Washington Economic Policy Conference", 24 March 2003. Full text available at http://www.sec.gov/news/speeches.html

[31] *The Conference Board Commission on Public Trust and Private Enterprise*, 9 January 2003, p. 16. This formulation goes further than that endorsed by the New York Stock Exchange proposals on corporate governance, which maintained that a simple majority of independent directors would suffice.

many of the behaviours and manipulations."[32] The Commission limited its radicalism to calling for a shift in shareholder culture toward long-term holding of stock. The SEC Chairman, a consummate Wall Street insider, also made it clear that the pressure to meet market expectations had roots beyond individual executives:

> Corporate America developed a short-term focus, fuelled by an obsession with quarter-to-quarter earnings and the pervasive temptation inherent in stock options. The game of earnings projections, and analysts who focused on achieving self-forecasted results (or a firm's failure to achieve those results) created an atmosphere in which "hitting the numbers" became the objective, rather than sound long-term strength and performance.

Noting the need for seismic change, Donaldson concluded that the gatekeepers of the system – lawyers, accountants, auditors, investment – "must redefine corporate governance with practices that go beyond mere adherence to new rules and demonstrate ethics, integrity, honesty, and transparency." For the new Chairman of the SEC therefore there is a responsibility to inculcate a new culture that transforms "the DNA of the corporate body itself." The key question is whether that is possible to achieve without using the stick of credible enforcement. Continuing the genetic metaphor, initial clinical trials suggest at best inconclusive results.

Nowhere was this more forcefully demonstrated than during the short-lived campaign by the New York Stock Exchange (NYSE) to ensure the rehabilitation of Sandy Weill, the CEO of Citigroup. The board of the NYSE recommended the appointment of Weill as a director representing the investing public, a move that would see the executive joining the Chairman of JP Morgan Chase on the board. Spitzer reacted with apoplexy.

> To put Sandy Weill on the board of the exchange as the public's representative is a gross misjudgement and a violation of trust. He is the chairman of the company that is paying perhaps the largest fine in history for perpetrating one of

---

[32] Ibid., p. 17.

the biggest frauds on the investing public. For him to be proposed as the voice of the public interest is an outrage."[33]

Aware of the public relations disaster unfolding, the Citigroup Chairman wisely decided to withdraw his name from the nomination process. Leon Panetta, a former White House Chief of Staff and a member of the NYSE executive board, broke collective silence to voice his unease at the nomination process. "[It] was pretty much operating by the standards they had for a long time and felt anyone who was an experienced C.E.O. can serve on the board representing the public interest. But we are at a different time. The last two years have changed the way we have to think about these positions."[34] The row over Weill's short-lived candidacy represented another victory for the Attorney General, but, in criticizing the decision by the NYSE nominating committee, Spitzer has taken an enormous political gamble. In effectively vetoing the nomination – and suggesting possible alternatives – he drew attention to the questionable judgement exercised by the NYSE in putting forward Weill for such a sensitive post at such a sensitive time.

Not only was the choice of Weill injudicious it also served to highlight how seriously the board in relation to its own membership was taking the substance of corporate governance reforms, a charge that suggested the collegiality of old retaining its potency.[35] The charge was all the more difficult to refute given the fact that one of the three positions available was vacated by Martha Stewart, the cuisine entrepreneur who was forced to resign over allegations that she had benefited from insider-trading while an NYSE director.[36] Nominating Weill was regarded as another attempt to rehabilitate

---

[33] Quoted in Patrick McGeehan, "Spitzer says he will fight Weill's NYSE nomination", New York Times, 24 March 2003.

[34] Patrick McGeehan and Jonathan Fuerbringer, "NYSE urged to reform process", New York Times, 25 March 2003.

[35] See Charles Gasparino and Randall Smith, "Behind almost-directorship of Citigroup CEO and NYSE", Wall Street Journal, 25 March 2003.

[36] For an excellent overview of the Stewart fiasco see Jeffrey Toobin, "Lunch at Martha's", New Yorker, 3 February 2003.

the banking colossus, a process that had already begun with lavish celebrations for his 70th birthday the previous week.[37]

While William Donaldson's appeal for a DNA transfusion is laudable, on the evidence that has unfolded since Enron's collapse the prognosis is bleak. Without paradigmatic change the corruption endemic within the American social, political and economic model will continue to incubate, destroying its legitimacy from within: the alleged hubris in American foreign policy accompanied by its domestic equivalent. In this context it has become irrelevant who controls the White House. The operation of power in the United States is so complex and contingent on trust networks capable of asset delivery in terms of contributions or private sector employment in the future that proving individual malfeasance is a difficult, if not impossible task.[38] It is therefore imperative that the analysis maps the connections to see how policy is enacted in order to ascertain how influence is peddled.[39]

This issue came to the fore with the resignation of Richard Perle from the chairmanship of the Defense Advisory Board after a devastating exposé of his business dealings in *The New Yorker* just before the war began.[40] The article claimed that Perle stood to gain financially from the outbreak of hostilities through his links to a venture capital company. Publicly available information states that the company Trireme specializes in technology investment for the secur-

---

[37] At the SEC's request, the NYSE agreed to revisit its own corporate governance procedures. It nominated William McDonough, the formidable Chairman of the Federal Reserve Bank of New York, to take Weill's place as the representative for public investors. He did not take up the position. McDonough was subsequently appointed Chairman of the Public Company Accounting Oversight Board on 15 April, where he will monitor the accounting profession as part of the new regulatory regime mandated by Sarbanes–Oxley. It was Harvey Pitt's injudicious choice of former CIA director William Webster to run the board that prompted his resignation from the chairmanship of the SEC in November 2002.

[38] See Dean McSweeney, "Parties, corruption and campaign finance in America", in Robert Williams (ed.), *Party Finance and Political Corruption* (Macmillan, Basingstoke, UK, 2000), pp. 37–60.

[39] See David Nelken and Michael Levi, "The corruption of politics and the politics of corruption", *Journal of Law and Society*, Vol. 23, No. 1, March 1996, pp. 1–17.

[40] Seymour Hersh, "Lunch with the chairman", *The New Yorker*, 17 March 2003.

ity and defence sectors. According to the *New Yorker*, Trireme made significant play of its connections to the administration in a letter sent to the Saudi arms dealer Adnan Khashoggi. "Three of Trireme's Management Group members currently advise the U.S. Secretary of Defense by serving on the U.S. Defense Policy Board, and one of Trireme's principals, Richard Perle, is chairman of that Board.[41] Perle launched a spirited defence in the *Wall Street Journal*, claiming he resigned because it was an unwelcome distraction to Donald Rumsfeld in the prosecution of the war:

> It is only natural that an intellectually curious cabinet officer will reach out to peers who have occupied similar positions, in the hope that their experience will help avoid mistakes or point the way to new ideas. When he does so, he must have confidence that the advice he receives is candid, that it is the product of serious deliberation, that it is free from advocacy reflecting private interests. The relationship between official and advisor is ultimately one of trust.[42]

An analysis of the business interests of the Defense Advisory Board carried out by the Washington-based Center for Public Integrity found that "of the 30 members of the Defense Policy Board, the government-appointed group that advises the Pentagon, at least nine have ties to companies that have won more than $76 billion in defence contracts in 2001 and 2002."[43] The question marks over how lucrative defence contracts are won have been intensified as a consequence of the Iraqi offensive.[44] It is this ability to network that creates the biggest single crisis of legitimacy facing American democracy: the perception, and in some cases the reality, of interest groups dictating policy. In the Perle case, his resignation was in reality little more than a charade. With battle enjoined, his political policy had been ensorsed, a development that guaranteed the success of his economic interests.

---

[41] Ibid, p. 76.

[42] Richard Perle, "For the record", *Wall Street Journal*, 31 March 2003.

[43] See "Advisors of influence", Center for Public Integrity, Washington, DC. Full text available at http://www.statesecrets.org/

[44] See Neil King, "USAID defends secret bids for rebuilding postwar Iraq", *Wall Street Journal*, 2 April 2003.

The biggest, single, clear and present danger comes not from without, but from within: the operation of the securities market. As Frank Partnoy, a former investment banker and now professor of law at the University of California at San Diego, has pointed out: investors remain "oblivious to the fact that they have dodged, not a bullet, but a nuclear meltdown. The truth is that the markets have been, and are, spinning out of control."[45]

The provision of a reassuring balm from government, encouraging people that it is now safe to re-enter the market, has been accompanied by a slew of conservative writing that places the blame for the bubble on the naivety and greed of the individual investor. In a robust defence of the integrity of the system, Holman Jenkins argued recently in the influential journal *Policy Review* that "in a classic fashion, investors encountered the enemy and it was … themselves … the mere existence of investors who are mad because they lost money is hardly an indictment of capitalism. Losers are an unavoidable consequence of the system that has made the country rich."[46]

Jenkins is correct in highlighting that the crisis in the markets does not comply with media stereotype. He notes with satisfaction that

---

[45] Frank Partnoy, *Infectious Greed, How Deceit and Risk Corrupted the Financial Markets* (London, 2003), p. 2. For Partnoy, three pillars of control were absent. Financial engineering made nonsense of stated accounts, managers exercised unbridled control over companies and, third, the regulators rarely punished offenders. He is scathing about the effectiveness of Sarbanes–Oxley to combat the systemic risk. In a vivid metaphor, he compares the markets with "Swiss cheese, with the holes – the unregulated places – getting bigger every year, as parties transacting around legal rules eat away at the regulatory system from within" (p. 394).

[46] See Holman W. Jenkins, "The new economy's sore losers", *Policy Review*, April–May 2003. Jenkins is relatively sanguine about the consequences of the malfeasance, arguing that what "the high risk economy giveth it taketh away." He accepts however that the explosion of executive compensation exacerbated the crisis. "Options are indeed a powerful form of behaviour modification, making the stock price a central consideration in every decision a CEO makes. In this way, the rise of stock-based compensation has been an important force in pushing companies to be more risk-taking to meet the risk appetite of public investors." Thus the downward spiral begins. Betting on a visionary CEO can solve a corporate governance problem by ensuring the delivery of profits, hence the justification of Steve Jobs option package for 2001, which included $870m in stock and a Gulfstream jet.

Ken Lay of Enron, Bernie Ebbers of WorldCom and Dennis Kozlowski of Tyco represent "cases of classic myopia complicated by personal neuroticism, in which executives managed to fool themselves about the wisdom and propriety of their action until it blew up in their faces." Yet his defence of the continued use of options is more questionable. Option payments are defended on the basis of encouraging innovation, with failure represented as the cost of capitalism. Yet, as resilient a defender of the markets as Jenkins does accept, however, that the agency problems associated by the elevation of the CEO through option payments pose systemic problems that have been studiously ignored by Washington.

When companies are valued on subjective assessments of future growth opportunities, the temptation to meet those remains high. The consequence is an emphasis on short-term betting on the "number", leading to the prevalence of short-term casino capitalism, which in turn plays havoc with economic fundamentals. It was a point underscored by the Chairman of the Federal Reserve Alan Greenspan in evidence to the Senate Finance Committee on 16 July 2002: "It is not that humans have become any more greedy than in generations past. It is that the avenues to express greed have grown so enormously."

It is a point belatedly understood by the legal community. Practitioners and scholars attending a recent conference in Paris entitled *The Awakening Giant of Anti-Corruption Enforcement* heard presentations on the need for effective compliance to ensure that reputational risk was minimized. Tellingly, however, the only reference to the responsibility of the legal profession to the problems associated with private or private-to-public corruption came in the closing comments of Homer Moyes, a leading corporate lawyer based in Washington, DC. The legal community has already ensured the rolling back of proposals for corporate attorneys to "noisily withdraw" by notifying the SEC of their concerns should they become aware of material violations of US laws.

It is the wider failure to deal with these systemic failures that makes the internal corporate governance structures mandated by Sarbanes–

Oxley at best tangential, at worst irrelevant. The continued aversion
to the stock market is predicated primarily on a suspicion that the
markets remain unreformed. The argument that equities remained
artificially depressed primarily because of geopolitical concern was
falsified when, after the fall of Baghdad, the collective response to
victory was apathy. The mood is defined by a continued belief that the
numbers cannot be trusted. Allied to this is continued scepticism that
the new legislation on corporate responsibility will have a demon-
strable impact on dealing with white-collar fraud.

The announcement in March 2003 by HealthSouth that its financial statements could no longer be relied on indicates the difficulties
inherent in a system where meeting Wall Street's expectations
remains the primary driver of corporate strategy. HealthSouth's
ignominious departure from NYSE listing is even more troubling
when one considers that the strict rules regarding disclosure and
harsh penalties for malefaction built into Sarbanes–Oxley were trumpeted as measures that provided a final solution to the vexed question
of corporate malfeasance.

The fiasco over HealthSouth can be read in two ways. On the one
hand, it indicated that regulatory bodies are determined to crack
down on crime and are using the legislation proactively in order to
prosecute white-collar crime. It is undoubtedly the case that prosecutions in real time are a policy imperative for the regulators. So, too, is
manipulation of the fear of imprisonment in order to break the resolve
of those who sign off on fraud. In a statement, the Chairman of the
SEC William Donaldson argued that "tougher criminal sanctions
make it much more likely that midlevel executives are going to
come in rather than take a chance on a long prison term."[47] On
the other hand, the fact that HealthSouth engaged in the fraud in
the first place and attempted to cover its tracks by certifying the
accounts indicates the temptation to meet the numbers remain undiminished. It also suggests that the calculation of detection *vis-à-vis*

---

[47] Ann Carrns, "HealthSouth case unveils 'shock and awe strategy'", *Wall Street
Journal*, 4 April 2003.

profit is still heavily calibrated in favour of corruption despite the reputational risk.[48]

Richard Scrushy, the flamboyant chairman, received more than $170m in stock option in the period of the claim. At the time of writing, Scrushy maintains his innocence, via pleading the Fifth Amendment. He is contesting all charges, despite guilty pleas for fraudulent behaviour entered by nine senior executives at the company, including the CFO and two senior vice-presidents.[49] Scrushy, who started work as a hospital janitor, developed a Fortune 500 company from scratch. In the process he transformed the landscape of Birmingham, Alabama from corporate backwater into a mirror reflecting his largesse. He sponsored the local baseball teams, bought corporate boxes at premier sporting events and spent prodigiously on educational endowments. His medical empire sprawled across 1,700 different operations. John Moscow, Deputy Chief of Investigations at the New York District Attorney's Office and one of the most experienced prosecutors on Wall Street, is convinced that HealthSouth could have – and should have – been exposed much earlier:

> I was down in Birmingham fourteen months ago and I saw all these new buildings and all these new constructions. I have to tell you that I was busy. I have too many cases to handle and I don't have the manpower to handle them all. If I had I would have gone after this one. Why? Here was a man who found the power to make gold out of lead. He was in the field of healthcare, a field of very smart people who have given a lot of thought to making money. There is a

---

[48] The most concise equation for describing the circumstances in which corruption thrives is that coined by Robert Klitgaard. For Klitgaard it is represented as an equation "$C = M + D - A$. Corruption equals monopoly plus discretion minus accountability." See Robert Klitgaard, "Cleaning up and invigorating the civil service", *Public Administration and Development*, Vol. 17, pp. 500–1. There is much truth in Klitgaard's pithy aside "corruption is a crime of calculation not passion" (p. 501).

[49] The SEC filed charges against Scrushy on 3 April 2003, alleging that he illegally profited to the value of $170m by trading on non-disclosed, price-sensitive information about the true state of HealthSouth's financial affairs. For details see Lisa Fingeret Roth, "SEC files charges against Scrushy", *Financial Times*, 5 April 2003.

lot of money there, the question is how to make a profit. People have calculated
seventy-five different ways of doing it – nursing schedules, this kind of provision
and that kind of provision. It was a low margin industry, high costs. You can do
better in areas with cheap real estate, cheap labour. But even so, there is a limit
to how much profit you can make from operations. But when you see one person
in a low yield business making huge profits the real question which should arise
is how is he doing it. In the era where the emperor was wearing no clothes, that
was considered bad taste.[50]

Partial extracts of transcripts played to the court pointed to an
attempt to rectify past fraud by engaging in a new one: improperly
adjusting future earnings downward to dampen the expectations of
Wall Street.[51] The former CFO, William Owens wore an FBI wire to
incriminate Scrushy in the web of deceit. The conversation turned on
Owens informing the now disgraced former CEO that his wife is
concerned he would end up in jail if he continued falsifying records:

Scrushy: I mean, hell yeah, I mean I can't sleep. . . . [inaudible] . . .
My wife is out of town. I got my little babies. I got my
little boy. I got a ballgame I got to go to. I got . . . you
know, I'm sitting here watching him play ball and I'm
thinking, hell, you know? Look at, look at, look at
we're, everything . . . I mean, look at all these people.
Look at . . . And do you know the reality is. Look at
how profitable this company is. Do we really want to
trash all this?

Owens: No.

Scrushy: Or do we want a chance to try and get on the other side of
it.

Owens: Oh, I agree.

Scrushy: [He lowers his voice]. You got accountants signing off on
all this. You've got everything set up. You can get . . .
You're smart, Bill. You can . . . If you can . . . But you

---

[50] Interview with John Moscow, New York City, 9 April 2003.

[51] For a concise precis of the HealthSouth fiasco see Adrian Michaels, Lisa Fingeret
Roth and Betty Liu, "Diagnosis of fraud", *Financial Times*, 15 April 2003.

got to lead your troops ... I mean I, I'll do whatever you want to. But I mean, I think that, I think that if you ... You ought to go down fighting, Bill. At least you ought to go down fighting ... Let me tell you why: I am convinced that there are 8,000 companies out there right now that got ... on their balance sheet.

Owens: Think so?

Scrushy: Hell yeah. ... Everyone I know. Everybody ... you know that.[52]

The fall of HealthSouth also turns attention back to the role played by outside advisors, most notably the auditors, KPMG, and the investment banking community. Unsurprisingly, the most bullish cheerleader for HealthSouth throughout its expansionary phase was Howard Capek of UBS Warburg, the corporation's principal investment banker.[53] It remains to be seen whether UBS will face further investigation or the statute of limitations will be invoked as a consequence of the global settlement.

That the changes occasioned by the wave of scandal have therefore proved incapable of eradicating the malaise in the system itself suggests the need not just for stiff penalties but for a paradigmatic shift in the power ceded to Wall Street as the intellectual progenitor of growth in the first instance. Encouraging development through financialization has done much to incubate the virus: an economic stimulus package based on a reliance on financial trading risks, therefore hothousing the virus and encouraging the short-term casino investment that fuelled the greed in the first place.

---

[52] SEC transcript quoted in "Do we really want to trash all this", *Wall Street Journal*, 12 April 2003.

[53] Ken Brown and Robert Frank, "Analyst's bullishness on stock of HealthSouth didn't waver", *Wall Street Journal*, 4 April 2003. Data from Thomson Financial, quoted in the story, revealed that UBS received $7m in commission from $2bn in underwriting deals. While there is no suggestion that Capek was in any way guilty of keeping his rating high for investment banking purposes, it is at the very least acutely embarrassing for the firm.

This strategic failing is obfuscated by the tactical success in expediting charges against HealthSouth executives and the apparent rise in the efficacy of joint SEC and federal investigations. HealthSouth like all the others before it are merely symptoms of a lack of ethical restraint. Christine Bruenn of the North American Securities Administrators Association in an interview with the *New York Times* underlined the extent of the problem facing investigators. "My sense among regulators and prosecutors is that we're all rather surprised as to how much fraud is out there."[54] The recurring emphasis on corrupted individuals misdiagnoses, therefore, a much more fundamental problem. The fascination with meeting the Wall Street number may provide the context for economic crime and the option payments the potential reward, but the opportunity is enhanced dramatically by a culture that elevates the primacy of technical compliance with the law rather than principled corporate governance. Unless the balance is reversed, any attempt to clean up corporations or Wall Street itself is likely to fail, according to Mark Ellias, a leading political lawyer in Washington:

> In Britain when you had mad cow disease, you killed the cows. In the United States our response would be to regulate the cows. It is a quintessentially American thing to do. One of the reasons why the system is so politically resilient, regardless of the crisis, is because there is a fundamental belief that if we just tinker with the way in which the law regulates the activity that has proved to be problematic that the matter will be solved.

In an interview with *BusinessWeek*, Robert Morgenthau, the influential District Attorney for New York, suggested this latest outbreak in corporate fraud was more dangerous and more disturbing than previous waves of scandal. "I think what we're seeing now is that the system of corporate governance, of checks and balances, has really broken down. In the past, you had a guy acting largely on his own. Now, you've got a lot of people involved, and that's the lawyers, accountants, executives, the board of directors. The kindest thing

---

[54] Alex Berenson, "A US push on accounting fraud", *New York Times*, 9 April 2003.

you can say is they have all been asleep at the wheel. Regulators have to take some of the blame for not analyzing what's going on. The whole system seems to have broken down."[55]

On 28 April 2003 the long-delayed global settlement was announced in a blaze of publicity at the SEC headquarters in Washington, DC. Each regulator spoke of the lessons of history. The Chairman of the SEC, William Donaldson, set the tone. He gave an at-times emotional account of how the securities industry and the intermediary gatekeepers had signally failed to protect the integrity of the market. He recalled that he first made his name in research:

> For that reason I speak very personally when I say that I am profoundly saddened and angry about the conduct that is alleged in our complaints. There is absolutely no place for it in our markets and it cannot be tolerated ... We have no choice but to conclude that the research system was broken. These cases reflect a very sad chapter in the history of American business – a chapter in which those who reaped enormous benefits based on the trust of investors profoundly betrayed that trust.[56]

All the rancour of the past 12 months was set aside as each regulator took it in turn to acclaim the integrity of the other. Richard Grasso, the Chairman of the NYSE, and Eliot Spitzer pointedly referred to each other as "my great friend." It was an indication that the earlier spate over the nomination of Weill would not deflect from what the New York Attorney General referred to as "an inflective moment for America." An opportunity existed, he maintained, to restore order to the market. What they were attempting was to rewrite the fundamental rules of the game, an enterprise he compared to the legendary attempts by Teddy Roosevelt to reform Wall Street a century before. With Spitzer basking in the reflected glory of the moment, the choice of role model was indicative of the shrewd politician's wider aspirations. Spitzer spoke about past slights and organized opposition,

---

[55] *BusinessWeek*, 23 December 2002. Full text available at http://www.busi nessweek.com/magazine/content/02_51/b3813011.htm
[56] William Donaldson, Press Conference, SEC Headquarters, Washington, DC, 28 April 2003. Full text available at www.sec.gov

similar obstacles that temporarily obstructed his predecessor on the path to create a just society by allowing fairer access to the American dream:

> A year ago, before we began this endeavour publicly by filing our first action against Merrill Lynch, we were living in a world where small investors were being laid astray, small investors were suffering huge losses because of the fraudulent research that was being placed into the market and unfortunately that was a reality that destroyed lives, destroyed college tuition for children, destroyed savings that were going to pay off mortgages and destroyed confidence that investors had placed in investment banks on whom they had relied.

Ever the tactician, he named a new elite apparently untainted by the lessons of past egregious behaviour, including Warren Buffet and Paul Volcker, former Chairman of the Federal Reserve. Small details, like the fact that Volcker had been a major architect of the very system now described as being responsible for the glorification of greed as corporate policy, were glossed over as Spitzer launched a formal attack on the entire legislative class for allowing the repeal of Glass–Steagall:

> We had been told "don't worry, trust us." Unfortunately, we have seen the result. The investment bankers who claimed that they were uniquely placed to handle these conflicts of interest have proven that they were uniquely incapable of handling those conflicts. I do not often quote Jack Grubman but when he said in his famous statement that "we have turned conflicts on interests into synergies", he was right. The synergies were for the investment banks. They were making money on both sides of the equation and the losers were the small investors who relied on the integrity of the research that was being placed in the marketplace.

While there has been continued sniping that the Attorney General's investigations have done little to restore confidence, there has also been little doubt that a further outpouring of evidence would reveal unpalatable home truths about how unequal the operation of the market had become. The opening of a veritable treasure trove of new information about the activities of Wall Street during the boom may not necessarily have cathartic qualities, but from the moment Spitzer had aquired the Merrill Lynch emails, this moment was foretold. Stephen Cutler, Director of Enforcement at the SEC, introduced a note of caution to the proceedings before the disgorgement got under way. He suggested, reasonably, that it would be wrong to attribute all the failings of corporate America to the egregious activities of the investment banks, noting a fair proportion of greed was also to blame for the irrationality that underpinned the lust for stocks in the late 1990s. In certain respects, just as Enron was symptomatic of a wider failure within the corporate model, the public humiliation of the financial powerhouses that had done so much to finesse its reputation was a necessary, if unedifying and somewhat distasteful reminder of systemic hubris.

The strength of Spitzer's investigation lay in the fact that it demonstrated how the entire model had become corrupted and how internal corporate governance and compliance programmes were rendered effectively meaningless. A corrosive compact that heavily discounted ethics in favour of investment fees, whatever the reputational risk, had degraded the concept of compliance. Spitzer was determined to effect structural reform by virtue of decimating the reputation of the firm most associated with the corporate culture: Citigroup, a conglomerate whose very formation had rendered any final legislative qualms about the consequences of repealing Glass–Steagall meaningless.

In the statement of claim, accepted by Citigroup, the Attorney General charged that the corporation was negligent. The company failed to manage conflicts of interest between its research and investment banking divisions; published fraudulent and misleading research that promoted investment banking clients and harmed investors, in a manner which violated New York's Martin Act; ignored internal warnings that its research product had become "basically worthless."[57] Throughout his presentation, Spitzer was determined that the focus should remain on the failure by management of Salomon Smith Barney to manage the conflicts inherent in the business culture inculcated by the time. "We have seen how crass this system was. What

---

[57] Office of the Attorney General (OAG) Press Release, 28 April 2003. Full text available at www.oag.state.ny.us/press/2003/apr/apr28a_03.html

we are releasing today is additional documentation about how far up the food chain that information had flown":

> One of the documents obtained from Salomon Smith Barney, from the head of global equity research, in the handwritten notes to his own presentation to the most senior management at Citigroup, says that their research is quote "ridiculous on its face." Ridiculous on its face. That's right in here. And yet what was the reaction? There was none. The reaction was to continue disseminating that research to investors who would rely on it and be subjected to the enormous losses that occurred.

In unpacking the relationship between investment bankers and research analysts, Spitzer made a mockery of internal controls at the firm. The head of Global Equities Research was the senior manager responsible for managing the conflicts of interest and ensuring the maintenance of the Chinese walls erected by the bank under the self-policing system engineered by Congress. As charted in earlier chapters, the collapse of the technology bubble in 2000 had prompted rising concern. Congress engaged in an exercise of hand-wringing, but absolved itself of responsibility. So too did senior managers at Solomon, even as a succession of internal and external red flags appeared and were ignored. As retail brokers with the conglomerate began to take flak from irate investors, the message filtered back to senior management. Comments forms submitted to the corporate headquarters in Greenwich Street's part of the annual review of all analysts provided the first sign that the aurora surrounding the company's star analyst was beginning to tarnish. In the rating exercise, Grubman accrued the most negative votes. The loss of the popularity contest did not unduly concern Grubman, who breezily shrugged off the slight. In an email to an associate outside the firm he even boasted about it:

> I never worry much about review. For example, this year I was rated last by retail (actually had a negative score) that to T [AT&T] and carnage in new names [technology stocks]. As the global head of research was haranguing me about this I asked him if he thought Sandy [Weill] liked $300 million in trading commission and $400 million in banking revenues. So, grin and bear it.[58]

---

[58] Jack Grubman to Cutler, 16 January 2001, cited in Assurance of Discontinuance (AOD), p. 18.

That is precisely the message that Hoffman conveyed to senior management to his own review of the unit's overall performance that year. He accepted there was a "growing noise level from retail because of technology and telecom's area in the second half of the year. Retail's attitude towards research definitely carries with the level of the stock market ... but I think there is a legitimate concern about the objectivity of our analysts which we must allay in 2001."[59]

This, however, was a secondary concern to the key performance target for the coming year: "to better integrate our research project with the business development plan of our constituencies, particularly investment banking." If Hoffman had spotted the warning flags and ignored them, so too did the personnel department. From reading a tabulated computer read-out of Grubman's salary, released as part of the global settlement, there can be no doubt of his value to the firm. Between 1998 and 2000 he was paid a basic salary of $200,000. His bonus payments advanced from $11.8m in 1998 to $14.8m in 1999 to $17.8m in 2000. Alongside, in a small box, personnel noted that the star employee "has gone from the most popular analyst ever to the most unpopular ever." There is no record that anyone in human resources attempted to question the rationale for the change and why the comments sheets contained so much personal and professional vitriol. It was clear that retail brokerage concerns did not feature on the corporate radar. It was an oversight that was to have disastrous consequences. The paper trail uncovered by the investigation revealed and put on public display a comprehensive failure of internal risk management that reads like a Harvard Business School case study. It was not merely retail that had become disillusioned with Grubman. The lucrative Private Client Group was also in a state of open revolt.

Hoffman compiled a list of stock calls from his group on 29 January 2001. It was this document that Spitzer quoted from in the Washington, DC press conference as evidence of systemic failure. Hoffman described stock recommendations as "the worst" and "ridiculous on

---

[59] John Hoffman to Michael Carpenter, 2000 Performance Review, 8 December 2000.

face". He observed that there was a "rising issue of research integrity and a basic inherent conflict between IB [investment banking], equities and retail."[60] A month later he apprised the troops of the problem. The handwritten comments appear to coincide with a conversation Hoffman had had with Jay Mandelbaum, the Managing Director of the Private Client Group. According to Hoffman, Mandelbaum "stated that our research was basically worthless because of limited discrimination in stock ratings, wide inconsistencies in rating and price targets, and . . . repeated occurrences of riding a stock down 50% or more and then, seemingly, capitulating at the very bottom." Most seriously, he threatened that the Private Client Group was considering whether they should contribute to the research budget (they currently pay about 25%, a considerable sum) anymore. But as Spitzer pointed out in his statement of claim, "Salomon Smith Barney did not change its rating system, however, and the de facto three-category rating system remained in place throughout 2001."

The Attorney General argued, "because of Salomon Smith Barney's and Citigroup's record of violations, those companies face additional requirements that go well beyond the global settlement. These provisions are necessary and appropriate and my office will be vigilant in ensuring full compliance by the company." Sandy Weill may have escaped investigation because of his cooperation with the Spitzer investigation, but his reputation has suffered irreparable harm.

As the press conference ended, the SEC lodged the settlement papers with the Southern District in New York, bringing to an end what the Lex column in the *Financial Times* disparagingly referred to as a circus. Common to all charges was the structural problem with the Chinese walls, which the financial performers found so easy to vault across. It may have been a spectacle for canny investors writing inside track gossip columns for the financial press. In reality, however, it was crime: concerted and repeated attempts to defraud within a structured framework that rewarded egregious behaviour, particularly in the cases of Merrill Lynch, Salomon Smith Barney and Credit

---

[60] AOD, p. 13.

Suisse First Boston, the three companies singled out for publishing fraudulent material.

According to the SEC complaint, "CSFB issued fraudulent research reports on two companies: Digital Impact, Inc. and Synopsys, Inc. In both cases, research analysts expressed positive views of the companies' stocks that were contrary to their true, privately held beliefs. In these instances, investment bankers pressured research analysts to initiate or maintain positive research coverage to obtain or retain investment banking business, and the analysts were pressured or compelled to compromise their own professional opinions by regarding the companies at the direction of the firm's investment bankers." To support its claim of fraudulent research to push the stock of Synopsys, the SEC published an email in which the research analyst complained about:[61]

> "Unwritten Rules for Tech Research: Based on the following set of specific situations that have arisen in the past, I have 'learned' to adapt to a set of rules that have been imposed by Tech Group banking so as to keep our corporate clients appeased." After the analyst downgraded a company, an investment banker informed him of "unwritten rule number one: that 'if you can't say something positive, don't say anything at all.'" The analyst further wrote that after issuing cautionary comments about another company, following which that company's CEO informed CSFB that he would never do investment banking business with CSFB, an investment banker informed the analyst of "unwritten rule number two: 'why couldn't you just go with the flow of the other analysts, rather than try to be a contrarian?'" The analyst applied these "unwritten rules" to Synopsys, a company that he had rated as a strong buy from July 1999–June 2000, but wanted to downgrade to a buy in light of a "down-tick in guidance." "By following rules 1 & 2," the analyst wrote, he "had successfully managed not to annoy the company."[62]

Merrill Lynch, the company that had prompted the investigation in the current form was also deemed responsible for publishing fraudulent material. Interestingly, in this instance the SEC complaint

---

[61] Memo from John Hoffman to US Research MDs, "Stock Rating System", 22 February 2001.

[62] SEC vs. Credit Suisse First Boston, fka Credit Suisse First Boston Corporation, 03 CV 2946 (WHP) (S.D.N.Y.).

suggests that Henry Blodget "aided and abetted" the corporation in its rating of GoTo:

> Merrill Lynch and Blodget published research on five other companies [24/7 Media, Inc.; LifeMinders, Inc.; Homestore.com, Inc.; Excite@Home; and Internet Capital Group, Inc.] that were not based on principles of fair dealing and good faith and did not provide a sound basis for evaluating facts, contained exaggerated or unwarranted claims, and/or contained opinions for which there was no reasonable basis.[63]

In all other cases, examples abounded of unwarranted and misleading research in which each participant was aware that the system was being gamed. JP Morgan Chase was charged with a unique variation – parcelling out research contracts with preordained outcomes to other investment banks to ensure that future stock received a boost. Among those who agreed to the conspiracy to misrepresent the market was the Suisse giant, UBS Warburg. In the Goldman Sachs litigation release, for example, the SEC quoted correspondence from the US Telecommunications Research Manager to his counterpart in Europe. It suggested insistent pressure from investment banking:

> The plan we have in place now is that in early September we are going to rerate most of the CLECs [competitive local exchange carriers], which is where the problem is most egregious. The ratings were a residual from [a former analyst], and I never changed them, not wanting to disrupt things too much. But it's ridiculous. I've already met with the bankers, and plan to move most of the companies down to M[arket]O[utperformer], from RL [the highest rating]. For the other segments the situation is not as bad, and where there is a problem, investment banking considerations have prevented me from making a change (i.e. AT&T, WCOM). I don't think I would end up leaving only 7.5% as RL, but the present 68% is ridiculous . . .[64]

There was no doubt, according to the regulators, who was going to be harmed by the activity. It was a concern shared by many working

---

[63] *SEC vs. Merrill Lynch, Pierce, Fenner & Smith Incorporated*, 03 CV 2941 (WHP) (S.D.N.Y.); *SEC vs. Henry M. Blodget*, 03 CV 2947 (WHP) (S.D.N.Y.).
[64] *SEC vs. Goldman, Sachs & Co.*, 03 CV 2944 (WHP) (S.D.N.Y.).

within the brokerage houses themselves, as evidenced by the following missive uncovered in the investigation into Lehman Brothers:

> In one instance an analyst who covered Razorfish Inc. told an institutional investor in an email, "well, ratings and price targets are fairly meaningless anyway ... but, yes, the 'little guy' who isn't smart about the nuances may get misled, such is the nature of my business."[65]

While the firms were accused of atrocious behaviour, there was unanimity from the platform that the aim of the investigations was not to destroy Wall Street, simply reform it. The corporate governance lapses were unfortunate, but there was to be a limit to the demonstration effect. Three individuals, in particular, became the whipping boys of the hour. As widely leaked, Henry Blodget of Merrill Lynch was fined $4m and banned from the securities industry for life. Fifty per cent of the total amount – $2m – was set aside for the disgorgement of ill-gotten gains. Jack Grubman of Citigroup was forced to pay $15m in fines and penalties in return for a settlement of fraud charges. Under the terms of a sidebar arrangement $15m of the fines cannot be written off against tax.

Frank Quattrone, the third stellar figure in the corrupted world of analyst research is now awaiting trial on charges of obstruction of a federal investigation following the unsealing of a US Attorney's claim in Manhattan the previous week. The US Attorney for the Southern District made clear that Quattrone was to be made an example of, because of his decision to ask subordinates to "clean up" their files, despite knowing that a criminal investigation was about to begin. Following his appearance in court, Quattrone's lawyers told reporters that his client would be contesting the charges. "Only prosecutors who see the world through dirty windows would take a one sentence e-mail supporting company policy [to purge computer systems] and try to turn it into a federal criminal case. The accusations are wrong and unfair."[66]

---

[65] SEC vs. Lehman Brothers Inc., 03 CV 2940 (WHP) (S.D.N.Y.).
[66] Randall Smith, Kara Scannell and Susan Pulliam, "Now, Frank Quattrone faces a criminal obstruction case", Wall Street Journal, 24 April 2003.

There is no doubt that the legal environment has changed dramatically as a consequence of the corporate scandals. Prosecutors have considerably more leverage over recalcitrant corporate behaviour, a fact underscored by the dissemination of new prosecutorial guidelines to all US Attorneys on 23 January 2003. The memo, written by the Deputy Attorney General Larry Thompson, acknowledges that while securing a successful prosecution against a corporation is laden with risk, "every matter involving business crime must assess the merits of seeking the conviction of the business entity itself." What is particularly striking is the tone of the Thompson memo. "Too often", it decries "business organisations while purporting to cooperate with a Department investigation, in fact take steps to impede the quick and effective exposure of the complete scope of wrongdoing under investigation. The revisions make clear that such conduct should weigh in favor of a corporate prosecution. The revisions also address the efficacy of the corporate governance mechanisms in place within a corporation, to ensure that these measures are truly effective rather than mere paper programs."[67]

While the Department of Justice can see the "important public benefits that may flow from indicting a corporation", a balance is, of necessity, struck between exposing egregious behaviour and winning Pyrrhic victories. This applies at every level in the interlocking judicial system. The investigation by the New York District Attorney into Tyco worked on the assumption that the corporation was a helpless victim, its board and shareholders hoodwinked by the activities of venal executives. A similar rationale underpins the continuing case against the Rigas family in the Adelphi case. In Health-South, a clean sweep of senior executives would suggest that the enterprise was run as a criminal enterprise and that under the revised federal prosecution principles corporate guilt would have to be assessed.

A corporation can only act through natural persons, and it is there-

---

[67] Larry Thompson, "Principles of federal prosecution of business organizations", US Department of Justice, 20 January 2003.

fore held responsible for the acts of such persons fairly attributable to it. Charging a corporation for even minor misconduct may be appropriate where the wrongdoing was pervasive. A corporation is directed by its management, and management is responsible for a corporate culture in which criminal conduct is either discouraged or actively encouraged. Pervasiveness is case-specific and [will] depend on the number, and degree of responsibility, of individuals [with] substantial authority.[68]

There is, however, no suggestion of indicting HealthSouth as a criminal enterprise or running a RICO case against the corporation itself. As one senior Department of Justice prosecutorial manager told the author recently, "there is no benefit to be accrued by the government gaining control via forfeiture of a busted company. RICO is the most draconian legislative tool we have and not necessarily the most useful. A balance has got to be struck." Exercising that judgement is even more acute when the investigation turns to the wider issue of the roles played by the investment banks in "gaming the system" in the first place.

The global lesson from the United States is that effective corporate governance structures require therefore a much wider focus than that traditionally utilized. As the Organization for Economic Cooperation and Development (OECD) recognized when drafting its widely cited definition in 1999, "corporate governance is affected by the relationships among participants in the governance system."[69] When the OECD itself highlighted the "synergy between macroeconomic and structural policies," it saw corporate governance as a way of maximizing growth through transparency. It is now abundantly clear that narrow definitions of corporate governance and ideological aversion to regulation can in itself form part of the problem. A similar failing

---

[68] Ibid., p. 5.

[69] OECD *Principles of Corporate Governance*, 1999, p. 12. While acknowledging the rights of stakeholders, the OECD itself relies heavily on the tripartite model to deal with agency problems. "The corporate governance framework should ensure the strategic guidance of the company, the effective monitoring of management by the board, and the board's accountability to the company and the shareholders" (p. 22).

surrounds the OECD convention on bribery and extortion, which omits mention of payments to political parties and downplays the importance of private-to-private corruption.[70] As the American example has so graphically demonstrated, the erosion of confidence in the integrity of the market has its roots in a political and economic model that glorified greed and rested on a deliberate erosion of the checks and balances necessary to ensure a level playing field.

To date, the unrelenting examination of individual units, companies and sectors has the same distorting effect as peering at a section of the Bayeux Tapestry with a microscope. The result of this myopia can be an intellectual confusion between cause and effect. We are left with an intricate, but partial, understanding of how the complex weave fits into a wider system of decision-making, policy formulation and societal structure. In those circumstances, advocating a return to the markets as an engine of growth, without a more balanced understanding of how and why policy is actually created, is nothing short of reckless. Without calling to account the gatekeepers of the system – the auditors, lawyers, the regulatory authorities and ultimately the politicians – meaningful reform is unlikely to provide an antidote to the poison that has led to a corrupted state. Wall Street remains on trial.

---

[70] See François Vincke, "Private to private bribery", in François Vincke and Fritz Heimann (eds), *Fighting Corruption, A Corporate Practices Manual* (International Chamber of Commerce Publishing, Paris, 2003), pp. 127–39.

Index